Ain't No Such Thang AS A PURDY GOOD Alligator Rassler

Mastering the 12 Absolutes essential for success in the "Swamps" of today's ever changing unpredictable landscape.

BOB FLYNN

To Austine, my precious gift from God and beloved Partner in the creation of our Love Based Vision.

BOB FLYNN

BOB FLYNN

GROWTH AND EVOLUTION

Table of Contents

Foreword

On a hot August day in 1986, my company sent me to Newark, NJ for a two-day seminar. This was the last place I wanted to be but there I was in the ballroom of a large hotel adjacent to the Newark Airport with about 200 of my "new best friends".

Those two days were unremarkable except for the two hours when an intriguing guy from North Carolina was on stage conducting his part of the program. I remember little else of those two days but I do remember going home that night and telling my wife I heard a guy speak today who really touched me and caused me to examine some behaviors that needed changing.

That "intriguing guy" was Bob Flynn the author of this book.

Fast forward three years when I joined a large national transportation company. In my second week of employment, I was sent to Virginia for a five-day workshop. The facilitator for this event was Bob, he had recently joined this organization as executive director of training and education. And thus, began an on-going thirty-year relationship with the person I first saw on that stage in Newark. Beginning as a business associate, Bob became a personal and professional mentor, spiritual advisor and most of all a trusted-friend.

Our relationship was unique, me being an "in your face" Northeaster, and Bob a "down-home" Southerner, but our kindred spirits were immediately aligned by our mutually focused desire to be the very best we could be.

Over the past thirty years Bob has Unequivocally changed my life in so many ways and on so many levels that I could never do his impact justice in this forward. But suffice it to say that it is his "body of work" and the manner in which he presents it that form the foundation for the life changing moments you'll experience when you become a participant in his teachings.

This book encapsulates many of the core fundamental lessons you must be willing to embrace if you truly desire to grow and evolve. Bob's teaching is based on Immutable Laws and is therefore irrefutable.

AIN'T NO SUCH THANG AS
A PURDY GOOD ALLIGATOR RASSLER

The "Twelve Absolutes" contained in this book have the potential take you on a life changing journey and if you take the action prescribed, will put you on a path to greater success in all aspects of your life.

While not for the casual reader, it is certainly for the person who seeks to take their life to the highest possible level.

Bob's unique gift comes to life as he teaches and coaches you through what he has learned in many years of painstaking research and practice. In this book, he has condensed his learnings into a format that is easily readable and understandable. His style of teaching, delivered through compelling stories, will capture and hold your interest and Bob's use of characters will undoubtedly help you personalize the lessons at hand. He weaves these stories with timeless lessons that are immediately actionable and success enhancing.

"Ain't No Such Thang as a Purdy Good Alligator Rassler" is vintage Flynn, it is life changing.

Bob Flynn changed mine, and many others as well, and for that I am eternally grateful.

So, if you're ready for the ride of your life, buckle-up, hang on – it's so worth it.

JIMMIE D'ALESSIO

Introduction

A Personal Statement

I watched him pace the floor and wondered what had brought him to this point. He had the appearance of a broken man, a distraught man, a man lost and alone, and a man in severe agony… I later discovered that he was, in fact, all these things, but he was mostly… a man on the brink of a colossal decision.

How long had he been in this state? What was going through his mind? I knew that intense emotional pain usually drives a person to intense introspection or surrender to their condition, so my ultimate question was… What decisions would he make, which road would he choose?

I watched him speaking to a group of sophisticated business people, coaching a sales executive, developing his next seminar, teaching at the university, counseling a Fortune 500 CEO. I observed him traveling the globe to conduct training, consulting, and speaking assignments. I saw him in his beautiful home enjoying his loving family. I saw him totally relaxed and fulfilled.

And suddenly, I realized both these men are the same man… both these men are me.

What happened the day that I paced the floor in misery pondering my options, and determining my fate, what conclusions were reached, decisions made? It started simply really; I decided I wasn't thinking and living right, and I decided that the reason I wasn't was because I didn't know how. I decided to learn the "secrets" of successful well-adjusted, happy people. Undoubtedly those were three major decisions, however, the most important decision I made that hot August day wasn't a decision at all, it was a conclusion. See, I surmised that I was where I was: alone, broke, and miserable because I put myself there. It wasn't my background, my parents, my former wife, the government, my friends, my schooling, the job or the boss, it was me! I guess you could say I finally decided to grow up, stop feeling sorry for myself and take personal responsibility for all aspects of my life.

I had made similar decisions in the past and basically lied to myself, but somehow this time I knew it was now or never. Somehow I knew that I was really going to follow through on the promises that I made to myself. Little did I know that as a result of those promises I was about to embark on the most exciting, challenging, and rewarding adventure imaginable; little did I know that a major restoration was under way.

And so it began, my adventuresome quest to learn all I could about how to become happy and successful. Having made the unequivocal decision to learn and apply all I could about how to achieve these timeless yet evasive goals I immediately got my first lesson...

> ## *When a person truly makes up their mind to commit, to become focused and open minded, teachers, helpers, and favorable circumstances appear as if by magic.*

Seemingly out of the blue, my company sent me to *The Dale Carnegie Course*. Later that same year they sent me to a Nightingale-Conant workshop entitled *Lead The Field*. Both these opportunities exposed me to information that caused my life to begin heading directly toward success and happiness, I was hooked! I began reading, studying, and applying everything that would perpetuate my self-improvement. As I learned, I applied, as I applied I began seeing results, as I experienced results, I continued learning and applying at increasing rates. Thus began the cycle that continues today. Decisions determine destinations and I thank God for the pain that led me to the decision to study and apply the wisdom of the ages, for my destination has far surpassed anything that I could have ever imagined.

Along my journey toward success and happiness people begin noticing that I was more focused, determined, and definitely becoming happier and more successful. Some asked questions, some even took my advice, and without even realizing it I began teaching the concepts and immutable laws that were changing my life, it was in the midst of this process that I discovered...

> ## *The more I helped others, the more I helped myself.*

It was that discovery that precipitated this book. Now, you are probably not at your rope's end as I was, in fact things may be going reasonably well for you. But... you may be dealing with a common malady that I call uncomfortable complacency. This is the feeling that your life is progressing okay but that there's still significantly more that you could be accomplishing. You're

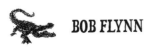

moderately happy but far from blissful. I've found many otherwise blissful and highly productive people in the uncomfortably complacent predicament, so many in fact that Jack Williams, the main character of our story epitomizes the uncomfortably complacent individual so prevalent in today's society.

Before I provide some basic insight into *Ain't No Such Thang as a Purdy Good Alligator Rassler*, let me quickly confess that the ideas contained in this work are not mine. Oh, I have put them in my words, and created a storyline to make them interesting and palatable. Their essence, however, have been borrowed from: Jesus, Solomon, David, Socrates, Plato, and The Bible.

In addition to these, many contemporary writers and teachers have edified and inspired the creation of the *12 Absolutes*, they include: David Burns, Tony Allasandra, Wayne Dyer, Robert Ringer, Jim Collins, Chuck Swindoll, Charles Garfield, Ken Blanchard, Brian Tracy, W. Edwards Deming, Og Mandino, Tony Robbins, Napoleon Hill, Ralph Waldo Emerson, Sarah Ban Breathnach, Dale Carnegie, Earl Nightingale, Oswald Chambers, Kahill Gibran, Vernon Howard, Aubrey Daniels, Norman Vincent Peale, Stephen Covey, Billy Graham, Joel Osteen, Bruce Wilkinson, John Eldredge, Rick Warren, Mihaly Csikszentmihalyi, Viktor Frankl, and David McCullough.

AIN'T NO SUCH THANG AS
A PURDY GOOD ALLIGATOR RASSLER

Benefits of Reading

Ain't No Such Thang as a Purdy Good Alligator Rassler

Over the past thirty years, my conservative estimate is that I have read 175 books containing 35,000 pages on the subject of success, happiness, and self-actualization. I have compiled over 400 pages of notes from classes, seminars, and tape programs on these same subjects. While it has most certainly been a labor of love it also represents a tremendous time and effort investment, an investment you won't have to make.

The information in this book is highly condensed and arranged in a simple easy to understand format. With a minimum of time and energy you will gain the knowledge and information it has taken me thirty years to compile.

By absorbing this material you will learn how to...

- Discover your *authentic* self.

- Maximize your time, energy, and efforts.

- Build a network of enthusiastic supporters.

- Program your mind to furnish the optimum answers to difficult problems.

- Capitalize on changing conditions rather than being victimized by them.

- Rapidly cause others to see things from your perspective.

- Identify and use your greatest fears as catalyst for exponential growth.

- Become happier than you ever dreamed possible.

- Bring into our life the things that you truly desire.

- Maintain the ideal emotional state in any situation.

- Use time to your maximum advantage.

- Take complete charge of your life.

Thank you for selecting *Ain't No Such Thang as a Purdy Good Alligator Rassler*. May it serve to take you to your highest calling and aspiration, and may God bring you the blessings of happiness and fulfillment.

Bob Flynn

Powhatan, Virginia
April 2019

CHAPTER ONE

Ain't No Such Thang AS A PURDY GOOD Alligator Rassler

The Weekend

You only get one shot at life but if you live it right – one shot is all you need.

RUSSELL JAMES

AIN'T NO SUCH THANG AS
A PURDY GOOD ALLIGATOR RASSLER

The Weekend

Something wasn't right…

Jack had looked forward to this weekend alone for quite some time. His wife Hannah had taken their two children to her parents' house for a visit, and he was caught up at work and around the house. All was in order, just like he had planned it, except for one thing: this uneasy feeling in the pit of his stomach. It wasn't worry exactly, more like a kind of foreboding, a mild aggravation like a puppy trying to pull a rag out of his master's hand. His first inclination was to busy himself by finding an activity to throw himself into. That always worked when something was bugging him. But wait a minute, wasn't this supposed to be a "lay around and do nothing" weekend? Hadn't he promised himself that he would totally relax and get his mind off the daily grind? I mean. what could be wrong, anyway? He had a good wife, two beautiful kids, a good job, two half-paid-for cars, and a home with a comfortable mortgage in a nice safe neighborhood. Yeah, of course there were a few problems, but nothing pressing. Really, things were as good as they had ever been, so why the weird feeling?

"Football, that's the ticket; there's some great games coming on in the next hour or so. I'll watch a game. That'll get me on track. Let's see who's playing. The Giants—man, I can't believe it! I thought they were playing tomorrow. I love the Giants. Let's see who they're playing. Oh no, the Redskins. This won't be much of a game; the Redskins are on the bottom of their division and when they win this one, the Giants are headed for the playoffs. Well, I'll watch the first quarter, maybe the half. The spread says it's the Giants by two touchdowns. I'd say the Giants have the potential to beat these bums by 20 at least."

This is hard to believe, Jack thought. With twenty seconds left in the first half the Redskins are attempting a 42-yard field goal. Yeah, right, in this wind and with Garcia kicking. He couldn't make a good high school team; there's no way.

"It's up, and it's good!" the commentator's voice boomed. "Redskins 24, Giants 0 as the first half draws to a close. Well, fans, it looks like the Giants' playoff hopes are in jeopardy. It's going to take a miracle for the boys from the Big Apple to get back into this one!"

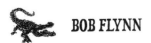 **BOB FLYNN**

Bradshaw, he's as lousy an analyst as he was a quarterback, Jack thought. How many concussions did that guy have in his playing days anyway? He thinks the last four words to the national anthem are gentlemen start your engines. He figures the French Rivera is a sports car, and a sub-division is a math problem. His mind ain't ever been cluttered with the facts!

Now that's peculiar, Jack thought, as the camera panned the Redskins bench. Those guys are jumping up and down, laughing joking, high-fiving and basically behaving like a high school team at homecoming. Despite what that hayseed Bradshaw said, you jokers have got another half to play.

"This thing ain't over yet," Jack yelled at the TV screen.

Heading off the field into the tunnel that leads to the dressing room, the Giants presented a total contrast to the Redskins, heads held high in defiance, teeth clenched in anger and determination. They looked poised and ready to turn things around.

"With twelve seconds remaining, ladies and gentlemen, the Giants line up on the Redskins' eighteen. Jenkins sets up under center, barks the signals, drops back to pass. He's in trouble, rolls right, there's O'Malley in the flat, touchdown Giants! In a stunning comeback, the Giants beat the Redskins 25 to 24--unbelievable!"

"Wow! What a game," Jack thought out loud. I'm going to see what that Redskins coach has to say at the press conference. *I'm going to enjoy watching him eat a little crow.*

"Ladies and gentlemen of the press, let me present Steve Starling, Washington Redskins' head coach. He will now take your questions."

"Yeah, Charlie," Coach Starling said in a remarkably calm though disappointed tone.

"Coach, you guys dominated in the first half. What happened?"

"Two things happened, Charlie, and both of them are my fault. First, we attempted to sit on our lead. We did just enough to get by. We didn't take calculated risks like we did in the first half. We played cautiously, almost fearfully, not with abandon like we did in the first half. We lost our drive, our hunger. We were just happy to be in the thing. Secondly, we were complacent, satisfied, and we figured all we had to do was play pretty good in the second half and we'd come out okay."

The coach continued, "When I spoke to the team at halftime, I had this weird feeling, but I couldn't really put my finger on it. It wasn't anxiety, really, more of an unsettled feeling, kind of like I had forgotten something and couldn't remember what. I know that anytime I get a feeling like that, I had better examine it and come up with some answers, a plan to do things differently, but in this case, I chose to ignore it and hope for a good outcome. As my daddy used to say, 'Hope ain't no winning strategy, boy.'"

Coach Starling concluded his comments by saying, "It all boils down to this: in the first half we really wanted it, we played up to our potential, we stretched our self-imposed boundaries, we pushed ourselves through fear and adversity, made no excuses, took total responsibility and accountability. In the second half we coasted, and there ain't but one way to coast!"

Jack was irritated by Starling's comments, but why? *He wasn't talking to me, or was he? Jack thought, Am I sitting on my lead, complacent, failing to push myself to the outer edge of my potential? Is that what's bothering me? I mean, I work pretty hard, I'm a pretty good husband and father, our finances are okay. I take the family to church most Sundays, and I know a lot of guys that are in worst shape than me. Naw, he couldn't have been talking to me.*

Coach Starling's comments kept resonating in Jack's head. Finally, he'd had enough. It was time for some tough questions and serious thinking.

Jack invested the remainder of the weekend in some rather intense introspection. While it wasn't the most relaxing weekend he'd ever spent, it was perhaps the most productive. He concluded that while he was doing okay in the key aspects of his life, he certainly had room for improvement, perhaps significant improvement. Jack invested the next hour and a half in identifying and prioritizing the most critical components of his life.

Jack's next question was *Where do I find proper instruction and coaching?* While pondering that question, he recalled a conversation with Tom Kearns, an acquaintance from work. Even though the conversation had taken place over three years ago, Jack vividly remembered the circumstances surrounding it. Jack had noticed a significant positive change in Tom. So had Tom's management, and they rewarded him with two major promotions in three years. Tom seemed more poised, relaxed, and happy. Jack asked him what had changed. Tom explained that he had felt stuck in all the important aspects of his life, not doing too badly, but not doing all that well either. Because of his inability to get free from the vice-like grip of mediocrity, he had decided to seek help and found a course called *The 12 Absolutes of Personal Effectiveness.*

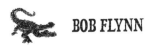

Jack could certainly relate. He was sorry that he had lost contact with Tom, as he would like to get more information on the course. *Hey*, Jack thought, *I'll bet Bill Hanks would know how to get in touch with Tom, since they were like best buddies. One of these days I'll give him a call and see if I can run old Tom down. Wait a minute--that's one of my challenges, I'm continually putting things off. If I'm going to do something about this, it's time to get off my butt and do it now.*

"Bill, it's Jack Williams. Got a minute?"

"Sure," Bill answered with a puzzled tone.

"Bill, are you still in contact with Tom Kearns?"

"Yes, why?"

"I've been thinking about a course he recommended to me over three years ago."

"You mean *The 12 Absolutes of Personal Effectiveness*?

"Yeah, that's it. I wanted to contact him and see if it's still available."

"Not only is it available, Jack, Tom joined the company that produces it. He conducts seminars, workshops, and does consulting work all over the country."

"That's incredible, Bill. I can remember when Tom couldn't lead a group in silent prayer."

"Yeah, me too, and you're right, it is incredible. Here's his number. Give him a call; I know he'll be delighted to hear from you. And by the way, if you are interested and can qualify for the program, there's a group of us that meets once a month to work on mastering *The 12 Absolutes*. We have a great time, and… it's made a big difference in every facet of a lot of people's lives."

"Thanks Bill, I'll be in touch," Jack said as he said goodbye and hung up the phone.

Man, Jack thought, *I wondered what became of Tom. Sounds like he's really doing well--and just think, less than five years ago he was stuck, just like me. I think I'll give him a call sometime. I'd call him now, but he's probably relaxing at home; I wouldn't want to disturb him, and besides, now that he's hit the big time, he probably won't even remember me. Even if he does remember me, he probably wouldn't have time to discuss the program. I'll bet that program is very expensive, anyway. I don't have a lot of money lying around these days. Yeah, it's probably that positive thinking crap, a bunch of nonsense like live with passion, walk on hot coals* junk that they promote on TV. Besides, I don't like that "if I can qualify" stuff. Sounds like a marketing ploy to me. I'll guarantee you they'll take anybody that can cough up the bucks.

Jack interrupted his thoughts. *There I go again, making excuses and being skeptical, going to the movies in my head, as my wife says, putting it off. I've closed my mind and I haven't even tried. I'm calling Tom. What have I got to lose?*

"Hello…this is Tom Kearns, thanks for calling." Jack breathed a sigh of relief at the voice mail message. The message continued: "Today Is Saturday, April 18. I'm traveling and will be returning Friday, April 24. I will be checking my messages every day twice a day, so please leave your name, number, and any message that you have, and I'll return your call within 24 hours. Thanks again for calling."

Responding somewhat reluctantly to the message Jack said, "Uh, Tom, this is Jack Williams. Bill Hanks gave me your number and told me you were now conducting *The 12 Absolutes of Personal Effectiveness* Program. I'd like to get some more information and catch up as well. Call when you can. My number is…."

Jack flipped through the TV channels, paced the floor, and tried to get interested in a Clancy novel, all in vain. He just couldn't seem to get his mind off his current state of affairs. Then the phone rang

"Jack?" It was Tom Kearns.

"Yes."

"Jack, this is Tom Kearns. It was a pleasant surprise to hear from you. How've you been?"

"Great, Tom. Thanks for returning my call, especially on a Saturday night."

"My pleasure, Jack. I was in a workshop all day, and sitting in a hotel room all evening isn't all that much fun or productive, so I thought this would be a good time to get back to you and see what's on your mind. Is this a convenient time for you to talk?" Tom's tone was sincere and down to earth.

"Yes, actually I'm home alone. My wife and kids are at the in-laws', so this is a great time to talk."

Tom went right to the heart of the matter. "Good. You mentioned your potential interest in *The 12 Absolutes of Personal Effectiveness* Program. What has piqued your interest after so many years?"

 **BOB FLYNN**

In an instant, Jack decided to be direct and not beat around the bush like he usually did. "Tom, I think I'm stuck; at least, that's the way it feels. Something has been bugging me and I have decided it has its roots in complacency … mine." Jack was somewhat shocked, yet pleased, at how up-front and on target his response had been.

In a truly interested tone, Tom asked. "What leads you to that conclusion, Jack?"

"It's a long story," Jack replied, "but let's just say it culminated today after watching the Redskins blow a 24-point lead. They became complacent and got whipped! When Coach Starling answered the press's questions, I thought he was talking to me." Again, Jack was surprised at his straightforward response, as he had always had trouble admitting any form of weakness, especially to another guy.

"Yeah, I saw the highlights about an hour ago; super game if you're a Giants fan. So, tell me more, Jack. In what aspects of your life do you feel complacent?"

Man, this guy is thorough, Jack thought before responding. "Funny that you should ask, Tom. After Starling's commentary I began to prioritize the key components of my life: family, career, health, finances, spiritual life. Man, I 'm telling you, I'm flat complacent in all of them. When I assessed how I was doing, the answer that kept coming back was pretty good, and that was a stretch in most of the categories."

"Yeah, I can relate; been there myself, Jack," Tom offered compassionately.

Jack's curiosity got the best of him. "So, Tom, how'd you do it? How did you break free from complacency and get on with it?"

"Well, Jack, I suppose you think I'm going to tell you that it was the course that did it, and if that's what you're thinking, you'd be exactly right. *The 12 Absolutes of Personal Effectiveness* was definitely the catalyst that got me off dead center and moving forward."

There was no doubt in Jack's mind that he had received an honest answer. "Okay, Tom, I'm sold. How do I get started?"

"Jack, I appreciate your enthusiasm." Tom chuckled. "You know, it's a person's drive, energy, and resolve at the beginning of anything worthwhile that has the most effect on the results. However, it's important that you fully understand the program and the personal commitment required, before you jump in."

Surprised at Tom's statement, Jack asked, "So how do I go about that?"

AIN'T NO SUCH THANG AS
A PURDY GOOD ALLIGATOR RASSLER

"Here's how I think we should proceed. Bill Hanks will be starting up a new group in two weeks. They will be beginning with a general overview of the entire program. Why don't you have a preliminary discussion with him, get the basics, and then attend the introductory session? By taking that approach, you'll be in a much better position to determine if this is what you're seeking. How does that sound?"

"That makes a lot of sense, Tom, but I got to tell you I'm a little surprised that you didn't put the sales pitch on me--you know, close the deal while the prospect is hot."

With a chuckle in his voice, Tom answered, "That's not the way we operate, Jack. We want all of our participants to receive great benefit from this program, and we know that the only way we can achieve that is to see if our prospects really want to break the chains of complacency and do something special with their lives."

Jack was incredulous. "Tom, wait a second. Are you telling me I've really got to qualify to invest my money and time in this program? Are you telling me I've got to make the team?"

Tom answered unhesitatingly, "Yes, Jack, that's exactly what I'm telling you. You see, this is a program for the men and the big boys."

Jack and Tom chatted for a few more minutes, small talk mostly; then they said their goodbyes.

Hanging up the phone, Jack thought about Tom's comment about this being a program for the men and big boys. *You know what?* he concluded. *Tom doesn't think I'm serious about moving ahead with my life--and you know what else? He may just be right.*

Jack spent what was left of his weekend thinking about whether or not to contact Bill Hanks for some more information about the program. Frankly, he was a little intimidated by the fact that he would actually have to qualify for the workshop. He decided to discuss it with Hannah when she returned Sunday afternoon.

The sound of the garage door opening signaled that Hannah and the children were home.

"Hi, Jack. Great to see you. How did your weekend go?" Hannah said, smiling as usual.

"Fine, dear," Jack answered half-heartedly.

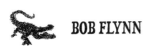 **BOB FLYNN**

"Were you able to relax and get your mind off things?"

"Yeah, well--not exactly."

"Oh, what happened?" Hannah asked as the children scurried up to their rooms.

"Hannah, I want to talk with you about something pretty important. When do you think we could make that happen?" Jack asked in a serious tone.

Jack definitely had Hannah's attention.

"The kids are worn out, so they'll be asleep in a couple of hours. How about we talk then?"

"Yeah, that sounds good." Jack sounded relieved.

"Okay, they're down for the night. What's going on, Jack?"

Jack told Hannah all about his weekend, Coach Starling's comments, and his discussion with Tom Kearns. She listened with keen interest, interrupting occasionally to gain clarification. Jack concluded by saying, "Hannah, really I don't know what to do. Do you think I'm making too much of this?"

Hannah pondered her response carefully. "No, Jack, I don't. I think you are finally listening to your feelings. I think you are getting in touch with the source of your anger and frustration."

Anger and frustration? Jack looked puzzled.

"Yes. I've noticed for some time now that you don't have your usual zip and drive, and your sense of humor seems to be on an extended vacation."

Frowning, Jack asked, "Really? Why haven't you brought this to my attention before now?"

"Oh, I've tried, but whenever I broach the subject, you change it fast."

"Has it been that awful?"

"No," replied Hannah cautiously, "but you are definitely not your usual self, and that concerns me."

"So, are you telling me that I should attend the program?" Jack asked with a touch of sarcasm.

"No, but I think Tom Kearns gave you some good advice. Call Bill to get the basic information and if it seems feasible, go to the first meeting. Then you'll be in a position to make an intelligent decision." Jack and Hannah chatted awhile longer.

Right before he fell asleep, Jack said, "I'll call Bill tomorrow."

The Encounter

When Jack arrived home at the usual time, Hannah greeted him at the side door. "How was your Monday, honey?"

"Okay, I guess. The usual fires to fight, customers to deal with; nothing special, just the typical Monday headaches. There was one thing that kind of caught me by surprise, though."

"Oh? What was that?" Hannah asked.

"Pete said he wanted to see me first thing tomorrow morning, can you believe at 7:00 a.m.?" Jack continued with slight concern in his voice, "He's been my boss for over five years now and never requested anything like that. Oh well, it's probably nothing; maybe I'll get a big promotion or raise or something. I could sure use a little good luck."

"Oh, I'm sure it's something good," replied Hannah reassuringly. "By the way, Jack, how did your conversation with Bill Hanks go?"

Slightly wincing, Jack stammered, "I, uh, decided not to pursue the program." He continued rapidly so as not to allow Hannah time to comment. "I just don't, uh, have time for that type of commitment. You know, uh, I'm busy at work, there's golf on most Saturdays, you and the kids need my attention. There's no time. Hannah, and besides, I haven't been feeling all that well lately. I think I need more rest. The program is just not in the cards right now."

"I see," replied Hannah with a touch of wifely disappointment.

Oh man, I'd better hurry, Jack thought as he scurried to the shower. *I've overslept again, no way I'm going to make it in by 7:00. I can't believe I've been so stupid. Pete ain't going to like this!*

Almost running, Jack hustled across the parking lot arriving at Pete's office at 7:50. The door was closed, so Jack knocked nervously. After what seemed like

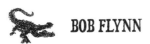 **BOB FLYNN**

an eternity, Pete opened the door. To Jack's dismay, the company president, Joe Holt, was seated across from Pete's desk.

"Sorry I'm late," Jack blurted out. "The traffic, you know."

"Jack, as you can see, I'm tied up at the moment. Stay close and I'll give you a call when my meeting has concluded."

"Yeah, sure, Pete. Oh, I have a customer appointment in less than an hour, so can we meet later this afternoon?"

Pete responded in an atypical authoritative tone of voice, "Jack, you'll need to reschedule with the customer. I need to see you right after this meeting so hang loose, okay?"

One hour passed, then two, as Jack contemplated every possible scenario from receiving a huge promotion to a "pink slip." Just when he thought he could stand the suspense no longer, the phone rang.

"Jack, it's Pete; come on down."

Jack took a deep breath and headed on down to Pete's office.

"Come on in, Jack," Pete said in his usual informal way. Jack felt relieved, but that relief was short lived.

"Jack, it gives me no pleasure to have this conversation with you today." Pete pressed on, "Your performance has slipped. I mentioned this to you three months ago, to no avail; in fact, things have declined even more. I need some reassurance, a plan, a change of direction, something or I'm going to have to take you out of this position."

Reeling as if he had been slugged in the gut, Jack sat silently for a moment, then responded. "Pete, I had no idea it was this serious. I mean you got to know the economy ain't all that great, the recent downsizing and that acquisition we made has caused more problems and less time to solve them. I don't get much of your time these days, and you know what, the lousy weather and new governmental regulations haven't helped matters either."

"What else is hindering your performance, Jack?" Pete asked sincerely.

Jack was on a roll now. "Programs, Pete. It seems every month we've got another program rolling out. Programs cause meetings, and meetings take time. I'm spending more and more time attending meetings and completing paperwork associated with them. There are just too many problems and not

AIN'T NO SUCH THANG AS
A PURDY GOOD ALLIGATOR RASSLER

enough time to do real work. Have you considered that at all?"

Pete allowed the silence to take effect. Then he spoke in a subdued tone, almost a whisper.

"What else, Jack? What else is keeping you from realizing your potential?"

Jack wanted to talk about his salary. He wasn't really happy about his last increase, but he decided he'd better save that for another time and so he said, "That's it, Pete, and from my perspective, that's enough."

Pete stroked his chin in contemplation. Then, making direct eye contact with Jack, he hit the issue head on. "Jack, I don't disagree with anything you've said. I'm in the same ballgame you are, and yet I'm quite concerned with your comments."

Jack interrupted, speaking apologetically. "Sorry, Pete, I guess I spoke out of turn, raised my voice a little too much, got emotional, I guess. I didn't mean any disrespect."

Pete smiled for the first time during the encounter. "No disrespect taken. Jack, I didn't personalize anything you said, and it's okay to get emotional. I know you're a passionate guy, or at least you used to be."

"So, Pete what did you mean when you said you're concerned about my comments?" Jack asked politely.

Pete was totally relaxed now, himself. "It's your focus, Jack. Everything you targeted as a reason for your declining performance is outside your sphere of control. I mean, come on. What can you and I do about any of the reasons you cited? This is the hand you've been dealt. You simply aren't taking any responsibility in this matter. You are placing the blame totally outside of yourself, and that's a terrible position to assume in any situation."

Pete was speaking with wisdom, conviction, and assurance that was definitely intriguing. Something had changed about him, but Jack couldn't put his finger on exactly what it was. Addressing Pete's last statement, Jack asked, "So Pete, why is pointing out the facts contributing to my situation such a terrible thing to do?"

Pete bristled slightly, then quickly regained his composure, sat erect in his chair, and looked Jack straight in the eye. "You're taking me out of context, Jack. This isn't about facts. I already agreed that everything you said is, to one degree or another, factual. No, the issue isn't the facts, the issue is what you're doing

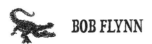 **BOB FLYNN**

about them, and what you're doing is taking zero responsibility for dealing with them. You're labeling facts as problems and using them as shields against taking personal responsibility. Unfortunately, this is a common approach, an approach that stifles productivity and subdues potential.

"Let me tell you something I've learned recently. The more I think about it, the more profound it becomes, and I think it applies directly to this discussion." Pete walked over to a flip chart in the corner of his office and wrote in bold letters…

YOU WILL ONLY BE REMEMBERED FOR TWO THINGS IN LIFE…

• THE PROBLEMS YOU SOLVED

• THE PROBLEMS YOU CREATED

Remaining at the flip chart Pete said, "Jack, you've defined the circumstances of our organization as problems, so what are you going to do about them? Will you focus on solving them or will you focus on avoiding them? It's your decision."

Pete flipped the page and wrote…

MAJOR PROBLEMS ARE CREATED AS A RESULT OF ATTEMPTING TO AVOID MINOR ONES…

Again Pete spoke, "Right now your problems are minor. You still have your position. You have simply been issued a warning, a wake-up call. You are held in good esteem within this company and you have tremendous potential. However, if you wring your hands, focus on the problems and not the solutions, you will be attempting to avoid the minor problems and major ones will result. This is not a theory Jack, this is a law, an absolute."

Turning the page, Pete wrote…

MOST PEOPLE, WHEN CONFRONTED WITH A CHALLENGE, FOCUS ON CHANGING THEIR CIRCUMSTANCES INSTEAD

OF CAPITALIZING ON THE REAL OPPORTUNITY,
CHANGING THEMSELVES...

"Jack," Pete spoke in a compassionate almost fatherly tone, "you have great potential, everyone in the organization recognizes that. However, I've got to tell you I'm concerned that you are going to squander it. Lately you've become lackadaisical, skeptical, and negative. Nothing is as constant as change Jack. Times aren't changing, they've changed. You can either use these changes as a catalyst for growth or an excuse for mediocrity, it's your choice."

Allowing his message to sink in, Pete remained silent waiting for Jack to respond. The seconds ticked by as Jack sat in deep thought. Finally he spoke. "I think I hear you Pete. I could argue but what good would it do? It just seems that the company has changed so drastically. I'll be glad when things settle down, you know get back to normal."

"This is normal," Pete quickly inserted.

"Yeah I guess that's true. So Pete, where do we go from here?"

Pete took a chair across from Jack, "That's up to you Jack. I'm going to do you a big favor and put this monkey squarely on your back. See, one person cannot take responsibility for another. That's like trying to teach a pig to sing. It angers the pig and frustrates the voice teacher. I'll be glad to point out the specifics of your behavior and give you some ideas of how to improve. Additionally, I can recommend some reading material. If anything is going on in your personal life I can point you in the direction of a good counselor. I'll help in any way I can; however, in the final analysis it's your job, your responsibility. As I mentioned Jack, you have great potential and to whom much is given, much is expected. I'm holding you accountable for making it happen."

Again Pete paused to capitalize on the silence. When he resumed speaking he could tell he had Jack's full attention. "Jack I have another meeting in five minutes but let me make one final comment. I've sat in the same chair you're sitting in. Less than two years ago I was on the bubble, not at work but at home. I won't bore you with the details, but suffice it to say that I was delivered a stern warning. At first it angered me. I put the majority of the blame outside of myself, like a whining child I kept saying, "this isn't fair, it's not my fault, they just don't understand". I was all set to pack my bags and head for greener pastures. Nobody was going to tell me what to do.

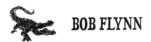

"In the midst of my funk and anger a friend recommended a personal effectiveness program. I saw it as something that might help me on the job, you know, advance my career, so I decided to sign up. Ironically they turned me down, said I wasn't ready yet. I persevered and when I was able to satisfy their requirements I was admitted. Sounds crazy, audacious really, but that's the way they operate. I now understand how they can claim that 100% of their graduates experience significant growth in their personal and professional lives, but I digress."

Jack sat in stony silence thinking how much guts it took for Pete to share such a private story. Pete's stock went up exponentially in Jack's mind.

Pete continued, "Now Jack, I want your plan on my desk by the 17th of next month. I want to know where you're going and how you're going to get there. Most importantly, I want to know what specific behavioral changes you are going to make. I'll be glad to consult with you any time I can, but remember Jack, this is your baby, your baby."

Realizing that Pete was dead serious and that the meeting had concluded Jack stood up, extended his hand and thanked Pete for his candor and concern. As he approached the door he turned and said, "Oh by the way Pete, what was the name of the program you mentioned, the one that helped you so much?"

"*The 12 Absolutes of Personal Effectiveness*", Pete answered.

Shocked, Jack stammered, "Do you recommend that I take it?"

"No," answered Pete immediately.

Surprised, Jack asked, "Why not?"

"You're not ready," replied Pete as he shut his office door.

AIN'T NO SUCH THANG AS
A PURDY GOOD ALLIGATOR RASSLER

The Answer

Not ready, not ready, not ready. Those words kept turning over in Jack's mind. Not ready for what? How do these people know I'm not ready? I might just quit this chicken outfit. I wonder if they're ready for that! I've done a lot for these people and now they want to send me down the road. It's not my fault. I can't help the economic situation; I didn't get a vote on whether we downsize or buy another company. It's not fair and it's not my fault; I've busted my butt, and look what it has gotten me!

Startled back into the moment by the ringing of his office phone, Jack collected himself.

"Hello, this is Jack Williams, how may I help you?

"Jack, glad I caught you. This is Marty Collier I just wanted to remind you that we have baseball practice this afternoon starting at 6:00 at Sims field. It's important that you make it because I've been called out of town unexpectedly. As a matter of fact, I'm home packing right now."

Oh great, Jack thought. *I'm in no mood to deal with a bunch of fourteen-year-olds. I never should have volunteered to help Marty coach fall baseball in the first place.*

"Okay, Marty, I'll be there."

"Thanks," Marty responded, sounding relieved. "Oh, and Jack, spend some time with Barney Corbin, will you? This kid has tremendous potential but I'm not sure if he's ready to realize it."

Marty's closing comment resonated in Jack's head. "This kid has tremendous potential, but I'm not sure he's ready to realize it." Is that what I'm not ready for, the realization of my potential? Man, I hope not. Jack shivered at the thought. Just then an idea flashed into his mind. I'm going to find out what I'm not ready for, he thought as turned on his computer. Okay, let's see what happens if I log on to www.12absolutes.com. Well, I'll be darned, Jack thought as he read the caption on his computer screen. Maybe I'll get some answers now.

 **BOB FLYNN**

Are You Ready To Make the Master Decision?

Most people never make it, the master decision that is, and as a result lead lives far below their God given potential. Decisions determine destinations, there's something empowering, almost magical about the words *"I have decided."* Not you have decided or they have decided but *"I have decided."* Until you can honestly and decisively without equivocation say *"I have decided"* you are forever caught in the web of mediocrity, that gray twilight where the icy fingers of **"IF ONLY I'D HAVE"** encircle your potential and limit your future. But what's on the other side of *I have decided?* What is the master decision? It's a decision the masses never make and so they forever march in the ranks of the average. They become the also-rans; never stretching, pushing or challenging. They remain bound by the confines of their self-imposed comfort zones, never daring to break free of self-imposed limitations. Ultimately, realizing that it is in seeking comfort and security that causes both to flee, the pursuer realizes that neither comfort nor security can be captured like a butterfly in a net for both must be attracted, not pursued. The attraction: the acceptance of complete personal responsibility for who you are and everything you will become. The acceptance without reservation that you are where you are and what you are because of yourself, your sowing and reaping to this point. You see when you think the problem is other than yourself that thought becomes the problem. If you want things to change then you must change first. You must come to the realization that the seeds you sow today are the only influence you will have on your future. Understand that you are programmed from infancy to believe that someone or something else is responsible for your accomplishments in life. This natural situation becomes a chronic, self-defeating problem when people come into adulthood with the unconscious expectation that somewhere, somehow someone is still responsible for them and their place in society.

The Master Decision?
You'll be ready when you make it.

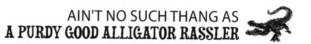

Huh, Jack thought. The message ended abruptly. There were no other screens, no more information, no phone numbers, addresses, nothing. And then the screen went blank. Jack was beside himself.

"Ready when I make it!" Jack was talking to his computer. "Wait a minute, how can I make the master decision when I don't even know what it is?" This is crazy, Jack thought. I'm tired of this mysterious crap!

In the midst of his tirade, Jack's phone rang.

Settling himself as much as possible, Jack feigned calmness and professionalism.

"Hello, this is Jack Williams. How may I help you?"

"Mr. Williams?" Jack didn't recognize the voice.

"Yes, this is Jack Williams."

"Mr. Williams, this is Steve Corbin, Barney's dad. We met briefly after last week's game."

"Sure, Steve, I remember."

Corbin continued, "I tried to reach Marty, but I understand he's out of town."

"That's right."

"I guess he told you I was less than happy when he pulled Barney off the pitcher's mound in the third inning. You saw what happened. It didn't make any sense. Barney didn't give up a run; there were two outs and a weak hitter at the plate. I know he threw his glove down and cussed when that last hitter doubled, but I don't blame him. That clown you've got playing right field should have held him to a single. I'm just calling to tell you guys that if you pull another stunt like that, Barney's going to find another team."

Jack couldn't believe his ears. He was in no frame of mind to be dealing with the likes of Steve Corbin. Quickly settling down, he responded, "Well, Steve, I'm sorry you feel that way. Barney's a good kid with a lot of potential, but we can't tolerate angry outbursts and language like he used."

Corbin was really hot now. "Are you threatening to kick my son off your silly little team?"

Keeping his cool Jack answered, "Steve, I'm not threatening to do anything. As I said, Barney is a good kid and potentially one of the best players in the

 **BOB FLYNN**

league; however, when he breaks the team rules, he's going to get the same treatment as anyone else."

His voice calmer now, Corbin asked, "What do you mean potentially one of the best players in the league?"

Whew, Jack sighed to himself, *I'm glad this thing didn't get out of control.* "Here's what I mean. Steve, Barney's got all the tools. He can run, hit and throw. He knows and loves the game, but he hasn't made the master decision."

"The master decision? What's the master decision?" Corbin asked sarcastically.

Jack hesitated. He had to think of something fast. "Steve, the master decision is when a person decides to take total responsibility and become fully accountable for all aspects of their life, no matter what's going on around them. I'm talking about their work ethic, career growth, behavior, physical fitness, health, relationships, attitudinal quality, education, growth, spirituality, everything. In Barney's case, it applies to whether or not he chooses to conform to team rules. It's his decision; the ball is in his court. You see, Steve, until he's ready to make the master decision, nothing is going to change no matter how many rules we give him."

In a disgusted tone, Steve Corbin grumbled something under his breath, said goodbye, and hung up. Jack, on the other hand was elated. *Bingo,* he thought, n*ow I've got my answer. I've had it all the time, now I know what the master decision is… And I can clearly see why Tom and Pete said that I'm not ready for* The 12 Absolutes of Personal Effectiveness *program. Until a person is ready, really ready, to take personal responsibility for his effectiveness no matter what the circumstances, there's no program that will benefit them; it would simply be a waste of time. Simple, so simple, he thought, so why doesn't everybody get it? Why doesn't everybody take full responsibility for his or her growth and effectiveness? Why don't I?*

Jack would have his answer soon, and he wouldn't like it….

Personal responsibility. This theme kept re-entering Jack's mind. Even though he tried to dismiss it, it kept coming back. A week passed, then two, and despite the nagging reoccurrence of the personal responsibility theme, Jack continued to avoid taking action relative to *The Twelve Absolutes* program. *Busy, I'm too busy,* Jack's mind raced on, *lots going on. I've read self-help books and it's all the same old stuff. I don't see how any program is really going to make a difference. It's all about who you know, not what you know. I mean, how can you take responsibility when everybody else is pulling the strings and pushing your buttons?* Then it happened….

The Admission

"Brian, that's great, man," Jack said after he heard the news. "I'm so happy for you and your family. Thanks for calling and letting me know. Sure—sure, buddy, we'll get together real soon."

Jack quickly pondered what he had just heard from his best friend from back home, Brian Thompson, who had just been promoted to an officer level position in his firm. While Jack was truly happy for him, he felt a twinge of jealousy course through his veins. *Shallow, shallow of me*, he thought, *not to be totally elated at Brian's news. I'm a better man than this; how can I feel jealous of Brian's good fortune?*

"Hello, this is Jack Williams."

"Jack." It was Hannah. "Isn't it super about Brian? Sally just called and told me that Brian had called to tell you the news. She was beaming with pride, and so am I. Brian's in the big leagues now and I know you are delighted for him."

"Yeah, yeah… I sure am," Jack responded in a subdued tone. "Hannah, I've got another call. I'll see you tonight."

"Sure. Is everything okay?"

"Yes—yes, of course, see you tonight. Hello, this is Jack Williams."

"Jack." He recognized his mom's voice immediately. "Sorry to call you at work, honey, but I just got off the phone with Betty Thompson. Did you get the news about Brian?"

"Yes, Mother, I did."

"Isn't it wonderful?"

"It sure is," Jack answered with limited enthusiasm.

"Well, I'll let you go. I just wanted to make sure you had received the great news. I've got so many people to call. This is big news for our little community, you know. Your father says hi; call soon. Oh, by the way, son, is everything okay? You sound a little down."

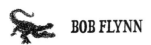

BOB FLYNN

"Yes, everything is just great."

Jack's slight feeling of jealousy had quickly escalated into irritation bordering on anger and self-pity. Even though he was quite disappointed in himself, he couldn't seem to shake his contempt for Brian's good fortune. In an attempt to break out of his downward emotional spiral, Jack decided to leave work and take a walk in his favorite park. Walking along, he continued his self-induced "pity party." *This is a fine state of affairs,* he thought. *Here's Brian hitting the big time with everybody singing his praises while I'm stuck and barely holding on to what I have. I just don't get it; Brian's no smarter than I am. In fact, I made better grades in school, was more popular, and got out of the blocks faster in my career. How is it now that he's left me in the dust?*

It was at that point that Jack made a very important decision.

He decided to go see his old pal Brian.

Jack said his goodbyes to Brian and his family, pulled out of the driveway, and headed out on his five-hour trip home. Jack could always get some good thinking done when he drove, and in this case, he certainly had a lot to think about.

Two days with his pal Brian and his family had proved very beneficial. He saw that not only had Brian enhanced his career situation, his relationship with his wife Sally and their three children had also greatly improved. Brian seemed to have a peace about him; he was assured and confident, yet in a humble, appreciative sort of way. No doubt Brian had grown, and no doubt Brian deserved all the good that had happened to him. As Jack thought about their conversations, he was glad that he had told Brian about his petty jealousy. It was hard, but that admission seemed to open Brian up to revealing some things about himself that Jack hadn't known.

"Jack," Brian had said, "I'm sure that if the situation were reversed, I would feel some jealousy and anger too. I think it's natural, since we have always been pretty competitive with each other. You asked me what prompted me to make the changes I've made. I don't know if I can confine it to a single event. It was more evolutionary than revolutionary. I can tell you this; it started with a feeling that seemed to dog me around for quite some time. It wasn't worry, really, more of a premonition, or a slight irritation like a child that won't stop pulling their parent's sleeve. I mean, really, things were going okay. I was doing pretty good on my job, and my marriage and relationship with the kids was fair to good. I knew guys my age that were in worse physical shape, and I took the family to Mass most Sundays. Like I said, things were okay. Finally, I realized that was the problem. Things were okay, average, but I was leading a boring, mediocre existence hoping at the least that things wouldn't get worse, and at the best that I'd run into a little good luck. I was stuck, man, as complacent as the Redskins in that Giants game last month. So, Jack, I can relate to your story-- been there, partner."

There were a few moments of silence. Then Jack said, "Brian, there had to be something that got you off the dime and on your way to realizing your potential."

"Come to think of it, there was one instance that seemed to be the catalyst for my first step toward changing things for the better. I was reading an article about how easy it is for anyone to be lulled into a dull, uneventful existence as a result of complacency combined with what the author termed entitlement mentality. I learned from that article that as human beings, once we get stuck in a rut, it's just a matter of time before we become status quo conditioned, and when that happens, it usually takes a significant event to get us up and moving toward our potential. An event like losing our jobs, going broke, a divorce, or loss of an important relationship, a stern warning, or even an accident or major illness--you know, something big, something physically or emotionally painful. Additionally, I learned that that's what it takes for the vast majority of us stubborn humans to seek our higher self—pain, man, with a capital P. The article also taught me that even with massive doses of pain, some people never get it; in fact, they allow the significant event to drive them deeper into their self-imposed limitations and their condition actually worsens. I'm telling you, it really got me thinking. I hate pain; I didn't want to wait until a serious problem replaced my nagging aggravation. I started moving toward the outer limits of my potential."

"Okay, that's what I came for. How did you start moving in the right direction?" Jack asked.

"I started pretty much the same way you are," Brian answered. "I asked some people whom I considered successful, people that were really enjoying their lives, people that were fully alive and vibrant. I found out that for every person who is approaching their highest potential, there's a different method of how they go about accomplishing it. For me, a book study club was most appealing."

"A book study club," Jack broke in. "What's that?"

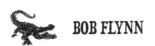

"Each month we read a powerful book that dealt with human potential. At the end of the month, we met for an entire day, usually a Saturday, to discuss how we would, not how we could, apply it to our lives and current circumstances. There were eight people in our group, and we got real close. We challenged each other to follow through on our commitments to take specific actions. I think it takes a strong support group to get us to do what we need to do to improve our conditions. I know it did for me. Anyway, the book study group was the primary catalyst for me. I'm still in it after all these years."

Jack looked slightly shocked, then asked, "Why didn't you tell me about this sooner?"

Brian smiled. "I did, but you told me you didn't have enough time and that you had already read several self-help books."

Jack hung his head slightly. "Guess I wasn't in enough pain, huh?"

Brian chuckled. "Could be, man, but I think you're about there now."

Attempting to get the focus off himself, Jack asked. "What are some of the books you read?"

"You really want to know?" Brian asked hesitantly.

"Yes, I certainly do," replied Jack with conviction.

"Here are the ones that I found most helpful:

- *The Seven Habits of Highly Effective People* by Stephen Covey
- *Man's Search for Meaning* by Victor Frankl
- *Living Above the Level* of Mediocrity by Charles Swindoll
- *The Sky's the Limit* by Wayne Dyer
- *Peak Performers* by Charles Garfield
- *Danger in the Comfort Zone* by Judith Barwick
- *Laws of Success* by Napoleon Hill
- *The Magic of Thinking Big* by David Swartz
- *The Secret of the Ages* by Robert Collier
- *The Man in the Mirror* by Patrick Morley

AIN'T NO SUCH THANG AS
A PURDY GOOD ALLIGATOR RASSLER

- *The Holy Bible"*

Jack looked skeptical. "You read all those?"

"Read and studied and applied, Jack," Brian responded with humility.

"Brian, I don't have time to read all those. I need to get going now," Jack pleaded.

"The book club approach is only one of many. There are some excellent courses out there that incorporate the principles of books like the ones I have cited," Brian said with an encouraging tone.

"Ever heard of a course called *The 12 Absolutes of Personal Effectiveness?"* Jack asked.

"No, but there are lots of great courses I've never heard of. Why do you ask?" Brian probed.

"It's one I'm considering, but it's weird because you've got to qualify to attend. What do you think about that?" Jack inquired.

"I don't know, but on the surface, I like the sound of it. You see, reading books and taking courses is only one-third of the equation. To be effective, you have to apply what you learn, get feedback, and keep on modifying until you achieve maximum results. My guess is the reason these people require you to qualify is they realize the absolute importance of commitment. They don't want to waste your time, their time, and the time of the other participants. Check it out, though; there's also a bunch of junk out there."

Suddenly, as if snapping out of a trance, Jack realized that he had been driving for over three hours. As he had replayed the majority of his conversation with Brian, the time and miles had flown, somehow deep within he knew he had assembled enough information to make some key life changing decisions....

The question was . . . would he?

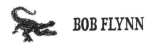 **BOB FLYNN**

NOTES

AIN'T NO SUCH THANG AS
A PURDY GOOD ALLIGATOR RASSLER

CHAPTER TWO

Ain't No Such Thang
AS A PURDY GOOD
Alligator Rassler

The Decision

*If you think education is
expensive,
try ignorance.*

DEREK BOK

AIN'T NO SUCH THANG AS
A PURDY GOOD ALLIGATOR RASSLER

The Decision

Arriving home, Jack was anxious to tell Hannah about his visit with Brian. "It was incredible Hannah. I'm telling you, the changes in Brian are nothing short of remarkable. He's got his priorities straight, he's totally focused and committed. Man, no wonder he's moving up so fast. He said it was the pain Hannah; the pain is what got him up and out of his comfort zone and on his way.

"You know what? I think I'm there, I've got me some big time pain, and I think I'm ready to do something about it. I think I'm ready to test the outer limits of my potential. Here's why: it's will do versus can do."

"Huh?" Hannah said with a puzzled look. Jack grabbed a piece of paper off the kitchen counter, took a felt tip pen out of the drawer and wrote in big black letters…

What you can do accomplishes nothing, it's only what you <u>Will Do</u> that matters!

"If I learned one thing from my visit with Brian it's that the world only rewards action; in other words, what we *will* do. When we take specific actions that are targeted at specific goals, what's when the fun begins. That's when we begin to cut ourselves out of the pack and start moving toward the truly meaningful things in life. Hannah let me tell you what I will do: I *will* call Bill Hanks and sign up, I mean I'll see if I can qualify for *The 12 Absolutes of Personal Effectiveness* program."

Hannah was pleased with Jack's enthusiasm and resolve. She encouraged him to pursue the program, but her woman's intuition told her that her man Jack had a lot to learn. Boy, was she right!

"Bill Hanks."

"Bill, Jack Williams."

"Yes, Jack, how have you been?"

 **BOB FLYNN**

"Oh great Bill. Listen, I know you started *The 12 Absolutes* program several weeks ago, but I was wondering if there's another one I could look into."

"Sure Jack, there's one starting in ten days on the 14th. It's an introductory session, and if you like what you hear you can take it to the next step which is qualification."

"Yeah, Bill, I'm definitely interested. Who should I call?"

"I'll have Dan Hardee the facilitator call you."

"Thanks Bill, it's much appreciated."

"Glad to do it Jack. Good luck and stay in touch."

"Will do Bill, will do."

"I've got that *will do* thing going on," Jack thought.

The Session

"Goethe once wrote: 'Nature understands no jesting; she is always true, always serious, always severe; she is always right, and the errors and faults are always those of man. The man incapable of appreciating her, she despises, and only to the apt, the pure, and the true does she resign herself and reveal her secrets.'"

There was no hello, no glad you're here, no welcome to *The 12 Absolutes*, no warm up at all just a distinguished looking man at the front of the room, exuding confidence and sincerity. The man continued: "People performing below their potentials have a difficult time with Mr. Goethe's statement because they are so accustomed to looking for excuses outside of themselves. They look for excuses that will fix the blame for their under-performance on someone or something other than themselves. In so doing they fail to come face to face with the only person on this earth who can better their circumstances, the man or woman in the mirror."

"My name is Dan Hardee. I was formerly one of those "fix the blame outside myself" people. Caught in the vice like grip of complacency and conformity

AIN'T NO SUCH THANG AS
A PURDY GOOD ALLIGATOR RASSLER

and performing far below my potential, I sought answers, solutions and hope. Perhaps you can relate; perhaps that's why you gave up your hard-earned Saturday morning and came here today. I clearly remember my introductory session. Being intensely practical, I was seeking clear explanations and reasons— not theories— for how I could better my life and realize my God given potential. I found that and more. Perhaps you will too… but I doubt it. What I must tell you is that out of the twenty eight of you who are in attendance this morning, twelve will not attempt to qualify, eight will fail to qualify, and of the eight remaining, three will fail to complete the program. That leaves five. Those are the odds, and since we keep close tabs, those numbers are accurate. Frankly, I hope I'm wrong, but I know I'm not. You see, there will always be the haves and the have-nots, winners and losers, disciplined and undisciplined, the can do's and the will do's. High achievers will always be in the minority because…

The price of exceptional achievement must always be paid and it must always be paid in advance.

That's the law, and the vast majority doesn't adhere to it, and as a result, they never come near their potential. *The 12 Absolutes of Personal Effectiveness* is advanced price paying and only five of you in this room will pay it.

"Now, let me tell you about the program. A gentleman named Russell James developed *The 12 Absolutes of Personal Effectiveness*. Some people study law and some people study engineering. Some immerse themselves in sports and become authorities on football, baseball, basketball or hockey. Others invest many hours learning about cooking, history, stamps, computers or a thousand other subjects. Mr. James studied success and personal effectiveness. From a young age he had a passion to know why some people became more successful than others. He was mystified by the disparities of wealth, happiness and influence. Perhaps his passion stemmed from the fact that in his youth he was poor and had somewhat of a behavioral problem. Who knows? The fact remains that Mr. James amassed the most comprehensive success and personal effectiveness base of knowledge on planet Earth. *The 12 Absolutes of Personal Effectiveness* is the very best that has ever been discovered about individual achievement. The program is free of jargon or complexity. All the student has to do is learn and apply.

"*The 12 Absolutes* are grounded in nature's laws, not concepts or principles, but laws. When learned and applied, these laws unlock your innate powers and drive you to your rightful place on the ladder of success. *The 12 Absolutes of*

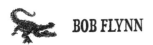

Personal Effectiveness operates from the fact that everything you are or will ever be is up to you. Your decisions and your actions up to this point in your life are totally responsible for where you are today in all aspects of your life. Similarly, your future decisions and actions will determine your happiness, well-being and ultimate peace of mind. In short, the program is all about making better decisions and acting on them.

"Your current level of knowledge and action binds you. This is because of two laws. Simply stated, these laws are… (Once again, Dan wrote in large letters on the flip chart)…

> *You are locked in place by your current level of action and skill… Your future depends on what you learn and apply from this moment forward.*

What you learn and apply will cause you to begin allowing yourself to take complete control of circumstances and your future. How can I be so sure? Mr. James proved that whenever a person's life is going well, it means that their thoughts and activities are aligned with one or more of the *12 Absolutes*. In contrast, whenever you and I are experiencing difficulties of any kind, it is invariably because we are to some degree in violation of these invisible mental laws.

"I know this program and these 12 laws work for two major reasons. First, I've tested and proven them to myself by personal application. Second, our organization has taught them to thousands of people from all walks of life, and they have worked for every single person who seriously applied them. Application is the key, *will do* versus *can do*. Learning is one thing, applying is another. It's not only what we know, but also what we do with what we know that really counts."

Dan walked briskly to the flip chart and wrote…

> *The* **12 Absolutes** *are nature's laws and nature is neutral. She is no respecter of persons, not you, not me. She plays no favorites. She gives you back what you put in, no more and no less.*

"We strongly believe in the small group concept. This means that you will be with the same group of five to eight persons throughout the twenty-week program. You have two options relative to meetings: Tuesday and Wednesday from 6:00 PM until 9:00 PM or Saturday from 9:00 AM until 6:00 PM. Once you choose an option you must stay with it so you won't disturb the dynamics of your group. Each session will feature one or more of the *12 Absolutes*. There will be lecture, discussion and exercises. Yes, there will be homework between sessions. The program is intense and the expectations are high. Remember, nature gives back what you put in, no more and no less. Ignoring that law won't change it or make it go away. Should you need assistance during the week, either another associate or myself will be available to work with you.

"A question most people have is how does the qualification process work? Let me explain. Basically, there are two steps. First, you will complete a comprehensive personal assessment called *The Blueprint for Personal Effectiveness*, the BPE we call it. This assessment will cause you to explore the specifics of what you want to accomplish in the key components of your life. This is critical to your success in the program because... (Again Dan wrote on the flip chart)...

To become exceptional, you must have a clear vision of your ideal self.

"As you learn the *12 Absolutes* you'll need specific areas in which to apply them. The clearer the vision you have of your ideal self, the more clearly you will see how, when and where to apply the laws. By completing the BPE you will take a huge step toward that end. Be forewarned, participants tell us they typically invest a minimum of 10 hours to complete this process. After you submit the completed BPE, our staff will review it to determine if you qualify for this final step. If you do, another staff member and myself will interview you for one hour to determine if the program is a good "fit" for you. During this interview we will answer all your questions concerning the program. Should we mutually concur that the *12 Absolutes* program is right for you at this point in your life, we will then assign you to your group and get started."

Dan concluded by saying, "Thank you for attending this briefing. Should you have additional questions I'll be glad to meet with you. On the table in the back of the room you'll find packets with additional program information and the *Blueprint for Personal Effectiveness* assessment. These must be submitted by next Friday the 21st. Thanks again for attending. Perhaps you are one of the few who will pay the

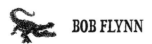

price in advance, and if so, we will meet again and it will be good. Whatever your decision, may God richly bless each one of you." Dan Hardee quickly packed up his briefcase and left the building.

The Struggle

Jack walked over to the table, picked up his packet and headed home. During the ride to the house he replayed the meeting in his mind. A common theme kept recurring in his thoughts. "These people are very serious, they mean business, this program isn't anything to half commit to. It's either get in completely or stay out, a game for the men and the big boys," as he had been so aptly told.

Arriving home Jack found the house empty. He had forgotten that Hannah and the children would be out until around 5:00. "Great," he thought, "this will give me time to knock out that BPE." As he was opening the packet, Jack noticed a quote on the envelope:

> *I know of no more encouraging fact than the unquestionable ability of man to elevate his life by conscious endeavor.*
>
> HENRY DAVID THOREAU

"Yeah, that is encouraging," he thought.

When Jack opened the envelope, his delight turned to shock. He almost dropped his glass of milk as he read the first assignment.

Write Your Epitaph

Vividly envision your wake, he was instructed. Friends, family, co-workers and acquaintances are gathered. What do you truly want the important people in your life to honestly say about you? In other words describe your ideal self. Identify each person. Include *precisely* what you want each of your immediate family members, business associates, close friends and anyone of importance in your life to say about you, your life and your relationship with them. What character traits would you like them to have seen in you? What contributions, what achievements would you want them to remember? Look carefully at the people around you. What difference would you like to have made in their lives?

"Hold it right there," Jack thought. "I don't want to think about dying and my funeral. That's morbid. Where do these people come up with this stuff?" Jack laid the paper down, walked into the kitchen and began preparing a sandwich. Trying to eat, his thoughts kept returning to the BPE document and a comment Dan Hardee made earlier that day:

> *The price of exceptional achievement must always be paid and it must always be paid in advance.*

"If this is really a law, I guess that BPE is a part of advance price paying." Jack threw the half-eaten sandwich in the trash and returned to the document.

The second major heading was:

BEHAVIORAL SELF- ASSESSMENT

Your epitaph should provide you with a graphic representation of your ideal self. Review your epitaph and identify specific actions and behaviors you will need to add, change or enhance to meet the criteria of your ideal self.

PERSONAL MISSION STATEMENT

Write your personal mission statement. The most effective method of accomplishing this is to break your mission statement into the major categories of your life, such as: spiritual, family, career and health, and then define the goals you want to achieve in each. Keep in mind that an effective goal focuses predominantly on the results you want to produce, not the activities leading to the results.

The Explanation

After reading the assignment, Jack paced the floor. He did battle with himself as he wrestled with whether or not he would actually begin work on the assignment. One minute it seemed silly to him, the next quite profound. Somewhere deep within, he realized that this was important stuff, stuff that most people never force themselves to do. An hour passed and then another, and Jack felt no closer to starting than he did when he first opened the envelope.

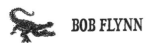 **BOB FLYNN**

Finally, he decided to call Dan Hardee.

"Dan, this is Jack Williams, I was at the session this morning."

"Yes, Jack. Bill Hanks referred you, is that correct?"

"Yes Dan, that's right. Say Dan, I have a question about the first assignment."

"The BPE?"

"Yes, the BPE."

"I'm not surprised Jack. You're the third person who's called."

"Dan, what's the purpose of this thing? I mean why the funeral and all that? And this personal mission statement? Isn't that for companies? I just don't get the reasoning behind it."

Dan was silent for several seconds and then he began to reply to Jack's concerns. "Jack, a basic tenet of the *12 Absolutes* program is to gain a clear understanding of your current reality and how you would like to enhance it. Most people when they set out to make changes, to improve their circumstances, have only a general idea of what they want to better about their lives. They know they want "things" to improve, but they haven't clearly defined the term "things". Through research and years of experience, our organization has discovered that the best way to clearly define the aspects of a person's life that need improving is through the completion of the BPE. Starting with the end of your life and working backwards defines a frame of reference relative to decisions and behaviors that will produce the life consistent with your ideal self. This occurs by having you identify specific behaviors that produce the outcomes you desire and comparing them with your current behaviors. By taking this approach, you will see the contrast between your current reality and your desired reality. This "gap of difference" is your challenge, your opportunity to ascend from where you are to where you want to go. The chasm may be wide or it may be narrow. Whatever the case, this process lets you see from here to there."

Dan continued, "Should you decide to complete the BPE, and you work on it diligently, you will clearly define what success is to you. It will no longer be something nebulous such as happiness, wealth, wisdom or security. This is something only 5% of the population will ever do. It would probably come as

AIN'T NO SUCH THANG AS
A PURDY GOOD ALLIGATOR RASSLER

no surprise to you that this 5% rise into the top 20% of the areas they consider essential to their well being. Ignoring a fact won't make it go away, and the fact is that you must first create something in your mind before you can make it your reality. The old saying is true, Jack:

What the mind of man conceives and believes, he achieves.

This is very important because if we do not take full responsibility for our own lives, we empower circumstances and give other people full reign over our future. You're either making your own dreams come true or you are making someone else successful. Happy, self-assured people, people with peace of mind, do what they should do, when they should do it, whether they want to do it or not, whether they feel like it or not, whether it's popular or not and they do it every time. People performing below their potential wait for the feeling, until they're in the mood, when the timing is right, when circumstances favor them, when they are being congratulated and encouraged, when success is assured. Said another way, Jack, successful people pay the price in advance.

"I hope I've answered your question Jack."

"You have Dan, thanks."

"Oh, one other thing Jack."

"Yes Dan, what is it?"

"Better go have a long talk with yourself."

"About what Dan?"

"Commitment Jack. For you to be accepted into the *12 Absolutes* program I must be totally convinced that you are truly committed to a "no holds barred" look at yourself. The BPE starts the process Jack, but without a clear picture of where you are and where you want to go, it's extremely difficult to pinpoint the necessary changes and behaviors required to take you there. I'll be taking a hard look at your BPE to determine the amount of thought and effort you put into completing it."

"Thanks for the trip out behind the woodshed Dan. I guess I needed it."

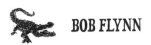 **BOB FLYNN**

"Don't be so hard on yourself. Almost everyone goes through the commitment cycle before they decide one way or another. I know I did."

"Thanks again Dan."

"My pleasure Jack. I hope we get the opportunity to work together."

Jack walked into the family room and sat down, gazing out the window as his thoughts began to solidify. "I'm still not committed. If it's not easy and if it doesn't happen fast, I bail out. Let's face it, I'm scared to death to take a real look at myself. I'm intimidated by this BPE because it's a lot of emotional work."

Jack's internal battle lasted the rest of the day. He thought about Hannah and the kids and his conversations with Pete and Brian, but most of all he thought about his hopes and dreams. Finally, the hard fought battle was over. Somehow, he sensed the timing was right. It was at that moment that he truly committed to ending his complacency and began realizing his God given potential. In the early evening he picked up the BPE and started working in earnest.

"Congratulations Jack, you have been accepted into *The 12 Absolutes of Personal Effectiveness* program." Jack smiled as he soaked in Dan Hardee's words." We'll be starting your program on Saturday the 14th. I'll email you all the particulars. If you have any questions give me a call, otherwise I'll see you bright and early on the 14th."

"Thanks Dan, I'm sincerely looking forward to it."

"Me too, Jack. See you soon."

"Hannah, I've been accepted to the program, we start on the 14th."

Hannah smiled and said, "Jack, that's wonderful. You worked so hard you put so much into it that I'm delighted that it worked out."

"I'm telling you Hannah, it's one of the toughest things I've ever done. Do you know that I put over fifteen hours into the BPE? But I'll tell you this: it was well worth the effort. It gave me the clearest look I've ever had at the person I truly want to be. Beyond that, it showed me the behaviors I need to stop and the behaviors I need to start to become my ideal self. And man, that interview was something else! Dan and a fellow named Al Sampson kept me on my toes, especially as it pertained to my commitment. They emphasized the easiest parts of the race are the beginning and the end. They emphasized that the most difficult is the middle where the energy and enthusiasm has worn off and you know you've got a long way to go to reach the finish line.

"Anyway, I'm glad it's over and I got accepted. I'm as ready for this as I have been for anything." About the time Jack uttered these words a resounding voice went off in his head….

"You'd better be ready Jack!"

Jack had no way of knowing this admonishment was a gross understatement.

ABSOLUTE #1

Jack looked around the room at the seven other students. He wondered what their stories were, how they got here and why. Before he could continue his thought, Dan Hardee began speaking. "Welcome to your first session of *The 12 Absolutes of Personal Effectiveness.* Before we meet each other I want to give you the title of our first Absolute…

NOTES

AIN'T NO SUCH THANG AS
A PURDY GOOD ALLIGATOR RASSLER

CHAPTER THREE

Ain't No Such Thang AS A PURDY GOOD Alligator Rassler

The Beginning

ABSOLUTE #1

Pre-Determine Your Focus

Man is made or unmade by himself; in the armory of thoughts he forges the weapons by which he destroys himself; he also fashions the tools with which he builds for himself heavenly mansions of joy and strength and peace.

JAMES ALLEN

The Beginning

Jack looked around the room at the seven other students sitting in a circle; he wondered what they were thinking, what their stories were, how they got here and why. Before he could continue his thought, Dan Hardee began speaking.

"Welcome to the first session of *The 12 Absolutes of Personal Effectiveness.* Before we get acquainted, I want to give you the title of our first Absolute. It is:

Pre-Determine the Focus

"In this first segment, you are going to discover that you are where you are today in all aspects of your life because of what you focused on yesterday. In summary, where you are and what you'll become tomorrow is totally dependent on what you focus on today. We'll invest all of today on this topic and I'll give you a related assignment for next week's session. After we meet each other and discuss how our group will interact, we'll get right into the components of this critical first Absolute.

"Now, let's discuss the small group concept and why we feel it is so important to your progress and success in this program. Effective small groups function in three basic dimensions. First, we learn from one another. Each one of you will be asked to discuss how you are working with the Absolutes, what's working and what's not. This will provide the group with several perspectives of how to best initiate the concepts and what traps to avoid. Second, we will support each other. As I explained in our one-on-ones, don't expect this program to be easy. You're going to identify and face up to many of your deep-seated fears and examine your limiting beliefs. Support from your group will help you push on in difficult times. Third, we will challenge each other. You also learned in our one-on-ones that excuses for inaction simply won't cut it. If you are not taking the actions we recommend, then you can't expect anything to change.

"One of our key responsibilities will be to risk confrontation and to challenge each other to take the actions required for improvement. You guys have all been indoctrinated to 'can do versus will do.' Challenging one another is part of the 'will do' phase, and as a group we're going to continually challenge

 **BOB FLYNN**

our individual comfort zones. This means that as our trust for each other builds, we will increasingly hold group members accountable for taking the sustained action necessary to maximize our personal effectiveness."

"Now, let's begin to get to know each other." Dan looked at the well-groomed middle-aged man to his immediate left and said, "Tony, why don't you lead off?"

The Group

What a feeling, thought Jack. Was it elation or exhaustion, confusion or clarity, satisfaction or longing? It was all of these things, Jack decided on his drive home after his first *12 Absolutes* session. One thing for sure, it had been a memorable, exciting, and very challenging day. There was a lot to sort out and ponder. There were major decisions to be made. I can't believe I sat in a classroom for six hours on a beautiful Saturday and was not bored for a second, Jack thought as he turned the car into his driveway.

"Hi honey," Hannah said in her usual upbeat, cheerful manner. "How'd it go today?"

Jack paused before responding, then answered with a serious tone in his voice, "I can't tell you, Hannah."

"You can't tell me? Why not?"

"I have to prepare my lesson first."

"Jack, what's going on?"

"Okay, here's the deal. As part of my assignment for next week's session I've agreed to condense what we covered today and then teach it to someone important in my life. Since you're the mother of my children, you qualify. Oh, and I've got to work hard on this because one of us will be selected to present an overview of today's Absolute to the group at our session next week."

"Okay, when does this lesson take place?"

"Next week's a killer at work, so it's got to be tomorrow evening. Let's have an early dinner start the lesson at 6 and end it at 8. How does that sound?"

"You're on, professor! But there is one stipulation."

"What's that?"

"You've got to tell me about the others in your group."

"Okay, we'll start at 5:30, I'll give you a thirty-minute overview of the group, and then we'll get into the first Absolute--fair enough?"

"Fair enough."

After a good night's sleep and church on Sunday, Jack began preparing his lesson. He had taken copious notes in his workbook, so he used them to organize his thoughts. Dan had emphasized the importance of teaching what we learn as soon after we learn it as possible. This seemed a little strange, since Jack didn't feel qualified to teach this newly learned material. Dan was insistent, however, that this was a powerful learning method, so Jack was determined to give it his best. As he worked through the material, it became obvious to Jack just how powerful yesterday's session had been. He hoped he could do it justice when he recapped it to Hannah.

"Well, Jack, I'm ready to hear all about yesterday's session and the people in your group," Hannah said with a truly interested tone in her voice.

"Okay, great. Let's start with the people." Jack seemed anxious to get going. "There are seven participants, and I gotta tell you, it's quite a diverse group. Tony is a fifty-something business executive and his primary motivation for taking the course is to determine his next step in life."

Hannah interrupted. "Jack, before you get right into the reasons the people are taking the course, give me the personal stuff, you know, the family info. Are they married, any kids? I mean, you did bring out that sort of thing, didn't you?"

"Oh yeah, sure. You know me. I want to get right into the facts, the heart of the matter."

"Yes, I know. Now Tony, does he have a family?"

"Okay, I've got it. Yes, Tony has been married for twenty-seven years. He has two grown daughters. One is married, and I think he said the other is fresh out of college. Is that enough personal background?"

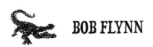

BOB FLYNN

Hannah grinned and said, "Yes, for now."

"Now, as I was saying, Tony stated that his primary purpose for taking the course was to determine what to do next in life. You know, he really didn't seem to be the kind of person who would need the *12 Absolutes* course."

"Why do you say that?"

"He seems to be all together, to me. Great job, financially secure, you know, the successful go-getter type. Anyway, he said it's time to reinvent himself and alter or perhaps change direction, and that's what he's expecting the *12 Absolutes* to help him with.

"Now, Joanne's different--talk about a contrast. She's a single mom, I'd guess early thirties, two kids, I'm not sure of their ages, but I think she said eight and ten. She wants to increase her income, that's her primary motivation for taking the course. She claims her ex is neglectful in sending the child support, practically makes her beg for it. She's hoping the *12 Absolutes* will help her become independent of him. She seemed really determined to stand on her own two feet. I can tell she's having a pretty tough time of it, and man, is she bitter. I think she hates this guy. How am I doing?"

"You're doing great. Please continue."

"Well, now there's Clyde, and he's a piece of work. Clyde's a southern guy, mid-fifties I'd guess. I think he said he was from South Carolina. Anyway, he's got this southern drawl and he is funny. He was kind of vague about his background, but I think he's been married a few times. He said there's a new bumper sticker out in his hometown that says, HONK IF YOU'VE BEEN MARRIED TO CLYDE! Clyde says he's ready to settle down, make something of himself, commit, quit being so sorry and be more like Tony, as he put it.

"William is a college professor, early forties Afro-American guy who is recently divorced, with two kids that he gets every other weekend. He says he's through the trauma of his divorce and wants to get on with his life. His goal in taking the *12 Absolutes* program is to find clear direction. He's kind of quiet and dignified. He didn't have too much more to say.

"James is a mid-forties guy and he had plenty to say. What a talker! Dan had to intervene several times to keep him on track. James has just been downsized and boy, is he angry! His reason for taking the course is to secure a better position than the one he had. He also said that he needed to improve things

AIN'T NO SUCH THANG AS
A PURDY GOOD ALLIGATOR RASSLER

on the home front. I think Dan was afraid to get him going again so he didn't probe further.

"Then there's Mary. She's probably in her mid-twenties, married about three years, no children, she's quiet like William. She claimed that her primary goal in taking the course was to advance her career. Now that could very well be true, but somehow I don't think that's her real motivation."

"Why do you say that?"

"Well, Mary seems hung up on her husband's lack of ambition and her job situation; she says she's underemployed.

"Hank is a university student mid-way through his final year. His dad took the course and Hank said it made such a positive change in him that when his dad suggested that he take it, he agreed. His main reason for investing his Saturdays is to get focused on the important things in his life. He seems like a kid with his head on straight to me. He has a girlfriend, and they plan to get married after graduation."

"Thank you," Hannah replied approvingly.

"That's the group, and that's what I know about them so far."

"Jack?"

"Yes?"

"You forgot one."

"Hannah, you know why I'm taking the *12 Absolutes*."

"Remind me; I forgot." Hannah mused.

"Okay… I told the group that the primary reason I'm taking the course is complacency in all aspects of my life."

"Thank you."

"Well, I told you they were a diverse group. I'll bet they planned it that way."

"Probably so, Jack. I think these folks plan everything."

 **BOB FLYNN**

Absolute #1

PRE-DETERMINE THE FOCUS

You will become what you think about.

EARL NIGHTINGALE

"Now, let me tell you about the first Absolute," Jack continued. "It's called Pre-Determine Your Focus. Hannah, this is very powerful stuff. I learned that until people determine the most important aspects of their lives and concentrate the predominance of their focus on those key components, they make minimal, if any, positive progress. It's a proven fact that the vast majority of the population exercises little or no mind control over their focus. By taking this approach, they remain in a constant state of what Dan calls 'situational focus.' That means that whatever pops into their mind, or whatever situation they find themselves in, that's what they focus on. If the situation is too painful for them, they change their focus to something they consider more pleasant. In many cases, that something they consider pleasant leads to even greater misery. In today's society, there are so many diversions that seem appealing. These seductions can sap our focus and lead us into actions that worsen our condition. That brings me to:

FOCUS POINT #1

Until a person pre-determines what they place their focus on, they dissipate their energy and spread their thoughts and actions over too many subjects and in too many conflicting directions. This leads to indecision, weakness, and mediocrity."

"I think I see the point, but I don't get how focus in and of itself changes anything."

"Good observation. The fact of the matter is, it doesn't."

"So, what's so potent about this focus stuff?"

Reading from his notes, Jack continued.

"Focus, correct or incorrect, is the catalyst for our attitudes, behaviors, and actions. In other words, Hannah, focus is like a powerful magnet it draws us toward it."

"That's a little clearer, but can you give me an example?"

"Well, let's see. Okay, I'll take something simple, something that occurred recently. Remember when I got the news that Brian got the big promotion?"

"Sure."

"Initially I was focused on how bad I felt, how jealous and angry I was because things were great for him but not going all that well for me. As long as that was my focus, I stayed stuck in my funk. I took no action, I just obsessed on 'poor me.' When I changed my focus from my self-imposed depression to what I could learn, I began to feel better immediately. By keeping my focus on what I could learn from Brian's good fortune, I got the idea to visit him and find out how he was able to advance so rapidly. Because I stayed with that focus, I made the trip, learned a lot, and ultimately got accepted to the *12 Absolutes* program, and now I'm here teaching the sucker. Man, this stuff is too cool!"

"See, it's just like it says right here in the workbook." Jack turned the *12 Absolutes* workbook toward Hannah so she could read the large bold letters…

What You Focus on Expands!

Good thoughts and actions can never produce bad results.

Bad thoughts and actions can never produce good results.

Jack waited a few seconds to allow the words to sink in, and then he continued. "From my perspective the common thread of the whole session really came to life in…

FOCUS POINT #2——————————————————————

Successful people focus their thoughts, energy and efforts on high-payoff items they can do something about. Marginally successful people squander their thoughts, energy, and efforts on things over which they have little or no influence or control.

"Dan told this great focus story, let me see if I can remember it… oh yeah, this guy said that he handled all the important things concerning his household. He concentrated on all the really important issues such as the economy, pollution, world hunger, crime, global warming, energy prices and interest rates. He said his wife, on the other hand, focused on the everyday things like paying the bills, getting the children off to school, grocery shopping, getting the family to the doctor, keeping the house clean and in good repair, and keeping everyone fed. Silly story maybe, but it made a clear point to me and that is we, I mean I, waste a lot of time concerning myself with low-payoff items that I can do little or nothing about."

"Well," Hannah interrupted, "don't we all worry about the broad issues of life? These things affect us. We can't just turn them off at will, can we?"

"That's a logical question, and it's basically the same one Joanne had. Here's how I recall Dan answered it. It's not about turning those kinds of concerns off. As a matter of fact, when you try *not* to think about something, to turn it off that is a sure way to bring it into focus.

"The key to eliminating thoughts about issues we can't control is to pre-determine what to focus on. If the topic of your pre-determined focus is compelling enough it will override the 'no control' issue.

"Hannah, it's incredible what it costs us to focus in low-payoff areas where we can have little or no effect. See, the sad part is that as long as we focus on things over which we have no control, we empower those very things to control us. This is critical to our effectiveness because…

"What we focus on saturates our entire subconscious mind and has tremendous influence over our behaviors and actions."

"Hold that thought," Hannah said. "I'm going to fix us a snack. This focus topic is interesting, and I want to hear more." Returning with Cokes and snacks, Hannah asked, "So, what's next?"

"We've learned that by not pre-determining what to focus on, we leave ourselves open to all sorts of thoughts that can impede our progress. Focus point #3 gets us pointed in the right direction…

FOCUS POINT #3

The person who refuses to change the very fabric of their focus will never be able to change their circumstance and will therefore make only minimal (if any) progress. Every significant personal breakthrough is first a break with focusing on trivial things.

"At this point in our session, Dan had us do a one-hour exercise. See, Hannah," Jack said as he turned in his *12 Absolutes* Workbook to Page 8, "we took fifteen minutes and identified all the important categories of our lives. It was a free-for-all, no scrutinizing, just think and write. Then we took another fifteen minutes and narrowed them down to a maximum of ten. Now, take a look at the next page," Jack said, turning to Page 9. "Here we identified the things we fret and worry about--you know, things that nag at us. We listed anything that was bothering us, anything that was trying to get our attention. This exercise really put me in touch with just how much of my time, energy, and emotions I waste focusing on areas that *I can't, or won't* do anything about."

Jack started to move on when Hannah spoke up. "Hold on, Jack, I want to take a closer look at both those lists."

"Okay, no problem."

Jack handed Hannah the workbook opened to Page 8. Her eyes surveyed the information, starting with the "Key Categories" list Jack had written…

- Relationship with wife
- Relationship with children
- Career
- Health / Fitness
- Finances
- Golf game
- Spirituality
- Continuing education

Turning to the next page, Hannah saw that under the heading "Things That Concern Me" Jack had written…

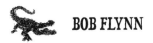

BOB FLYNN

- Job situation
- Future of the company
- Economy
- Terrorists
- Cost of living
- Private school for Tim
- Declining energy
- Relationship with my brother
- Dad's poor health
- New roof for house
- Recurring pain in stomach
- Disagreement with Paul
- Marsha's braces
- Linda's drinking problem
- Back up computer files
- The dangerous intersection at entrance to neighborhood

The Robber

Several minutes passed, and then Hannah said, "Jack. I think this exercise, as simple as it is, could have great benefit. I mean. there it is in black and white--your key life categories and the nagging items that can take your mind off them, get you out of focus, so to speak."

"Yeah, just getting this stuff down on paper has already helped me clarify my focus and identify what is hurting my progress. It especially helped me to learn about The Robber."

"The Robber?" Hannah asked in a confused tone.

"Look at the next page." Jack turned to Page 10. "See where I've taken some the items that concern me and put them under the column that Dan defines as… CLUTTER."

"Yes, what's that all about?" Hannah asked.

"Here's the definition Dan gave us for clutter…

"Clutter is any recurring concern that we can control, influence, or get help with but have chosen to avoid…

"We learned that there are two categories of clutter. Category One includes the things we have little or no control over. Category Two is things we can control or influence but are putting off. Take my list, for example--the economy, terrorists, cost of living, Dad's declining health, my sister Linda's drinking problem, even the future of the company. These are Category One issues. There's little or nothing I can do about any of these things. They're almost entirely out of my hands. Worrying or concerning myself about them has no effect except to take my focus off my key items."

Jack continued, "Now all the other items that are left, private school for Tim, my lack of energy lately, my lousy relationship with my sorry brother…."

"Jack!"

"I know, I know, don't be so judgmental… New roof for house, my stomach aches, the big blow out I had with Paul…."

"You didn't tell me about that, Jack."

"Ah, Hannah, it's a guy thing. Paul thinks he knows everything about everything, so when he shot his big mouth off, I had to straighten him out. Can we save that for another time?"

"Yes, yes by all means, but you and Paul have been friends for a long time, so I hope you do get it worked out."

"Okay now, where was I? Oh yeah, Marsha's braces; you know what the orthodontist said. My computer files, it bugs me every day that I haven't backed them up. And the intersection, there was another accident there last month. Hannah, all these items are Category Two issues. I can do something about them but have chosen not to. As a result, they keep recurring in my thought process and keeping my eye off the ball, cluttering up my mind, so to speak."

"So, other than making lists, how do we effectively deal with clutter?"

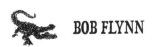 **BOB FLYNN**

"I'm getting there, if you'd just give me a chance!"

"Sorry, I'm just interested."

"Sorry I snapped at you. I'm still hung up on that Paul thing. He can be such a jerk!"

"Careful, Jack; you're letting it take your focus," Hannah said with a grin.

"No kidding," Jack replied. "See the negative power of this clutter stuff? It really is a robber. Anything hanging, anything unresolved interferes with our ability to focus on our key issues. Oh, and I almost forgot, unresolved relationship issues, especially when they're family-related, tend to be the most harmful. They need to be cleared up if possible, as soon as possible. I know, Hannah, I need to talk with Paul."

Jack continued, "Clutter is a 'robber'--it robs our focus often without us even realizing it. Remember the weekend that started me thinking about getting off my butt and changing some things?"

Not waiting for a response, Jack continued. "That nagging feeling I had was my clutter trying to get my attention. I tried to get rid of it by busying myself, losing myself in the football game, but thank goodness it didn't work that time. Finally, it got my attention. There's no telling how long this has been going on, no telling what it's cost me. Anyway, I'm convinced that If we do not have an effective strategy for identifying and dealing with clutter, it will jump on us like 'white on rice,' like a 'chicken on a June bug.' I learned that last phrase from Clyde."

"I wish you hadn't," Hannah quipped.

"So, we have a strategy for identifying clutter. We get alone in a quiet place, relax our minds, and start writing down the things that bubble up. We don't leave out a thing. It can be something as simple as cleaning out the garage. If that comes up, jot it down."

"Like the exercise you did in class."

"Exactly. But we might have to do it several times, because some of our clutter may have been suppressed so long that it will take a little coaxing. Denial is a powerful thing, and most of us are in some form of denial. That denial can sabotage our potential. Fear is also a potential killer. There's some stuff we may

AIN'T NO SUCH THANG AS
A PURDY GOOD ALLIGATOR RASSLER

not want to deal with because it scares us, but deal with it we must, if we are to maximize our potential."

"Jack, you really learned a lot!"

"I've got to tell you Hannah that I'm surprised at what I'm able to recall. I'm sure glad I listened and took good notes, but you know what?"

"What?"

"Teaching this stuff is a super way to really see what you retained, what you truly learned. When Dan insisted on it, I didn't see how it could really help, but now I do. I guess he was right when he said, 'It takes a minimum of fifteen exposures to anything new before it has any effect on our behavior.' Teaching the 12 Absolutes is just another method of getting us the exposure we need to take action.

"Okay. So, Hannah, we've got our strategy for identifying the clutter items in our lives; now here's our strategy for dealing with them. Remember the Category One items?"

"Yes, those are the things we have little or no control over."

"Right, and every second we spend worrying about those items is time, energy, and effort robbed from our key categories. Dan taught us a method called transference and attachment. Here's how it works… anytime a Category One clutter item pops into our mind, we transfer and attach that thought to a key category. An example would be anytime I catch myself thinking about the economy, I transfer and attach that thought to ways that I can improve my relationship with you. Or anytime I start worrying about the future of the company, I transfer and attach that thought to what I will do to get in better shape. In a relatively short period of time, this process will become automatic. And in about a month the Category One clutter item will practically cease its incessant nagging."

With a touch of apprehension in her voice, Hannah said, "Sounds to me like this transference and attachment method requires us to always be thinking about what we're thinking about. Isn't that a lot of work?"

"Initially that's true. It takes a little work, you know, concentration, but after a short while our subconscious mind takes over and does most of the work for us. Now, let's move on to the Category Two items; remember those?"

 **BOB FLYNN**

"Sure. Those are the items that we either have control or influence over."

"Perfect. Now here's how we get on top of those. We treat them like action items. Dan said it should be like making a contract with yourself. He advised us to write down the Category Two item, describe the action we would take, list the date by which the action would be taken, and leave a space to check when the item was completed. Here's mine. Take a look."

CATEGORY 2 ITEM	ACTION TO TAKE	START DATE	COMPLETED
Job Situation	Complete improvement plan. Meet with Pete to review	4/12	
Private school/braces	Meet with to discuss	3/20	
Stomach pain/energy level	Make Appt. Dr. Clark, checkup	3/12	
Relationship w/ brother	Arrange get together	5/23	
New roof	Call contractor/estimate	5/23	
Disagreement/Paul	Take to lunch/apologize	3/18	
Intersection	Arrange neighborhood meeting	6/4	

Hannah glanced admiringly at her husband and said, "Jack, I'm impressed. You've got all your Category Two clutter items covered. It won't be long before they'll be former clutter items."

Jack said, "Thanks Hannah, but no doubt there will be more to replace these. The process is dynamic, not static, but now I have a process to stay ahead of the 'clutter curve.'"

"Okay, we've got a proven process for keeping our focus on our key issue items, so what about the Key Issue areas?"

"What do you mean?" Jack asked.

"All we've done is written them down. Isn't there more to it than that? I mean, these are the major issues of our life; what are we going to do about them?"

"Funny; we had the same question at the end of the session."

"So how was it answered?"

"It wasn't."

"It wasn't?" Hannah asked turning both palms up.

"No, Dan just smiled and said we'll get into that next week. So, my guess is we'll get our answer next Saturday in Absolute #2."

"I'll be quite interested to learn more about what to do with our Key Issues."

"Yeah, me too."

"What else did you cover yesterday?"

"That's about it. I did take some more notes and there are some nuggets in the workbook. Want to go over them?"

"Sure," Hannah answered.

"All right, let's do it this way: I'll read out all the bold print items that we haven't previously covered, and you tell me what they mean to you, okay?"

"You're on."

"Cause and effect is just as much an absolute in the realm of thought and focus as it is in the world of visible and material things."

Hannah thought for a moment. "I'd say that means we're going to become what we keep our focus on. What we sow in our mind, we are going to reap in our circumstances."

"The outer conditions of your life are always in harmony with your focus."

"What we focus on is going to transfer itself into our life's conditions."

"As long as you believe you are a product of your circumstances you give them complete control. It's only when you take command of your focus that you become the master of yourself and your conditions."

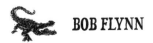 **BOB FLYNN**

"That one's a little harder. Let's see, if you keep the focus on a circumstance you remain in it. When you change your focus from your current reality to your desired reality, you begin moving toward it."

"When you apply yourself to focusing on the 'right things,' you make swift and marked progress."

"Progress and correct focus are joined at the hip."

"You will attract the predominance of your focus, that which you love, that which you hate, that which you fear."

"What we focus on becomes our reality, good or bad."

"Where you spend your time and your money is where your heart is."

"Your actions clearly reveal what you really care about."

"You are bound forever to the essence of your focus."

"Jack, it's what we've been discussing all evening. Focus is the catalyst for cause, and cause produces effect. We are tied directly to and responsible for the causes we produce. In other words, we are free to focus on anything we choose, but we are not free to choose the consequences of our focus. Consequences are governed by natural law."

"Hannah, you're so smart."

"Well, thanks honey," Hannah said, smiling. "This session sure has made me think. Oh, yes Jack, that reminds me, there's another book that came in your *12 Absolutes* packet. I saw it on your desk. What's that all about?"

"Thanks for reminding me; I almost forgot. The name of the book is *As a Man Thinketh*, written by a guy named James Allen. As part of our assignment for next week Dan asked us to read it. He said it would take about an hour. He also issued a warning."

"A warning?"

"Yeah, he said it could be life changing." Jack stretched. "Hannah, I've had enough, let's turn in."

AIN'T NO SUCH THANG AS
A PURDY GOOD ALLIGATOR RASSLER

"Let's do that. My head is still spinning."

Jack and Hannah chatted a little while longer, then went to bed. Shortly after they retired the phone rang. "Yes, he's right here. Jack, it's Pete."

"Pete?"

"Jack, sorry to call you on Sunday night, but something important has come up. I'm leaving town at 8 in the morning and I'd like to see you prior to leaving. Will 6 a.m. work?

"Yeah, okay, but can you give me a hint now?"

"Not really; it wouldn't be appropriate. We'll discuss it in the morning."

Absolute #1

PRE-DETERMINE THE FOCUS

Man is made or unmade by himself; in the armory of thoughts he forges the weapons by which he destroys himself; he also fashions the tools with which he builds for himself heavenly mansions of joy strength and peace.

JAMES ALLEN

KEY POINT

Personally effective people focus their thoughts, energy and efforts on high-payoff areas they can do something about. Mediocre people squander their thoughts, energy, and efforts on insignificant things over which they have little or no influence or control.

❏ Where you are today is due to what you focused on yesterday.

❏ Where you'll be tomorrow depends on what you focus on today.

❏ Dissipated / situational focus is a major source of wasted potential.

❏ Our focus is the catalyst for our attitudes, behaviors, and actions.

❏ Our natural inclination is to focus on trivial things.

❏ You must saturate your mind with self-determined, meaningful focus.

❏ The outer conditions of your life are always in harmony with your focus.

❏ When you take command of your focus you master your outer conditions.

❏ Focusing on the "right" things leads to swift and marked improvement.

❏ Where you spend your time and money is where your focus is, period!

❏ "Clutter" is a major focus robber.

AIN'T NO SUCH THANG AS
A PURDY GOOD ALLIGATOR RASSLER

MAJOR POINT ——————————————

The person who refuses to change the very fabric of his/her focus will never be able to improve his/her circumstances and will therefore make only minimal progress.

EVERY SIGNIFICANT PERSONAL BREAKTHROUGH IS FIRST A BREAK WITH FOCUSING ON TRIVIAL THINGS!

You are Bound FOREVER to The Essence of Your Focus.

ABSOLUTE #1

EXERCISE

(A) What are the top five priorities in my life? What is the goal of each?

1. _____
2. _____
3. _____
4. _____
5. _____

If I could select only one priority, which one would I select?

1. _____

Why? _____

(B) What are the top five items I spend my time and money on?

TIME	MONEY
1. _____	1. _____
2. _____	2. _____
3. _____	3. _____
4. _____	4. _____
5. _____	5. _____.

Where do my time and money investments "fit" with my top 5 priorities?

1. _____
2. _____
3. _____
4. _____
5. _____

AIN'T NO SUCH THANG AS
A PURDY GOOD ALLIGATOR RASSLER

Where don't my time and money investments "fit" with my top 5 priorities?

1. _____

2. _____

3. _____

4. _____

5. _____

What will I do about the time and money investments that don't fit?

When will I do it?

    1. Identify the item.

    2. State the actions you will take.

    3. State the date you will take the actions.

_____

_____

_____

_____

_____

(C) "Clutter" is any recurring concern that you can control, influence or get help with but have CHOSEN to avoid.

    1. Identify any areas of "clutter" in your life that you are not dealing with.

    2. State your plan for dealing with it.

    3. State the date you will take the actions.

_____

_____

_____

_____

_____

NOTES

AIN'T NO SUCH THANG AS
A PURDY GOOD ALLIGATOR RASSLER

CHAPTER FOUR

Ain't No Such Thang
AS A PURDY GOOD
Alligator Rassler

The Dilema

ABSOLUTE #2
Take Action

*Delay is the deadliest
form of denial.*

C. NORTTHCOTE PARKINSON

AIN'T NO SUCH THANG AS
A PURDY GOOD ALLIGATOR RASSLER

The Dilemma

What lousy timing, Jack thought as he sat in his office contemplating his recently concluded meeting with Pete. *This is a tough decision, lots of pros and cons. There's potential opportunity on one hand and significant risk and aggravation on the other. I'm happy for Pete. He certainly deserves the promotion to divisional vice president, and he's definitely the man for the job. My deal—well, that's another story altogether. I'm flattered and a little shocked that Pete wants me to assist him on a temporary basis, especially since I'm not performing all that well in my current capacity. I guess he really meant it when he said I had a lot of potential but no more money and three or four nights away from home each week for an unspecified length of time? As for my current job, I don't like the sound of "someone else" handling it until I return. And there's one other major consideration—the* 12 Absolutes *program. Man, that thing is demanding! Great, but demanding! I don't know how I can keep up. Dan isn't going to accept excuses. He expects total commitment. Have I got myself a dilemma going or what?*

Dilemma, dilemma, why is that word sticking in my brain? Jack scratched his head as he continued his contemplation. *Oh yeah, something we discussed last week in the program.* Jack dug into his briefcase and pulled out his *12 Absolutes* workbook. Thumbing through the pages, he came to a passage in dark bold letters:

> *Real growth opportunity rarely appears as a positive "bolt out of the blue" or a fortuitous occurrence... it is often disguised as a problem, an inconvenience, hard work, an aggravation or a dilemma....*

Ha! Jack thought. *This one meets all the criteria. It looks like I'm on my way to "real growth," either that or a nervous breakdown. I wonder if real growth is the way Hannah will see it?*

"Hi, Hannah, it's me. I just wanted to call and tell you everything went okay concerning my meeting with Pete. You were right, I didn't get fired or demoted or anything like that. Pete has presented me with a proposition that could be an opportunity, but frankly I'm a pretty skeptical. Anyway, I'll tell you all about it tonight. Got another meeting. See you then."

 **BOB FLYNN**

Arriving home that evening, Jack got right down to business. "So that's it, Hannah. That's what Pete wants me to do, and he wants my decision by week's end. What do you think?"

As predictably as the sunrise, Hannah did not respond with a direct opinion, but instead put the ball squarely in her husband's court. "Jack, I think you have assessed it right. Pros and cons, possible opportunity, possible risk, significant short-term aggravation. Here's a suggestion. Why don't you refer to your key categories list that you compiled at last week's *12 Absolutes* session?"

"Why should I do that?" Jack replied.

"Because if I heard you right last night:

"*The process of a pre-determined clear focus leads to prompt and accurate decisions.*

"Well, isn't you career one of your key category items?"

"Yes," Jack answered a little sheepishly.

"It seems to me," Hannah continued, "that this is a definite career decision. The determining factors relating to whether you accept or decline Pete's offer should be based on the effect your decision will have on your overall career--right?"

"Yeah, that's right, but all I have at this point is simply a list of my key life's issues. They aren't supported by any plans or strategies because Dan said we'd handle that at our next session, remember? I don't see how I can make a major decision based on a one-hour exercise, especially an exercise that's not even finished."

Hannah carefully pondered Jack's statement, then replied, "Why don't you give Dan a call, explain your dilemma, and see if he can give you some guidance?"

"Well, sure, I can do that."

"Can do or will do? That is the question, huh Jack?"

AIN'T NO SUCH THANG AS
A PURDY GOOD ALLIGATOR RASSLER

"You love that Shakespeare stuff, don't you, Hannah? Okay, let me find Dan's number."

"Thanks again Dan, this has been quite helpful. I'll follow the process you have given me and see where it leads. This is a tough decision and I need to give it thorough consideration. No, I haven't read the *As a Man Thinketh* book yet, but I will by our next session."

"Jack," Pete said in a sincere tone, "I'm indeed delighted with your decision to take me up on my offer. Thank you for your very prompt decision. I really wasn't expecting to hear from you until the end of the week. Your rapid decision and strong commitment will speed up progress, and believe me, from what I've seen so far, we need all the strong commitments and progress we can get. And yes, you do the job I know you're capable of and you have my commitment that good things will happen. By the way, how were you able to reach your decision so quickly?"

Jack set the stage by answering, "Oh, I just followed a recently learned lesson."

"What lesson was that?" Pete asked.

Jack smiled as he responded…

> *"From the time you crystallize your focus, your mind begins both consciously and unconsciously gathering and storing away the information required for you to make intelligent and accurate decisions."*

Pete chuckled as he said, "Seems like I've heard that somewhere before. Oh, and Jack, because you have made such a total commitment and prompt decision, the company will pick up the cost of the *12 Absolutes* program. Just send me the invoice upon your completion."

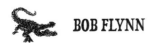

BOB FLYNN

The Recap

In his usual on-task, businesslike manner, Dan Hardee opened the second session of *The 12 Absolutes of Personal Effectiveness*. "Before we move on to Absolute #2, we're going to accomplish two things. First, we're going to recap last week's session, and then we're going to put some plans around our key issues list. Any questions before we begin?"

Not surprisingly, James spoke up immediately. "Dan, this focus concept is great, but I was hoping we would get right into Absolute #2. Why so much emphasis on pre-determining our focus? I work hard every day to try to do the right things. I think I'm already pretty good at being focused."

Without hesitation, Dan responded, "I want to make certain that everyone understands that we will invest considerable time in Absolutes One and Two. We'll take more time on these than any of the others because these two absolutes represent the foundation that all of the other ten will build on.

"Now James, in response to your comment, let me say that:

> *"People who labor without a clear vision backed by plans and goals are like ships without rudders, they meander around and don't take a straight path toward their port of call. Hard labor and good intentions are not sufficient to carry you to success. We all know hard-working, good people who aren't particularly successful. Until you have clearly defined what success means to you, the best you can hope for is to be pretty good at everything."*

Clyde jumped in. "Reminds me of a saying we have back home...**Ain't no such thang as a purdy good alligator rassler.** See, when you fixin' to rassle a gator, you'd best be clear about your focus. or the boys down at the store are gonna be calling you 'Stumpy.'"

Dan laughed and said, "Well, Clyde, you definitely have a way with words. What you say makes sense though. When we carefully select our key life's issues, there's no way that being pretty good at any of them will bring us satisfaction, much less personal effectiveness. And in this age of rampant attention deficit, a

AIN'T NO SUCH THANG AS
A PURDY GOOD ALLIGATOR RASSLER

clear focus on pre-determined areas is no less than critical."

"Yes Joanne?" Dan said in response to her upraised hand.

"I really learned a lot from last week's session. I've got a lot of clutter to deal with in my thinking. But there's one thing that's really bothering me. I can see how pre-determining our focus can help with almost any aspect of our lives except child raising. How does it apply there?"

Again, Dan answered immediately:

> *"Nowhere is the lack of a pre-determined, sustained focus more noticeable or more detrimental than it is in the relationship between parent and child. Children sense very quickly the wavering attitude of a parent, and they take advantage of that attitude quite freely. It is true in all other aspects of life as well – men and women with a clear focus command respect and attention at all times."*

Panning the circle with his eyes, Dan asked, "Any more questions or comments? Okay, great. James, you'll be delighted to learn that the entire recap will take less than thirty minutes. Here's what I'd like each of you to do. In fifty words or less, define the meaning you derived from last week's session. This should be something you truly believe, not just a quote from the workbook. You have fifteen minutes, so let's get started. Time's up. William, why don't you take the initial plunge?"

In a very clear, determined, and intellectual tone William began, "As I told everyone last week, my goal in taking the *12 Absolutes* is to clarify my direction. The stress of my divorce and all that entails has definitely gotten me off track, so far off I'm not sure where or what the track is anymore. Here's what I derived from last week's session:

> *"We can only achieve quantum improvements in our lives when we stop wallowing in our misery, stop beating ourselves up over what's past, and get to work on the causes. By pre-determining our focus toward our key life issues, we spawn the actions that if taken, will set us free."*

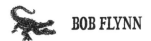

"Clyde, your turn."

"Well now, William, you're a tough act to follow, you being a college professor and all, but here's what Absolute #1 meant to me. First let me tell you a story. Now Dan, this doesn't count as my fifty words, okay?"

"Sure, Clyde, it's okay."

"Thank ya, Dan. There were these two ol' boys from down home. Actually, they was only ten years old, and Cooter and Earl was their names. Well, ol' man Booger Perkins accidentally locked them in a stable full of manure. Perkins was gone all day, and when he returned, he discovered that he had locked the chaps in that stable. Poor ol' Earl was a-sittin' in the corner crying and whining like a dying calf in a hailstorm. Perkins said, 'Boy, what in the world is the matter with you?' To which Earl replied, 'It's hot in here, it stinks in here, and this is an awful place.' Upon hearing that, Perkins flung open the stable door and out ran ol' Earl. Now ol' Cooter, on the other hand, was a-jumpin' up and down on that big ol' manure pile, laughing, throwing the stuff up in the air and digging in it like a hound dawg looking for a bone. Observing this, ol' man Perkins said, 'Boy how can you be havin' such a good time in a place like this?' Cooter replied, 'Mister there's gotta be a pony in there somewhere!'

"Now my goal for taking this course is to improve every aspect of my life, personally, professionally and spiritually. See, I've sown enough wild oats in my lifetime to make a wheat deal with Russia. I mean there ain't enough closets to hold all my skeletons. Here's what last week's session laid on me:

> **"The manure pile in the story represents the clutter we bring into our lives through uncontrolled focus. We can sit in the corner cogitating on our present situation and just whine about it like ol' Earl or... we can make the thing an adventure by digging into that clutter in search of our 'pony' (which is our key life's issues.) Then we can ride that hoss out of the mess that we focused ourselves into. Just like my daddy used to say, 'The worst enemy any man or woman can have is usually the one walking around under their hat.'"**

"Like I said, Clyde, you've got a way with words. Mary, you're up."

AIN'T NO SUCH THANG AS
A PURDY GOOD ALLIGATOR RASSLER

"I went through all we had to go through to get accepted to this program to advance my career. I'm far too educated and qualified to be stuck in the position I'm in. I also wanted to get my husband motivated. He's a good guy, but in my estimation, he needs more ambition. I've got to tell you that last week was eye-opening for me. Here's my bottom line, and I'm going to personalize it.

> **"Trying to motivate my husband to be more ambitious and convince my employer that I am underemployed is 'clutter.' The only things I can truly control are my thoughts and behaviors. If I wisely choose to focus on improving myself in my key life's issue areas, everything around me will improve. My job, my husband, and all the other things I'm fretting over and trying to control will improve in direct proportion to my improvement."**

"What about you, Tony? How would you describe your key take-away from last week's session?"

"I've been pretty good. Yeah, Clyde, I know there ain't no such thing as a pretty good alligator wrestler. Anyway, as I was saying, I've been okay at periodically reinventing myself, but it's time now for another reinvention. That was my goal in taking this course: to help me determine where to go from here. I felt like last week got me off to a good start. I'd sum up my key take away like this:

> **"We must carefully examine the lens through which we see the world, because it's the focus of our lens that determines our view of the world. Our future is achieved through organized mental focus because our actions are always aligned with our focus. What we focus on is the catalyst for personal effectiveness or ineffectiveness."**

"Joanne, what did you take from last week's session?"

"I struggled with last week's session. I think I understand the theory--focus on yourself and the things you can control and keep the bad thoughts out--but my situation is different. I've got two kids, my ex-husband will not pay child support, and he's going out of his way to overcomplicate everything, especially

my life. I've got to concentrate my focus on him and getting him to do what's right. It's very hard for me to concentrate on myself because my kids have to come first! I guess if I took anything from last week's session it was this:

> **"What matters most in life is how we respond to what we experience in life. And how we respond is controlled by our focus, and supposedly we can control the things we focus on."**

"Joanne," Dan said, "I can tell you have serious doubts about your ability to pre-determine and stick with your focus. Given your present circumstances, that's certainly understandable. Stay with the program; it will start making sense to you if you stay with it. Jack, what in last week's session was most meaningful to you?"

"If you guys recall, my primary reason for perusing the *12 Absolutes* program was to effectively deal with my complacency, you know, being pretty good at most everything in my life but not really being excellent at anything. In highly condensed form, here's what last week's session meant to me:

> **"We can have anything we truly want in life; we just can't have everything. In not clearly specifying what success means to us, we guarantee mediocrity, because we will spread our energies and actions over too many areas and never really master anything. Because of this, most people should choose no more than five key life issues. Also, we have to identify and get rid of the clutter in our thinking or it will destroy our focus."**

"Hank, it's your turn."

"Well, I guess you all remember that my purpose in taking the course was to define and focus on the important things in my future. After last week's session, I can see why and how the *12 Absolutes* have made such a difference in my dad's life. I called him after last week's session and told him that in fifteen minutes I had discovered that 'clutter' was really hampering my focus. He asked how many clutter items I identified, and I told him eight. He said, "When you really start getting in touch with this concept, you'll triple that number.

"Here's what I took home last week:

> **"My future will have an annoying habit of arriving whether I'm ready or not. I'll definitely not be ready if I fail to clarify my key life issues, build solid plans and strategies around them, and determine and eliminate the 'clutter' that is hampering my focus."**

"Well done, everyone," Dan said as he rose from his chair. "Now let's move on to…."

"Dan?"

"Yes, James?"

"You are a graduate of the *12 Absolutes* course, right?"

"Yes," Dan replied in an apprehensive tone.

"So, Dan, how did you summarize your key learning after completing the first session?"

"Glad you asked, James, because it so happens that I have my original workbook right here." Thumbing through the tattered workbook, Dan went to the board and wrote:

> **No undesirable environment is strong enough to hold the man or woman who understands <u>and applies</u> the power of clear focus. This is true because the subconscious mind is like a powerful magnet. When it has been vitalized and thoroughly saturated with a clear, compelling focus, it will attract into your life the people and circumstances that can bring the desired condition into fruition.**

"Also, James," Dan continued, "there's one important point that I didn't hear in any of your recaps. That leads me to believe that I didn't put enough emphasis on it during last week's discussion. Does anyone remember the study Russell James did regarding the most common forms of 'clutter'?"

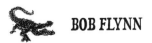 **BOB FLYNN**

The Killers

After a few seconds of silence, William spoke up. "Yes, Dan, I have it right here in my notes. Mr. James conducted an extensive study and discovered that there are seven categories of clutter that are the most common in men and women. He called them 'focus killers.' He concluded that your personal effectiveness is in direct correlation to the way in which you manage each one of these killers." He went on to list the seven categories.

1. **Intolerance**. This focus killer, if not controlled, will cause you to obsess about the beliefs and opinions of others, especially the ones that contradict your own. The effect of intolerance is a closed mind. We must not be easily swayed from our beliefs and opinions, but we must be open to the possibility of better, more productive ones. Intolerance prevents this.

2. **Revenge.** The killer of self-focus, revenge gives the power to the other person or circumstance and takes your focus off the one thing you can control…yourself.

3. **Greed.** This is the "dark side" of self-focus. Greed has at its roots the desire to take as much as we can while giving back as little as possible. It violates the law of reciprocity. People who suffer from greed believe the things they desire are in short supply.

4. **Envy.** Again, this is a focus outside oneself. When envy is allowed to occupy our thought processes, our focus is dissipated to the degree that we desire something that someone else possesses, be it tangible or intangible.

5. **Egotism.** An insidious focus killer, egotism gives the appearance of self-love, but in reality, it is an attempt to mask varying degrees of insecurity. Egotism kills the initiative to work on self because it has tricked the egotistical person into believing they have no need to improve. Additionally, it tends to drive away people and circumstances that could prove beneficial.

6. **Suspicion.** This is another form of closed-mindedness. The suspicious mind is constantly second-guessing itself and the intentions of others, making it extremely difficult to make decisions and to focus on your own improvement. Suspicion causes over scrutiny and cautiousness.

7. **Procrastination.** This is the mother of all clutter. The longer we put things off, the larger they grow, and the more room we make for other clutter items to accumulate.

AIN'T NO SUCH THANG AS
A PURDY GOOD ALLIGATOR RASSLER

The ability to take action is the most important attribute an effective individual can possess. Procrastination is the killer of focus, and it's our focus that is the springboard to action.

"Great recap, William, thanks!" Dan continued. "Sorry I didn't emphasize these focus killers strongly enough. I challenge each one of you to search yourselves and see how many of them are hampering your focus. Then the next challenge is to override them with your key issues."

Clyde interrupted with a contrived tone of seriousness. "Dan, do you know what we call gittin' rid of that kind of stuff back home?"

"No, Clyde, what do you call it back home?" Dan answered.

"Taking a mental enema; that's what we call it back home! You don't want me to go on back home, do you, Dan?"

"No, I don't want you to go on back home; not yet, anyway." Continuing, Dan said, "Okay, we have one more exercise to complete before moving on to Absolute #2. I want you to go back to the Key Categories list in your workbooks and do two things, both of which are extremely important. First, I want you to select one most important item. This may seem difficult, but as I said, it's quite important. The best way to select your most important item is to choose the one that in your estimation *will have the most impact on all the rest.* For example, if you are a spiritual person, your spirituality or your religion would take precedence over all the rest of the items. Another suggestion is that you review your BPE. This should prove indispensable in selecting your most important item.

"Yes, Clyde?" Dan said, responding to Clyde's raised hand.

"Say, Dan, speaking about religion…."

"Yes, Clyde," Dan answered, "what about it?"

"You're from Canada, right?"

"Yes, I'm Canadian."

"Whereabouts in Canada you from?"

 **BOB FLYNN**

"I'm from Edmonton."

"Yeah, that's what I thought. Did you hear about that preacher from Edmonton, the one that run off with all that money from the church?"

"No, I didn't hear about him, but I'll bet I'm going to."

"Yeah, you are. You see, this boy run off with ten thousand dollars of the church's money. He invested nine thousand of it in whiskey and wild living and just wasted the rest of it…you ain't gonna kick me out, are you?"

"No, I'm not going to kick you out--not yet, anyway," Dan said with a grin.

Getting back on track, Dan continued, "Okay now. When you finish selecting your number one item, I want you to take each item in your Key Categories list, including that number one item, and describe the actions you *will* take to make it a reality. For example, let's say you want to improve your job performance. List the actions that you surmise will cause improvement. Then go back and select the ones that you *will* do.

"You have an hour and a half to complete this assignment. Don't be concerned if you don't get all your planning completed, since this is a preliminary step. I'll provide you with other planning tips in Absolute #2. I'll be available to help if needed. If there are no questions, let's get started."

Checking his watch, Dan addressed the group. "All right folks, time's up. I think I answered your questions as we proceeded through the exercise, however, I do want to emphasize several points before we move into Absolute #2

"• POINT #1. Make certain you select a 'most important' item. This is the issue that has the most effect on all of the others.

"• POINT #2. All items in your key categories list must have action plans. The item is the 'what,' the plans are the 'how.'

"Your homework for next week is to clarify the work you have begun in class today. This means that by next Saturday's session you should have your specific written plans for each of the items in your Key Categories List. Any questions? Great, let's move on to Absolute #2."

The Response

Dan concluded the second session by saying, "Okay you guys, remember your assignment for next week. Put some specific action plans with timelines under each one of your key category items. Hopefully after today's class you see the vital connection between your key category items, planning and taking action. Thanks for a great session, and I'll see you next Saturday."

Jack waited for the other members of the group to leave, and then he approached Dan. "Dan, I'd like to visit with you for a minute. I have a slight problem."

"Sure, Jack, what is it?"

"First, thanks again for helping me sort through the decision as to whether or not to take the temporary assignment. When I weighed up its importance relative to my career aspirations, the decision came quickly. I'm going to take it."

Dan smiled approvingly, nodded, and said, "You're certainly welcome for the help, and I'm glad you reached your decision rapidly and decisively."

"Now that I have made the decision, I'm concerned about keeping up with the demands of the program," said Jack. "I think it would be a good idea to pick it back up at a later date, you know, when things have settled down."

"I see," Dan responded in a thoughtful tone. "Jack, I can see where the temporary assignment adds complexity to your life, and I appreciate you sharing it with me. The easy decision is simply to move you into a later class, but I don't believe that's in your best interest."

"Oh, why is that?" Jack asked.

"It's been my personal experience as well as observing participants in past programs:

> *"Whenever we set out to make improvements in our lives our commitment gets tested.*

"Now Jack, I don't have any data to support that statement, but I can cite numerous examples of a person's circumstances changing and becoming a challenge to their commitment to improve their lives. Ironically, these challenges

 **BOB FLYNN**

seem to occur almost simultaneously to the person's stated desire to improve himself. In our current class, for example, five of our class members have already had unexpected changes that are potentially threatening to their continuation in the program. So, having said all that, I suggest that you stay with the program and work through this inconvenience. If your desire for improvement is strong enough, you'll find a way."

"You know what he said, Hannah? If my desire for improvement were strong enough, I'd find a way. I'm finally beginning to see the absolute importance of true commitment. You just can't get 'half pregnant' with this commitment business. I learned that from Clyde."

"I wish you hadn't."

"So anyway, I'm committed to the program, so I'll figure it out. Cut out some TV, get up a little earlier, and I'm there. Like I said, I'll figure it out."

"I know you will," Hannah replied with assurance.

Hannah and Jack agreed that since he could count on being at home on the weekends, they would follow this schedule. Jack would attend the *12 Absolutes* class on Saturday, prepare his recap on Sunday afternoon, and present it in a two-hour session to Hannah Sunday evening.

Absolute #2

TAKE ACTION

The great end of life is not knowledge but action.
THOMAS HENRY HUXLEY

"Action is the key, Hannah. After yesterday's session, I'm absolutely convinced of it!" Jack began teaching Absolute # 2 as enthusiastically as Hannah had ever seen him.

"It's action and action alone that produces results. Nothing can take its place and there isn't a substitute. Yesterday Dan opened the program by stating that:

> **"The goal of the 12 Absolutes *program is not so much to educate us as to get us to take action.***

"He continued by saying that we know a lot of this stuff already and that it's not so much in the knowing as in the doing. The *12 Absolutes* just gives a process for applying much of what we already know. See, what we're talking about here is mostly common sense. Oh yeah, Hannah, know what Clyde said about common sense?"

"No, and I probably don't want to, but I'll bet I'm fixin' to."

"He said the reason that common sense was so common is cause ain't nobody using it."

"Ha ha," Hannah replied, faking laughter. "But he might be right," she added as an afterthought.

Jack continued, "The most intriguing and beneficial lesson I got out of the session was this:

"Motivation results from taking action, not the other way around.

"See Hannah, I had it backwards; most people do. They wait until they 'feel' motivated and then they do something. A motivational 'feeling' is very elusive, and we can't count on it. We have to get ourselves to take action, and then we'll feel motivated. In his studies, Russell James proved conclusively that the most effective people on the planet consistently take action in their *self-determined focus* areas. They take this action whether they 'feel' motivated to take it or not. They've learned that taking action is a 'pump primer,' and once they begin taking action, it motivates more action.

"The greatest attribute of the highly effective individual is their ability to get themselves to take action.

"Not just action for action's sake, Hannah, but productive action generated by a predetermined focus and aimed at one or more key categories. That's the ticket to freedom. Most people idly talk about what they're going to do, and they may even develop intricate plans and strategies. Planning and strategizing are fine—prudent, in fact--but in and of themselves, they produce nothing."

"Will do versus can do, Jack?"

"Will do versus can do, Hannah."

 **BOB FLYNN**

The Guarantee

"So, are you saying that taking action guarantees success in your key issue areas?"

"Not exactly."

"Not exactly? Then why all this hype about action?"

"To guarantee success, you have to take the correct action. Productive action, Dan calls it. That's a major purpose of planning, to determine the actions we think we need to take. However, there's speculation involved in all planning, even the best, and the only way we can test its validity is by doing what, my dear?"

"Taking action," Hannah answered in an enlightened tone.

"Correct. By executing our plans, we gain the information we need to modify our actions, and we sustain the process until we reach our goals in our key issue areas."

"Sounds like trial and error to me; lots of wasted time and energy. It sounds painful."

"A very astute observation, my dear. So, unless we want to be pioneers--oh, know what my man Clyde says about pioneers?"

"No, Jack, what does he say?"

"You don't want to be no pioneer, hoss, because them's the boys that takes the arrows."

"Very colorful, Jack, very," Hannah said, rolling her eyes.

"So, we have to try and avoid taking the pioneer route because the pain of the arrows might cause us to stop taking any action and then we're stuck, see what I'm saying?"

"Yes, yes--I see."

"Anyway, unless we want to be pioneers and take the arrows, we can initiate

a course of action that has the ability to enhance our success ratio considerably. We can locate a book, a course, or someone who has already produced the results we're aspiring to and ask them how they did it. Dan advised us that once we select our key life issues, we should get help planning the actions we should take. He said this is a step that's often neglected because our pride and ego get in the way. He also said that if we take this route at all, it's usually after our plans have failed to produce the results we're after. And that's the hard way. The key is to get good instruction on the front end, create a model, and then execute. By taking that course of action, we are very likely to produce positive results, results that will motivate additional action. Dan ended this part of the session by saying you can and should get all the appropriate advice and help you can, but ultimately…

> **"You are responsible for taking the action, so what are you going to do about it?"**

The Saboteurs

As usual, Hannah had questions. "Jack, taking action is so obviously correct--it's cause and effect, right? So why in the world don't people just figure out what's important to them and start taking action to make it happen?"

With a sly grin on his face, Jack responded. "Remember the focus killers?"

"Sure I do."

"Well, let me introduce you to the action saboteurs. Perhaps that will help answer the question of why people fail to take action."

"Let's hear it, Professor."

Reading from his workbook, Jack began. "There are five predominant action killers. They include:

"1. Poorly defined key life issues.

"It's the emotion, commitment and purpose behind the key life issues that determine the level of action a person will invest. When the key life issues are selected haphazardly, your heart won't buy it, at least not for long. You simply won't put forth the sustained effort required for success.

 **BOB FLYNN**

Our key life issues are the fuel that drives the engine of action, and they must be powerful enough to surmount all the inevitable hardships that we will encounter. Questions stimulate our thought processes, and the most important question you can ask yourself relative to your key life issues is why"? Why have I selected this as a key life issue? A common trap that many people fall into is selecting key life issues on an 'ought or should' basis. Searching your 'heart of hearts' is essential to determining key life issues that, in your estimation, are worth the effort required to reach the goal.

"2. Inadequate plans and strategies.

"Ill-conceived plans and strategies serve as action killers because the results they produce are disheartening. When we take the wrong course of action, the feedback we receive can cause us to believe that we'll never reach our goal. If planning and strategizing are not reasonably on target, our actions will take us away from not move us toward our goals, and we will eventually give up. Staying out of the inadequate planning and strategizing trap requires that we locate a mentor, model, or process that is proven, and build our plans and strategies around the recommended actions. By taking this approach, the initial feedback we receive from our actions will be mostly positive. Encouraged by our early successes, our motivation increases, producing the energy to sustain our efforts. All the feedback we receive even from the best of plans and strategies will not be positive. In the case of negative feedback resulting from your actions, simply modify the action until the desired result is attained.

"3. Unrealistic expectations.

"Certainly, we should aim high relative to the success we plan to attain in each of our key life issues. Problems occur, however, when we develop grandiose short-term expectations and then fall considerably short. There are cases of short-term exponential gains for sure, but combining consistent incremental gains secures most key life issue goals. Avoiding the trap of unrealistic expectations is easy when we break the desired end result into bite-sized bits. By taking this approach, you'll see rapid progress, and your energy and enthusiasm will follow proportionately. Progress is a vital catalyst for sustained action. Unrealistic expectations are action saboteurs because progress toward goal will be minimal or nonexistent.

"4. Overexposure to negative influences.

"We are most influenced by the people with whom we associate and what we read and watch. Unfortunately, our society is replete with negative

media and people. A large percentage of the people we come into contact with on a daily basis are to a large degree negative. Much of the written material, television, radio, movies etc. are either blatantly negative or contain negative undertones. Overexposure to these types of negative influences creates doubt, blurs focus, and diminishes or kills the action initiative. Success in achieving the goals of your key life issues is dependent on your state of mind. Negativity puts you in a negative state and delays or prevents progress. The most self-destructive aspect of a negative attitude is that it destroys self-discipline. Guard carefully what you put into your heart and mind or forget high achievement in your key life issues. Friends and family members can often be the most pronounced negative influences. Often inadvertently, family and 'friends' can have tremendous negative influence on you and your progress. It is your responsibility to determine who and what you will allow to influence you. Choose carefully!

"5. Failing to hold yourself strictly accountable.

"Changing non-productive habits and mastering the fine art of doing better isn't easy. Far from it. It's plain hard work, but my-oh-my, what a payoff! Despite what the New Age gurus claim, self-discipline and accountability are still and forever will be essential ingredients to success in any endeavor. There are only two pains in life: the pain of discipline or the pain of regret. Again, the payoffs for disciplined actions are huge, the effort well worth it! Along with clear, well thought out key life issues, goals for each, plans and strategies for achievement, you will need a method to measure your progress. The old saying is true: 'What gets measured gets done.' It's imperative that you establish benchmarks, timelines, and measurements in each of your key life issue items. Measurements should be quantifiable whenever possible, and they should at the least be qualified. When measurements are established, you must commit to holding yourself accountable for staying on track and on task.

"So, Hannah, does that give you a better idea of why most of us are so reluctant to take action?"

"Yes," Hannah answered, "and I can see several of these action killers alive and well in my life."

"Yeah, me too. I suppose most everyone can if they're honest with themselves. The question is what will we do about it?" Jack continued, "We also learned and discussed at length that even though these five killers are destroyers of our action initiative, there's one more that is...

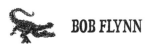

BOB FLYNN

"The Godfather."

"The Godfather?"

"Yeah, we call this one the Godfather because it is behind all the others. This one is the essence of the other five. It's the one behind the scenes masterminding our acceptance of mediocrity. Lurking in the darkness ready to do us in are the other five. Not the Godfather; he's sitting back running the show."

"Okay, okay," Hannah exclaimed, "who is the Godfather?"

> **"Expedience, Hannah; that's the baddest of the bad guys. He's the one that makes expedience look like an offer you can't refuse."**

"You're going to explain, right?"

Jack turned to a dog-eared page in his workbook, glanced down at it, and began reading the bold print.

> **"Expedience is the root cause of most frustration, anger, disillusionment, disappointment, broken relationships, and sub-par lives.**

"As you might imagine, when Dan led off with that statement, he got our full attention. And you know what? I've been pondering it almost non-stop since yesterday afternoon, and the more I think about it, the more I agree. Dan went on to explain that expedience is so devastating because it is in direct violation of the law of cause and effect… and nobody but nobody violates that law and sustains productive action."

"Expedience is simply trying to reap before you sow… and it will absolutely destroy your action initiative!

"Attempting to avoid up-front price-paying and expecting a favorable outcome is ignoring nature's law. Ignoring a law does not weaken it or make it go away. It weakens you and makes you go away! Cause and effect, reaping and sowing are just as powerful and absolute as the law of gravity. When we attempt to get before we give, take a 'Give me money and then I'll give you

AIN'T NO SUCH THANG AS
A PURDY GOOD ALLIGATOR RASSLER

work' approach, our end result is always frustration. To achieve every goal in our key life issues, there are prices to pay. The prices must be paid in advance, and until we pay them through our actions (causes), nothing changes for the better."

Turning several pages ahead, Jack continued, "We completed a very powerful and revealing exercise yesterday that really brought this business of expedience up close and personal."

"Tell me about it," Hannah said with keen interest.

"Dan gave us fifteen minutes to list as many instances as we could think of where we had allowed expedience to rule. He then asked us to list the consequences of succumbing to the vice-like grip of expedience. Here's my list--take a look," Jack said as he handed her his workbook.

Expedience	Consequences
Began exercise program to lose weight and get in better shape. Overdid it during the first two days.	Got tired and sore. Quit program after ten days.
Took on new project at work. Attempted to demonstrate immediate progress. Did not gain facts and adequate background info. Launched right in.	Repeated mistakes of prior mgr. Delayed progress. Produced marginal results. Lost credlbility with my management.
To appease children arranged vacation we could not afford.	Created debt and family tension. Unable to take vacation for two years.
Got raise, bought wanted, but not needed car. Payment exceeded increase.	Unable to increase savings. Irritated wife.
To avoid a messy confrontation failed to discipline under-performing staff member.	Hurt personal credibility with management, peers and other staff members. Caused anxiety. made excuses for their poor performance. Diminished self-esteem. Reduced overall performance of dept. Gave employee false sense of security. Probably could have saved, but had to dismiss.

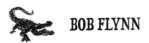

Rather than taking responsibility for my marginal job performance, I took the expedient way of whining and complaining about circumstance beyond my control and Influence. Expended energy and effort "fixing the blame" on conditions and others and generally feeling sorry for myself.

Got passed over for promotion. Created doubt concerning my competence. Gave my power to circumstances. Became overly cautious and fearful. Got poor performance rating and no Increase. Put on "notice."

In a rush to mow grass so I could play golf. Failed to check oil in mower.

Did considerable damage to engine. Wasted day trying to get engine repaired. Missed golf game. Ended up replacing mower.

Took an easy job I really didn't want.

Two years of misery doing work I was not suited for.

Instead of dealing with a misunderstanding I criticized and gossiped behind the back of a peer.

Peer found out, confronted me. My reputation was damaged. Caused unnecessary tension. Created an adversary.

Yelled at kids over a trivial matter.

Hurt relationship with kids. Set poor example. Failed to use Incident as a teachable moment. In "doghouse" until I made humble apology.

Hannah completed her reading, paused contemplatively then said, "It took a lot of courage to list your expediencies and the consequences they caused. I'm proud of you, Jack. This is real growth, and most guys just wouldn't have done it."

Nodding his head, Jack responded by saying, "Thanks. This stuff is pretty revealing, Hannah. It brings the penalty of expedience out of the conceptual and right into your living room. I hope I've learned that expedience is a mean son-of-a gun. It's nothing to take lightly. I think it's like that infamous philosopher Clyde says: 'When you mess around with that ol' law of expedience, boy, you done pulled the tail of the wrong dog.'"

"I don't know, Jack. I think this character Clyde's getting in your head."

"Oh, Clyde's cool and he's a lot of fun. He keeps the class in stitches, but there's more to him than grins and giggles."

AIN'T NO SUCH THANG AS
A PURDY GOOD ALLIGATOR RASSLER

"How so?"

"He's dead serious about the program. He's working extremely hard, and he's setting the pace and raising the standard. Behind all his corny jokes and down-home sayings is a guy totally committed to improving his personal effectiveness."

"Okay, Professor, if you say so."

"Dan concluded the section on expedience by pointing out that the initial expedience items we listed in the exercise are usually the ones on the surface. He advised us to dig deeper and identify the expediencies that have had the most significant negative impact on our lives."

Hannah jumped right in. "Why would he want you to do that? It seems to me that looking back is a strange way to look forward."

"Some of the group had the same misgivings that you do. Dan explained that it is absolutely essential that we make the connection between expedience and negative consequences. By examining past expediencies and their corresponding negative effects, we accomplish three major things. First, we make a permanent connection between acting expediently and the pain it causes. Second, we solidify the law of cause and effect in our thinking. And third, we release the power that negative consequence of past expediencies may be holding over us.

"We finished up absolute # 2 by learning two more productive action strategies. The first one is:

"The Secret."

"What secret? Hanna asked.

"The secret of getting ourselves to take productive action."

"So, what is it?"

"It's simple but powerful. We get ourselves to take action by asking ourselves questions."

"Questions?"

"Yes, questions. See, when we ask ourselves questions, we put our brain in gear, so to speak. They stimulate our thinking and rev up our creativity. We won't get the results we're after if we ask ourselves just any old questions. The questions that we ask must be open--that is, they cannot be answered with a simple 'yes' or 'no.' Typically they would begin with how, why, what, when, where, who, and which. To maximize their effectiveness, these open questions must be aimed at a specific target. Now in our case we aimed our questions at our key life issues. Let me give you a few examples. Let's take my career, for example. Here are some of the questions I could ask.

"What specific action will I take today to advance my career?

"What are the five most potentially effective actions I could take this month to meet my production goals?

"Who will I contact this week and seek their guidance relative to my career?

"Why was I overlooked for promotion last year? What will I do to better my chances next time?

"What can I do to fast cycle the learning process on my new assignment?

"See, questions generate options, and options give us choices. They're great for helping us develop plans and strategies as well as assisting us in solving problems and capitalizing on opportunities. We're using this methodology in conjunction with developing plans and strategies for our key life issues. I used to hate planning, but this actually makes it fun and interesting."

"How are using the open questions going to help you develop your plans and strategies for your key life issues?" Hannah asked.

"Simple. We take our key life issues, then generate a series of open questions aimed specifically at each one. The answers we generate are our options. From our list of options, we select the ones we feel are most viable. The selected options then become our plans, our 'will do's.'

"Questions--I can see their potential for igniting productive action. So, Jack, you said there were two final action strategies. Questions are one, but what's the other one?"

"Dan called it . . .

AIN'T NO SUCH THANG AS
A PURDY GOOD ALLIGATOR RASSLER

"The Vision."

"Okay, let's get on with it.

"As we continue developing and scrutinizing our key life issues and the plans for their achievement, the vision of our ideal selves will become clearer. This vision is very important, because in order to determine our most advantageous actions, we must have our ideal self clearly in focus. As the picture of our ideal selves clarifies, we once again employ our open-ended questions. Here are some examples:

"How will my ideal self behave?

"How will my ideal self-talk?

"What will my ideal self stop doing?

"What will my ideal self start doing?

"What types of people will my ideal self avoid?

"Who are the types of people that my ideal self will form relationships with?

"What will my ideal self read? Watch? Listen to?

"How will my ideal self continue learning?

"What current behaviors are in line with my vision of my ideal self?

"What current behaviors are not in line with my vision of my ideal self?

"These types of questions will help lead us to specific actions and decide which behaviors to start and stop. Dan calls this 'pinpointing.' He went on to explain that pinpointed actions are productive actions and far superior to the trial and error variety."

Hannah pondered Jack's comments and then said, "I guess this will sound like a glaring statement of the obvious, but getting a clear vision of our ideal selves is very important, huh Jack?"

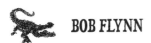**BOB FLYNN**

101

"Yeah, Hannah, it's really critical in molding ourselves into highly effective individuals. And to add even more potency to creating the vision of our ideal selves, we should clarify that vision in each of our key life issue categories. We just have to keep asking ourselves…

"What does this person do?

"What do they look like?

"How do they take care of themselves?

"How do they behave in relationships?

"How do they handle stress?

"How do they assert themselves?

"How do they handle money?

"Each person is charged with the responsibility of developing, adding to, and modifying their questions to themselves. By taking this action the vision eventually becomes crystal clear:

> ***"The clearer the vision the more obvious becomes the productive actions required to convert the ideal self-vision into reality."***

"The *12 Absolutes* really is a well thought out process, isn't it?"

"That it is, and according to Dan, the best is yet to come. Frankly, I'm pretty anxious to find out what Absolute # 3 is. Dan won't tell us until next week's class, because he says it might take our focus off our homework assignment."

"So, honey, what pain and suffering did old Dan inflict on you for this week?"

"He's assigned us the privilege of completing our key life issue plans and identifying any current or potential future expediencies. Also, we are to plan a review of Absolute #2."

"That should keep you out of trouble while you're on the road."

"Oh yeah. Well, Hannah, the old professor has about had it. I've got a big day tomorrow. Pete says he's going to give me the specifics of my assignment. I'll be gone all week and I'm sure going to miss you guys."

"We're going to miss you too. I'll bet you'll have a very interesting and adventuresome week."

Absolute #2

TAKE ACTION

The great end of life is not knowledge but action.
THOMAS HENRY HUXLEY

KEY POINT

The greatest attribute of the highly effective individual is their ability to separate the relevant from the irrelevant and a keen sense of urgency to take action. It's action and action alone that produces results. Nothing can take its place. There is no substitute.

❏ Motivation results from taking action, not the other way around.

❏ Trying to reap before you sow is the major killer of action.

❏ Actions should be relevant to your priorities.

❏ Pursuit actions provide sensory acuity.

❏ Plans, analysis, hopes, dreams, etc. in and of themselves produce 0.

❏ No one can take action for you; it's your responsibility.

❏ Poorly defined priorities prevent action.

❏ Inadequate plans and strategies prevent action.

❏ Unrealistic expectations prevent action.

❏ Negative influences prevent action.

❏ Not holding yourself accountable prevents action.

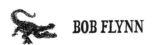 **BOB FLYNN**

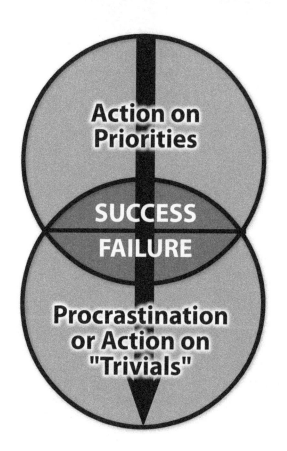

MAJOR POINT ──────────────────────────

Attempting to avoid paying the price up front, i.e.: failing to take action, is ignoring nature's immutable law of cause and effect. Ignorance of a law does not make it go away.

THE PRICE OF ACTION MUST BE PAID, AND IT MUST BE PAID IN ADVANCE. THE VIOLATION OF THIS LAW IS A MAJOR CAUSE OF FRUSTRATION, ANGER, AND FAILURE.

The price (ACTION) must be paid in advance.

There are NO exceptions.

AIN'T NO SUCH THANG AS
A PURDY GOOD ALLIGATOR RASSLER

ABSOLUTE #2

EXERCISE

What are key actions you will take in the top five priorities of your life? When will you take them?

MY #1 PRIORITY IS: _____

The ACTION(s) I will take is: _____

_____
_____
_____
_____
_____
_____
_____
_____
_____

I commit to take each of these ACTIONS by: *(list the date you will initiate each action).*

_____
_____

MY #2 PRIORITY IS: _____

The ACTION(s) I will take is: _____

_____
_____
_____
_____
_____
_____
_____
_____

I commit to take each of these ACTIONS by: *(list the date you will initiate each action).*

_____
_____

 **BOB FLYNN**

MY #3 PRIORITY IS: _____

The ACTION(s) I will take is: _____

_____
_____
_____
_____
_____
_____
_____
_____
_____
_____

I commit to take each of these ACTIONS by: *(list the date you will initiate each action).*

_____
_____

MY #4 PRIORITY IS: _____

The ACTION(s) I will take is: _____

_____
_____
_____
_____
_____
_____
_____
_____
_____
_____

I commit to take each of these ACTIONS by: *(list the date you will initiate each action).*

_____
_____

AIN'T NO SUCH THANG AS
A PURDY GOOD ALLIGATOR RASSLER

MY #5 PRIORITY IS: _____

The ACTION(s) I will take is: _____

_____
_____
_____
_____
_____
_____
_____
_____
_____
_____

I commit to take each of these ACTIONS by: *(list the date you will initiate each action).*

_____
_____

NOTES

_____
_____
_____
_____
_____
_____
_____
_____
_____
_____

BOB FLYNN

NOTES

AIN'T NO SUCH THANG AS
A PURDY GOOD ALLIGATOR RASSLER

CHAPTER FIVE

The Reflection

ABSOLUTE #3

Serve Others

*If there is anything you
don't like out there, there
is a need to change
yourself.*

LESTER LEVENSON

The Reflection

Pete was very concerned; he got down to business immediately.

"Jack, I'm glad you're here. I was hoping to be able to break you in slowly, but we have big opportunities masked as serious problems at the plant. I need you to troubleshoot the situation and give me some answers. Not only is production behind schedule, we also have escalating morale problems as well. The plant manager, Fred Rawlinson, has been on vacation, so I have not met with him. I suggest that's where you start. I was planning to be with you this week, but that's not going to happen since I'm leaving for Dallas this afternoon. I'll be back Friday morning. I hope you will have some answers for me, because we've got to turn this thing around quick!"

Pete handed Jack a stack of files, wished him good luck, and headed to the airport.

Jack was in shock. He wasn't expecting this. He had realized that there would be challenges, but not of this magnitude. It all seemed so unfair. His mind raced on. *Pete just dropped a major problem in my lap and left town, and he's putting the entire burden, the total responsibility on me. Man, have I ever made a bad decision! I don't even know this guy Rawlinson, and now I've got to find out why he's not cutting it. This is bad, really bad!*

In the midst of his internal tirade, Jack reflected on several key points of the *12 Absolutes* program:

- It's not what happens to us, it's how we respond.
- The subconscious mind believes everything we tell it, and I'm only giving it bad news.
- Opportunity often comes in the form of problems.
- Responsibility cannot be given… it must be taken.
- What I focus on expands, and I'm focusing on the negative.
- I must master my emotions, or they will master me.
- The only aspects of this situation I can truly control are my thoughts, and I'm letting mine run wild.

Much calmer now, Jack began reading Fred Rawlinson's file. The more he

read, the more encouraged he became. Fred had been with the company over seventeen years. This was the third plant he had managed, and while he wasn't a superstar, his track record was good--no serious problems with personnel or management. He had struggled with production and morale issues in the past and had always come through with a reasonable degree of success. Jack felt confident that Fred would have a good handle on the problems, and that between the two of them they should have some viable options for Pete on Friday.

Jack's enthusiasm ended abruptly.

As he entered Fred's office, Jack observed a large man in his mid-forties with dark, curly hair. Extending his hand, Jack introduced himself as Pete's assistant.

"Didn't know Pete had an assistant," Rawlinson responded curtly.

Jack explained his temporary assignment, and the fact that Pete was called to Dallas unexpectedly. He then asked when it would be convenient for him and Fred to discuss the production and morale issue.

"Now wait a minute," said Rawlinson, "I've never even met Pete Morrison, and now he sends his temporary assistant in to discuss the issues of my plant? This is strange, Williams, very strange. I'll meet with Pete on Friday, when I will have a major item to bring to his attention."

Feeling defensive, Jack muddled on. "Sure, Fred, I know Pete is anxious to meet with you too. However, he has suggested that we discuss the plant issues and come up with some strategies for getting back on track."

"You know, I'm really surprised that you and Pete don't already know the root causes of our problems here at the plant, but since you don't, here are a few for starters. We've got a lousy economy going, the plant pay is sub-par-- just ask the workers—and the recent acquisition we made ain't working. Throw meetings, the crummy weather, and the new government regulations into the mix, and you guys ought to be smart enough to see why productivity is hurting."

Jack listened attentively, but he couldn't help reflecting on his recent encounter with Pete. It was almost a mirror image. He saw his former self in Fred Rawlinson's refusal to accept any responsibility.

Fred continued. "John Richardson, the guy Pete replaced, I hardly ever saw him because he was always off to somewhere and didn't want to get involved. Now it looks like Pete's going to take the same approach."

Jack was contemplating his next move when Fred dropped the bombshell.

"But you know what? It doesn't matter anyway, it's all a moot point and there's no sense in wasting your time or mine, because I'm resigning. I've accepted a position with a competitor, and I'll be out of your hair in two weeks. Pass that along to Pete, will you?"

Jack tried to hide his dismay and engage Fred in additional conversation. He hoped he could get him to reconsider his decision, but it was to no avail; Fred's mind was closed, his decision was final.

After several attempts, Jack finally reached Pete on his cell phone.

"Pete, I hate to disturb you, but Rawlinson has resigned. He's gone in two weeks. I tried to get him to reconsider, at least until he met with you, but he wasn't interested."

In a calm tone, Pete responded, "Why is he leaving? He's been around over fifteen years, and this isn't the first time he's faced a little adversity."

"Remember our conversation, Pete, the one in which I fixed the blame on everyone and everything but myself? Well, he cited the same reasons. I was planning to see if he would accept any personal responsibility, but I never got there. He wouldn't let me."

There was a long silence on the other end. Finally, Pete spoke. "If he's not willing to accept a degree of personal responsibility, we're better off without him. Frankly, I think Fred checked out over a six months ago. I'd be willing to bet you can trace the slump in productivity to the day he stopped holding himself personally accountable. Once people begin focusing outside of themselves, the problems cease becoming opportunities, and they rapidly become overwhelmed.

"Okay, here's what I want you to do. Get in touch with Alan Simmons in HR and tell him that we need some top candidates for the plant manager's position. I'd like you to start interviewing as soon as possible. I'll call Mickey Kelly, Fred's assistant. I've known him for years, and he's very competent and a great guy. I'll arrange for him to meet with you in the morning and update you

on the plant problems and advise you of any potential internal candidates for the plant manager position. Stay positive, Jack. This will all work out."

Jack spent the rest of the day talking with Alan Simmons and lining up prospective candidates for the plant manager position. There were four solid prospects, and it looked like they would all be available to interview with Jack prior to the week's end. Mickey Kelley also stopped by to tell Jack he'd be glad to meet with him first thing in the morning. By the time he got back to the hotel, it was almost 8:00. It had been a long and difficult day. The day was far from over, however, as Jack had committed to investing an hour each night in completing his *12 Absolutes* assignment.

The Breakthrough

6:00 a.m. came early. Jack hustled to get ready, grabbing a quick bagel and coffee and heading over to the plant to meet with Mickey Kelly. Promptly at 7:30, Kelly walked into Jack's office. He was a portly, friendly mid-fifties guy with thirty years' experience in plant management. Mickey was the consummate "second man," a get-it-done kind of guy, good with the workers, good with management, and totally loyal to the organization.

"Well, Jack," Mickey began, "how can I help?"

Jack and Mickey chatted the rest of the morning. Mickey was very open and willing to answer all of Jack's questions. The rapport between them was good. Jack was beginning to get the picture. Fred had been an adequate manager, in Mickey's estimation; very technically competent but weak with people. Fred spent a lot of time in the office poring over spreadsheets and production schedules, and looking into the computer. According to Mickey, the only time Fred came out on the floor was when there was a problem. "One day I asked him why he spent so much time reviewing reports and doing computer work, and do you know what he said? Reports and computers don't talk back." Mickey surmised that the morale problems were real and somewhat longstanding, but with effective management, this thing could be turned around pretty fast. Then Mickey said something very astute. "It's been my observation over the years that…all problems can be traced back to the manager's office."

Enlightened, Jack mentally summarized his assessment of the existing situation. *Morale is down predominantly because our plant personnel have received only negative feedback. They are feeling neglected and underappreciated. They*

AIN'T NO SUCH THANG AS
A PURDY GOOD ALLIGATOR RASSLER

are inadvertently withholding their best efforts in an attempt to bring attention to the lack of leadership. The next plant manager must have excellent people skills to bring out the best in people. The old saying is far too mushy for guys like Fred, but it's so true: They don't care how much you know until they know how much you care.

After spending all of the next day on the plant floor talking to the people, Jack felt he had even a better understanding of what it would take to get the plant on target. It would be difficult but possible. The people held the key. Win their hearts and you win their minds. Armed with viable information, Jack began clarifying the attributes he would be looking for in the candidates for the plant manager position. It was going to take much more than a nice people person to get the plant back on schedule. It was going to take a strong leader, someone with drive and a keen sense of urgency combined with patience and empathy. A managerial hiring mistake at this point could spell disaster.

Jack scheduled all four interviews for the next day. That evening, he prepared his interview questions and continued to visualize the ideal leader to manage the plant to excellence.

Pete arrived at 9:00 Friday morning. After quickly checking his emails, he went directly to Jack's office.

"Well, Jack, sorry I've been out of contact, but our meeting turned out to be more important than I expected. Before I get into all of that, bring me up to speed on the status of things."

"Pete, between Mickey and myself, I feel we have things stabilized. He's been a tremendous ally, and the people trust and like him. We have both spent as much time on the plant floor as possible. Frankly, I sense the people are glad for a change, so I'd say things are better from a morale perspective."

Pete was obviously pleased, and he asked, "What's your recommendation regarding Fred? Should we try to retain him?"

"My gut says no, but you may see things differently."

"I'm meeting with him this afternoon and I'll make the call after our conversation. How did your interviews go?"

"Really good. I think we have the ideal candidate."

 **BOB FLYNN**

"Great. Tell me about it."

"Pete, let me hedge on that until you meet with Fred. It may not even be an issue if you guys come to terms."

"Fair enough, I'll see if he's available now. I'll catch up with you after our meeting."

The Surprise

Picking up the phone, Pete dialed Jack's extension. "Jack, let's grab an early lunch, and I'll tell you about my meeting with Fred."

"Wow, that was a quick meeting! Are you ready now?"

"Yeah, I'm anxious to hear about this ideal candidate. We're going to need someone who's totally competent and available immediately."

"So, Jack, that's it; Fred's had it, he's soured on everything. No telling how long this has been going on. Looks like we inherited a mess. I told Fred there's no need to work out a notice. Today is his last day and I really don't want him around the people any longer. He can say his goodbyes this afternoon. You and Mickey will be in charge of the plant until we can locate his replacement. I know that's not what you expected, but this is by far the most pressing need. Nothing is more important than getting this plant straightened out, especially given the fact that we just acquired another company--but more about that later. Now, tell me about your candidate. He must have really impressed you in the interview."

"I didn't interview him."

"Jack, wait a minute. I thought you told me you had a great applicant for the job!"

"I do, Pete; it's me."

"You? Jack, you don't have any experience managing an operation of this magnitude. This baby is a monster. Listen, I'm impressed that you want to step up to the plate and one day you may be ready, but not now."

AIN'T NO SUCH THANG AS
A PURDY GOOD ALLIGATOR RASSLER

"Pete, I want you to hear me out, and I want you to withhold your decision until next week. All I'm asking is that you give my proposition consideration. How about it?"

"Let's hear it, but it had better be good."

Settling back in his seat, Jack felt the plane lift off the runway. For the first time all week, he felt a slight sense of relaxation and relief. What a week it had been! The drama unfolded so fast, with so many ups and downs and so much unpredictability and potential opportunity!

Jack felt good about his discussion with Pete. He was glad that he had invested the time and effort to really think through his decision to seek the plant manager's position. He felt equally good about the proposal he made to Pete and was confident he'd get a fair shot at the job. Pete even admitted that the way in which the proposal was structured made the decision relatively low risk.

Jack chuckled at the fact that Mickey Kelly had really been the one who suggested he seek the position and then advised him how to go about it. It seemed to Jack that this whole thing was ordained. He could almost hear Mickey saying, "Jack, why don't you apply for the plant manager's position? Pete was right when he said that you've got great people skills and a solid background in the business. This would be a great opportunity for you, and you'd be crazy not to pursue it. See, I don't think one of our current managers is what we need.

"My concern is that it will simply be more of the same. I know them all they are cut from the same cloth. What we need is some drive and energy, some new ideas, and someone who will get to know the people and pull this thing together. That's you, man! Pete's biggest concern will be your lack of experience. You can rely on me to offset that. I've been at this plant for eleven years, and I know every nook and cranny, so I can bring you up to speed real fast. Why don't you ask Pete to let you and me manage it on an interim basis? Give us six months, and we'll have this baby humming."

"Please return your seats and tray tables to their upright and locked position in preparation for landing." The flight attendant's admonishment broke Jack's thought pattern. He smiled at the thought of being home and having a weekend with Hannah and the kids.

Five miles from home, Jack's cell phone rang.

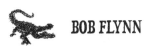 **BOB FLYNN**

"Jack, it's Mickey. I couldn't wait till Monday, man. How'd it go with Pete?"

"Good, I think. It was pretty hard to read him, but I'd say we've got a fifty-fifty shot."

"I'm gonna up the odds. Pete's staying the weekend, and at his request I'm having breakfast with him in the morning. I'm going to pitch him hard, because I'm tired of watching this thing flounder! See you Monday, Jack."

The News

Laughter abounded in the Williams' household. Hannah and the children were elated to have Dad home for the weekend; it had been a challenging week for them as well.

Jack was about to discover just how big a challenge it had been.

Hearing Hannah's footsteps coming down the stairs, Jack knew the children were down for the night.

"Well, Jack, you've had an extraordinary week to say the least. Tell me about your meeting with Pete."

"He seemed interested in my proposal. Mickey is meeting with him in the morning. They've known each other a long time, and Mickey's going to try and close the deal. There's significant mutual respect between the two of them. We might just pull this thing off. There's another factor as well."

"Oh? What's that?"

"We just acquired another company. Pete's going to have his hands full working on the integration. He needs to put this plant manager thing to bed, and that could work in our favor. Pete won't act out of expedience, though. He's too much of an advocate of the *12 Absolutes* to take that route. So that's where we are, little girl."

"Jack, you know that everything always works out for us. I'm confident that Pete's decision will be favorable. Well, old boy, I've had a challenging and exciting week myself. With all that was going on with you, I decided to wait until you got home to give you the news."

"The news?"

"With all the excitement on your end, you probably forgot that I had a doctor's appointment Wednesday."

"Sorry, Hannah. Is everything okay?"

"Jack, you're going to be a daddy again."

Absolute #3

SERVE OTHERS

Your returns in life come back to you as a result of your contributions to others.

RUSSELL JAMES

Dan had each *12 Absolutes* participant recap Absolute #2: Take Action. He accomplished this by having each class member give personal examples of when failing to take action had proven to be costly and when taking action had proven advantageous. Their personal stories validated the critical importance of the action absolute. Additionally, each class member identified areas in which they needed to take action, executed an action plan complete with timelines and deadlines, fashioned it into a contract, and signed it.

"Absolute #3, Serve Others, is probably the most controversial of the *12 Absolutes*." Dan Hardee began discussing this absolute in a serious determined tone. "Serve Others is quite counterintuitive. Even if we agree with it, it's difficult to live day in and day out, but when we do, the results are outstanding. First, let's discuss some principles surrounding this absolute."

Dan went to the flip chart and wrote:

The Law of Indirect Effort

- **The best way to get someone interested in you is to get interested in them, first.**
- **Don't try to impress, be impressed by them.**

- **To be happy, make others happy.**
- **Give respect to get respect.**
- **Get admiration by giving admiration.**
- **Believe in them, and they'll believe in you.**
- **Show confidence to gain confidence.**
- **Raise their self-esteem and you raise yours.**

Dan discussed each one of the highlighted points in detail and arrived at this bottom-line conclusion:

What you sow in the lives of others you reap in your own.

Surprisingly, Hank took immediate exception to Dan's commentary.

"Dan this all sounds great, you know the good old golden rule, and I agree to an extent. But what about when you're dealing with the jerks of the world, the know-it-alls, the irritators, the obstinate, the ones that will only capitalize on your kindness and take advantage of you? Are you telling us that this applies to that breed as well?"

By now they all knew what to expect. Dan threw Hank's question back at the group.

"How does everyone feel about Hank's analogy?" Dan asked.

Dan listened carefully as everyone shared their thoughts and feelings.

"Well," Dan responded, "let me tell you what I'm hearing. You all seem to agree that it's a great concept and has application, but the application is situational. In other words, if we're dealing with nice, cooperative, open-minded, rational, reasonable individuals it's potentially effective. However, when we encounter people who need mental enemas, as Clyde puts it, the law of indirect effort won't work."

"Yeah," James agreed, "that's about it. I mean, you've got to protect yourself out there. You can't let people push you around and take advantage of you. If you come on like the Good Samaritan in every situation, you're going to wind up like that pretty good alligator wrestler Clyde's been talking about. Turning the other cheek may work in your world, but it'll get your butt kicked in mine!"

"If you think I'm going to behave toward my ex-husband according to those dots on the board, you've lost it Dan," Joanne chimed in with her usual disdain. "Nice people, yes; mean people, no!"

William pondered his words carefully. "I know it's the way we should behave. I also believe it's effective most of the time, but this is supposed to be an absolute, and I'm struggling with that. I find it hard to believe that all people will absolutely respond in kind to the behaviors you're advocating."

"Good point, William," Jack responded. "I feel pretty much the same. I think I know some people that aren't going to respond favorably no matter how we set it up on the front end. As a matter of fact, I had to deal with one last week."

"Well, I been standing loose in the traces, keeping my mouth shut," Clyde chimed in with his usual sly grin "I been takin' all this in and I gotta tell ya, there's some people got a look on they face like they're doin' a commercial for embalming fluid. You know, the kinda people ain't smiled since their honeymoon. I just don't think those type folks gonna git it when we do those things you got up there on the board."

"So, Mary, what's your opinion?"

"I've been trying to think beyond the obvious, the obvious being that sometimes entering into the behaviors on the board will work, and sometimes they won't. It all depends on the people we're dealing with. While you guys were responding, I tried to take my emotions out of it. I asked myself, so what if they don't respond with the same respect I'm giving them? Why is it so important that the score be even? I'm beginning to think we should execute those behaviors with everyone in every situation, no matter what response we're receiving."

"Mary, you're making me crazy with those comments."

"How so, Tony?" Mary asked.

"I think you're on to something, but I don't want to accept it. When Dan first wrote them on the board, I immediately began picturing the most adversarial people I know, and my mind said no way. No way those type yo-yos are going to respond positively to anything. Now, Mary, you've put a completely different spin on things. Your questions—so what if they don't respond with the same respect we're giving them? And why is it so important that the score be even? —have prompted me to look at things from a modified point of view."

"What do you mean?" Hank asked.

"Well, Hank, when we assume that some type of people aren't going to respond to the Law of Indirect Effort from a positive perspective, where's the focus?"

"Oh yeah, I see where you're going. The focus is off us and on them, and anytime we think the problem is 'out there,' that is the problem."

"Right, Hank, and here's another consideration. I think we all agree that practicing this law is the right thing to do. I mean, by obeying the law we are on the right side of the master law of the universe, the Law of Cause and Effect, right? So, by doing the right thing, i.e. producing the right causes, we will gain positive effects. Whether or not we get those effects from the people that we are exposing to the Law of Indirect Effort is beside the point. In order to receive good effects, we must produce the right causes."

Dan interrupted. "Mary and Tony are definitely on the right track. Anytime we do the right thing, we will be rewarded for it. The only uncertainty is when and how. It's this simple uncertainty that keeps the multitudes from examining and disciplining their actions.

"The plaintive hordes want instant gratification, value for value on the spot. If they don't get it they quickly abandon their actions and proclaim, 'This stuff doesn't work.'"

The Trickster

"So, Dan," Mary asked, "what keeps us from staying with it? Why do we abandon the process so quickly?"

"In a word, Mary, ego. See, our need to be right, to have justice, to be heard, to receive immediate value for value, and to write off people who do not rapidly respond in kind to the implementation of the Law of Indirect Effort, is simply our ego stomping its feet and whining for attention like a spoiled child."

Dan handed out a sheet of paper with the heading:

AT THE FEAST OF EGO EVERYONE LEAVES HUNGRY

- The ego's first response is to attack or control.

- The ego justifies every fight.

- The ego overwhelms our desire to listen to reason.

- The ego keeps us too busy to evaluate our words and actions.

- The ego labels the other person unworthy.

- The ego creates our greatest problems when we're in its control.

- The ego lies when it convinces us that we'll be more secure by putting it in charge.

- The ego tells us that we can and should change the actions of another.

- The ego loves anger, and when it gets us in that state, it has total power over us.

- The ego exposes our vulnerabilities.

- The ego is the trickster that makes life difficult.

- The ego has a strong voice, and we will never be at peace when it interprets our experiences.

- The ego never wants what's best for us.

- The ego loves to make comparisons, to keep us feeling separate, superior or inferior, competitive and alone.

- The ego manufactures fear-inducing data to control us.

- The ego prevents us from being compassionate with ourselves.

- The ego strengthens selfishness and focuses our attention on scarcity and blame.

- The ego constructs the barrier to love.

- The ego inspires jealousy.

- The ego prevents us from helping others, forgiving others, and loving others.

- The ego prevents us from tapping into the power of the Law of Indirect Effort.

 **BOB FLYNN**

After allowing a few minutes for the group to review the ego handout, Dan discussed the enormous downside of allowing our egos to rule our associations with others. One of his major admonitions was:

Work hard at not arousing the ego of others. This is accomplished by keeping your ego under control.

The group learned that when two or more egos become entangled, our relationship with that person quickly takes second place. Petty disagreements, useless arguments, hurt feelings, damaged and sometimes ruined relationships result.

"Adhering to The Law of Indirect Effort on a continuing basis will turn even hard-core antagonists around. The key word is continuing. Be reminded when you focus on the other person's negativity you give them the power, and you give up taking personal responsibility. Certainly, by now you know that until you take full responsibility in every situation and every relationship, you're stuck." Dan concluded the morning discussion by advising that until we master our ego, we will never fully tap into the magnificent power of The Law of Indirect Effort.

The Bomb

The class reconvened after lunch and Dan handed out a document and asked each participant to read it.

Dear Dan and Class,

Due to the ineffectiveness of The 12 Absolutes workshop, I have decided to leave the program. From day one I have struggled with most of the concepts. They sound good, but in the real world of today, and especially given my personal circumstances, I see almost no validity in their potential. The straw that broke the camel's back was a statement Dan made this morning:

Your ability to find true success, happiness, and to maximize your personal effectiveness is in direct proportion to your willingness to forgive all people who have hurt you in some way. The bigger the hurt and the closer you are to the person who hurt you, the more important it is for you to forgive. Most unhappiness and psychosomatic illness

are caused by the unwillingness to forgive. This insistence on holding on to grudges and the desire for vengeance is a self-imposed prison. The very act of forgiveness totally liberates you from the person and the incident. The bottom line is... FORGIVENESS IS THE GIFT YOU GIVE YOURSELF.

When you have experienced continual betrayal, abuse, and now borderline poverty at the hands of someone who pledged to love and protect you forever, forgiveness is simply not an option; in fact, it's ludicrous. I wish each of you the best of luck in the future. If you are counting on this program to lead you to enhanced effectiveness; you are going to need it.

Sincerely,
Joanne

A pronounced silence engulfed the room. Finally, Dan spoke up. "I'm not totally surprised that Joanne has decided to leave. She has struggled with the course from day one. What is a little disconcerting to me, however, is that I explained the importance of forgiveness to her when she was qualifying for the course. She seemed to understand the importance of letting go and moving on. How is everyone else feeling?"

More silence, and then William spoke up. "I'm in a situation similar to Joanne's, so I can relate to a degree. However, I'm beginning to see how debilitating the inability to forgive can be. When you said forgiveness is the gift you give yourself, that struck a chord with me. I suppose it's the responsibility thing again. I mean, it's up to each individual to take personal responsibility for forgiving any and all who have hurt them."

"You said this would be the most controversial of the Absolutes," Tony began. "That prepared me to be open-minded. You also prepared us by conveying that all of the Absolutes were to some degree or another counterintuitive. I'm learning to suspend my first intuitive inclination and get the full picture. We've really just begun this Absolute and even now it's starting to make sense."

Everyone agreed to wish Joanne the best and move on.

Dan continued. "Suspending our own agendas is one of the most important and difficult lessons we can ever learn, but when we learn and practice it our personal effectiveness expands exponentially."

 **BOB FLYNN**

Dan displayed the following slide:

> *The most successful people in our society are those who have helped the greatest number of people to get the things they want. These people build up a reservoir of good will and create a propensity in others to help them, to reciprocate for having been helped in the past.*

"When we help others get the things they want, we are operating on the positive side of the Law of Reciprocity."

Dan advanced the next slide:

People are internally driven to be even, to reciprocate for anything done to or for them. They will be willing to help you achieve your goals only when you have demonstrated a willingness to help them achieve theirs.

Jack's mind raced back to the plant, to Fred Rawlinson and his management style. Fred was competent, knowledgeable, and experienced, but he didn't have a clue when it came to executing the Law of Reciprocity. No wonder the employees were withholding their best efforts!

Dan's voice brought Jack back to the moment.

"The Law of Reciprocity and the Law of Compensation work together to determine our level of personal effectiveness."

Dan brought up the next slide:

> *THE LAW OF COMPENSATION... Other people will help you achieve your goals only if they feel compensated for their efforts in some way.*

"When we're first introduced to this law, our natural inclination is to define compensation in financial terms. Money perks, benefits, etc., are compensation, but compensation also comes in many forms. These are but a few:

- Positive feedback.
- Recognition.

- Interesting assignments.
- Advancement.
- Sincere appreciation.
- Made to feel part of the team.
- Raising self-esteem.

> **Next to physical survival, the greatest need of a human being is psychological survival-to be understood, to be affirmed to be validated, to be appreciated."**

Clyde jumped in. "I got two old hound dogs, Catfish and Cornbread, and when they run a rabbit you better rub 'em, scratch 'em, and tell 'em they the best dogs in the county otherwise, hoss, you ain't gonna catch many rabbits."

"It's as simple as this," Dan continued. "People, and hound dogs, simply won't work for nothing. Steven Covey, author of *The Seven Habits of Highly Effective People*, calls this investing in people's emotional bank account. He uses the analogy of a personal bank account by saying if you continually make withdrawals without making deposits, you'll go bankrupt. The same is true with others. If you make withdrawals without making deposits, you'll bankrupt the relationship. It's all about service to others."

Dan pointed to the next PowerPoint slide:

> **You can serve others to the degree that you look deliberately for the good in each person and situation. If you first look for the bad in people and circumstances, you will not be motivated to serve them.**

"This is a critical point. Think about it. If we don't think a person is worthy, we're not going to want to serve them or to move them ahead in any way. It's easy to help nice, cooperative people, people who share our same perspectives, those agreeable, positive, open-minded, progressive types. But what about people who push back, people who challenge us and cause us to re-examine our plans and strategies, even our values?"

Dan touched the scroll key on his computer.

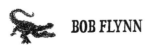

Insecure people think that all reality should conform to their view of the world, their opinions and paradigms. They have a need to control others, to mold them toward their way of thinking.

However, the very strength of a relationship is allowing another point of view. Sameness is not oneness; uniformity is not necessarily unity.

"We must learn to look past what seems to be disagreement and obstinacy. When we don't like someone, even when we feel offended by them, we must ask ourselves: What is it about this person or this situation that I don't like? What is the lesson that I'm supposed to be getting?

"We live in a world of hypersensitivity. If we join the hypersensitive crowd, we're going to miss many valuable lessons. We'll fail to look for the good in the person and the situation, and we'll severely limit the number of people we can get along with."

Dan pointed to the next slide:

The inability to get along with a wide variety of people is the primary reason for personal ineffectiveness, frustration, and unhappiness in life and work. More than 95% of people let go from their jobs are fired because of poor social skills rather than lack of competence or technical ability.

"There's no such thing as a pretty good alligator wrestler, and there's no such thing as independence. We are all interdependent. We need each other and we simply cannot survive of our own initiative. Should we desire to move beyond mere survival and seek outstanding results, we must obey the Law of Organized Effort."

Again, Dan pointed to the screen.

The most important and the most highly paid form of intelligence in North America is social intelligence, the ability to get along well with an expanding sphere of people. Fully 85% of your personal effectiveness is going to be determined by your social skills, by your ability to interact positively and effectively with others, and by your success in getting them to cooperate with you in helping you to achieve your goals.

"Serving others is not altruism. Frankly, it's good business. When you go through life raising the self-esteem of others, opportunities will open up before you, and people will help you in ways you can't imagine. Even knowing this, people who do not feel good about themselves cannot serve others. You can always tell how together a person is by the manner in which they relate to others, especially others who are different and have contrasting opinions. The more a person likes and respects himself or herself, the more they will like and respect others regardless of the differences. The most effective and happy men and women in our society are those who make other people feel good about themselves. However, this can only happen to the degree that they feel good about themselves.

"Personal effectiveness and the ability to influence are inseparable. Again, ego often comes into play and interferes with or totally destroys our influential capabilities."

Dan walked over to the flip chart and wrote:

Being influenceable is the key to influencing others.

"Ego often blocks our ability to be influenced by another, especially if that person is younger; a relative; holds a lower position; or has less education, experience, or clout. When we become wise and mature enough to interpret all of life's experiences in terms of opportunities for learning and contribution, we defeat the ego and open ourselves up to being influenced. As a result, we begin to influence others.

"Seeing the world in terms of what you can do for the world and its people causes you to be more authentic. The more authentic you become, the more genuine is your expression, particularly regarding personal experiences and

 **BOB FLYNN**

even self-doubts, then the more people can relate to your expression and the safer it makes them feel to express themselves. This causes them to relate and feel closer to you and opens the door to expanding levels of influence."

Dan concluded the teaching part of the session by discussing the Law of Overcompensation.

> **The Law of Overcompensation is triggered by the habit of always doing more than you are paid for. Effective people and effective businesses are those that habitually exceed expectations.**

"If you want to increase the quality and quantity of your returns, you need but to increase the quantity and quality of your service to others. People who assume the attitude of 'I don't get paid to do that, and if they want me to do more they must pay more,' simply don't get it! They are trying to gain the effect before producing the cause, reap before they sow. It's never worked, it never will."

The rest of the day was invested in completing exercises that substantiated the 3rd Absolute.

Tired but excited, Jack headed home. His excitement stemmed from the fact that as a result of today's lesson, he felt he knew exactly what to do to get the plant back on track. He couldn't wait to share the lesson with Hannah and get back on the job. He was quite anxious to put this stuff into practice. After learning that Mickey was going to put the "pitch" on Pete, he was feeling very confident that he'd get his shot at the plant manager's position. This was more important than ever with the new baby on the way!

Monday morning came fast. Arriving at the plant, Jack hurried excitedly to Mickey's office. To his shock and surprise there to greet him were Pete, Mickey, and Fred Rawlinson!

What he heard next was unbelievable.

AIN'T NO SUCH THANG AS
A PURDY GOOD ALLIGATOR RASSLER

Absolute #3

SERVE OTHERS

Your returns in life come back to you as a result of your contributions to others.

RUSSELL JAMES

KEY POINT ⎯⎯⎯⎯⎯⎯⎯⎯⎯⎯⎯⎯⎯⎯⎯⎯⎯

The concept of serving others is counterintuitive. Even if we agree with it in principle, it can be difficult to live day in and day out, but when we do the results are phenomenal.

❑ Obey the Law of Indirect Effort.

❑ What you sow in the lives of others you reap in your own.

❑ Any time we see the problem as "out there," that is the problem.

❑ Obey the Laws of Compensation and Overcompensation.

❑ At the Feast of the EGO Everyone Leaves Hungry.

❑ Being influenceable is the key to influencing others.

❑ The very strength of any relationship is allowing another point of view.

❑ You can serve others to the degree that you look for the good in all.

❑ Insecure people think that all should conform to their views.

❑ The greatest needs are to be understood, affirmed, validated, appreciated.

❑ No deposits, no withdrawals; obey the Law of Reciprocity.

 **BOB FLYNN**

MAJOR POINT ———————————————

Characteristics of the EGO: first response is to attack or control, justifies every fight, overwhelms our desire to listen to reason, keeps us from evaluating our words and actions, labels others unworthy, creates our greatest problems, tells us we'll be more secure by putting it in charge, tells us we should change others, loves to take complete control by getting us angry, exposes our vulnerabilities, never wants what's best for us, makes comparisons, keeps us feeling separate, inferior, competitive, alone, selfish, prevents us from being compassionate with ourselves, inspires jealousy, constructs barriers to love, prevents us from reaching our full potential... *MASTER YOUR EGO!*

THE MOST SUCCESSFUL PEOPLE IN OUR SOCIETY ARE THOSE WHO HAVE HELPED THE GREATEST NUMBER OF PEOPLE GET WHAT THEY WANT.

AIN'T NO SUCH THANG AS
A PURDY GOOD ALLIGATOR RASSLER

ABSOLUTE #3

EXERCISE

(1.) Identify five people that can assist you in becoming more effective in your top 5 priorities.
(2.) Identify actions you will take to adhere to The Law of Reciprocity.
(3.) Commit to a date that you will begin taking these actions.

1ST PERSON: _____
PRIORITY: _____
ACTIONS/DATE: _____
_____
_____
_____
_____
_____
_____
_____
_____
_____ / _____

2ND PERSON: _____
PRIORITY: _____
ACTIONS/DATE: _____
_____
_____
_____
_____
_____
_____
_____
_____ / _____

BOB FLYNN

3RD PERSON: _____

PRIORITY: _____

ACTIONS/DATE: _____

_____

_____

_____

_____

_____

_____

_____

_____

_____

_____ / _____

4TH PERSON: _____

PRIORITY: _____

ACTIONS/DATE: _____

_____

_____

_____

_____

_____

_____

_____

_____

_____

_____ / _____

5TH PERSON: _____

PRIORITY: _____

ACTIONS/DATE: _____

_____

_____

_____

_____

_____

_____

_____

_____

_____

_____ / _____

AIN'T NO SUCH THANG AS
A PURDY GOOD ALLIGATOR RASSLER

CHAPTER SIX

The Switcharoo

ABSOLUTE #4

Questions are the Answers

ABSOLUTE #5

Embrace Change

*Real opportunities
lie within setbacks,
disappointments,
problems, and hurts.*

RUSSELL JAMES

AIN'T NO SUCH THANG AS
A PURDY GOOD ALLIGATOR RASSLER

The Switcharoo

Jack could feel it. It was in the air. It was big, AND it wasn't good.

Upon entering Mickey Kelly's office, Jack sensed a high degree of uneasiness and tension. Mickey, Pete, and Fred Rawlinson were obviously not expecting him, as they all had a look of shock on their faces.

"You're early," Mickey said.

"Yeah," Jack replied. "I took an earlier flight. I'm ready to get going."

There was a deafening, seemingly interminable silence as the tension grew.

Taking charge, Pete quickly escorted Jack out of the room and into his office.

"What's up, Pete? What's Rawlinson doing here?"

"Jack, let me bring you up to speed," Pete began. "As you know, I met with Mickey for breakfast Saturday morning. He expressed his total support for you and pitched me real hard. He was almost insistent that you be promoted to the plant manager position. I'll have to admit it was a tempting consideration. I can't honestly say I wasn't overwhelmed by the validity of the plan, but it was feasible--risky but feasible. I told him I'd sleep on it, and then something happened."

"Oh, what was that?" Jack asked.

"Rawlinson called me right after Mickey left and said he wanted to meet. It seemed urgent, so I asked him to come over to my hotel. We spent the rest of the day talking. Basically, he convinced me that he should remain as plant manager."

"What!" Jack interrupted. "After he's screwed up production, has morale at an all-time low, and announced to everyone he's leaving, you're going to reinstate him? With all due respect, Pete, that's a very weird decision."

"I'm sure it seems that way on the surface. However, there are some

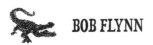 **BOB FLYNN**

extenuating circumstances that I wasn't aware of. When Fred brought them to my attention, I began to see his position. Frankly, if I'd been through what he has, I would probably have considered quitting myself. And by the way, he never told any of his people that he's leaving."

"So, what are these extenuating circumstances?"

"At this point I'm not at liberty to discuss them. It will all come out in due time."

"So where does that leave me?"

"Honestly, I haven't been able to give that much thought. There's significant change taking place in the company. We're continuing to make acquisitions, so there's going to be plenty for you to do, important things. I just have to get my head around it."

"Pete, I've got to tell you that this is quite a shock. One minute I think I'm going to run this plant, and the next minute I'm in limbo again. I'm beginning to question the fairness of all this. I feel set up, betrayed!"

"Jack, I can honestly relate to what you're saying. I know you're hurt and disappointed; however, you set yourself up. I made no promises. I told you I would give your proposal fair consideration, and I did. You had to know that this was far from a done deal. I can empathize, but your feelings are your responsibility."

Jack allowed a few seconds for Pete's words to sink in. As much as he hated to admit it, Pete was right. No promises had been made except that fair consideration would be given, and knowing Pete, that was probably the case.

"Jack?"

"Yeah, Pete?"

"You okay?"

"Yeah, I'm okay. I'm not all that happy, but I'm okay."

"Jack, I want you to get with Mickey right away. As you might imagine, he's quite concerned that you might think that he rolled over, just went along with

AIN'T NO SUCH THANG AS
A PURDY GOOD ALLIGATOR RASSLER

my decision. Let me assure you that's not the case. Mickey rarely shows anger. He's quite amiable, as you know, but when I told him of my decision, he lost it."

"What do you mean he lost it?"

"He basically told me I was weak and stupid. Those weren't his exact words, but I got the message loud and clear, same as I got it from you."

"It's a strange decision, Pete. It's just not like you to waffle."

"Well, if I've learned anything about leadership, it's that to be a strong leader you have to make hard decisions, unpopular decisions, decisions that may not seem logical on the surface. Occasionally, leadership requires that you make gut-wrenching decisions that may alienate people you care deeply about, good people, smart people, people like you and Mickey."

Pete's comment stopped Jack's pouting dead in its tracks. He was so wrapped up in his own anger and disappointment that he hadn't even considered how Pete and Mickey might be feeling.

He felt a twinge of remorse course through his body.

"Okay, Pete, I hear you. I should suck it up, be a big boy, and take full responsibility."

"That's what you can do."

"That's what I will do."

"Thanks; that means a lot to me. I won't forget it."

"There's just one more thing, Pete."

"What's that?"

"Those extenuating circumstances that caused you to reinstate Fred--are you ever gonna tell me about them?"

"Probably not."

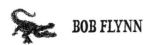 **BOB FLYNN**

As Jack entered his office, Mickey Kelley quickly rose to his feet and extended his hand. "Well I really put that plan together, huh partner?"

"Don't sweat it, Mickey. Pete told me you fought like a banshee."

"Fought but lost. I'm sorry, man. I had no idea Fred would want to reconsider, much less that Pete would take him back."

"What do you think happened?"

"I've got a theory, but it's sheer speculation."

"Let's hear it. It's a hundred per cent more than I've got."

"Pete's predecessor John Richardson and Fred didn't get along at all. He kept Fred under his thumb, made all the meaningful decisions, and if they didn't work out, which most of them didn't, Fred got the blame. Richardson was a hands-off guy, hardly ever visited the plant. He mostly called or emailed Fred and gave him his marching orders. You could just see Fred taking less and less initiative. He just sat and waited for his orders. The plant personnel assumed that Fred was calling the shots and continued to lose confidence in him. For most of the past year, Fred pretty much just stayed in his office, staring into his computer. He'd come in late and leave early. He did just enough to get by. I tried to get him to open up, but to no avail. By the time Richardson got the ax, Fred had already committed to another job. He took vacation time and waited for Pete to show up so he could drop the bomb."

"That sounds logical, Mickey. So why do you think Fred had a change of heart?"

"Again, this is strictly a guess on my part, but I think Fred assumed Pete would gladly accept his resignation and be done with it. As you know, that's not Pete's style. He probes deeply into all decisions, especially important ones. He strives to understand the root cause of everything. I'm sure Pete tried to get to the bottom of Fred's decision, and he did it in his usual compassionate way. Fred's mind was made up, he had decided to leave no matter what, and so he followed through and quit. Then he began to think about Pete's approach, and that's when his second thoughts began. So, he decided to give Pete a call, tell him the real story behind his resignation, and see how Pete would respond. When Fred told him his story, the fact that he was never allowed to manage the plant the way he thought best, Pete believed him. Pete believed him because he's heard all the Richardson stories. He's been checking behind Richardson's decisions and he's seen a consistent pattern. Pete told him things would be different and that the micromanaging and the blame-fixing are over. He assured him that he'd get a real shot at turning things around. Fred bought it, and here we are."

"Yeah, I think you're right. I'll bet that's about what happened. Pete didn't want to see all that experience walk out the door, especially since Fred never really had the opportunity to put his mark on the operation."

"Whatever the reason Pete left Fred in the job, you can be sure that he didn't soft sell it and that there's no doubt in Fred's mind that he is expected to get the job done, and fast. You know how Pete is about taking responsibility."

"Do I ever, Mickey--do I ever."

Jack lay back on the motel room bed and ruminated on the day's events. What a day it had been! Even though it had started badly, it had ended on a positive note. He now had a specific assignment at the plant. He would serve as the first shift Operations Manager and help Fred and Mickey get morale and production back on target. Fred had seemed like a totally different person. Now he had energy, drive, and focus. He apologized openly in front of Pete and Mickey regarding the comments he made when Jack attempted to assist him. Pete spelled out his expectations, pledged his support, and suggested that the four of them meet for a planning session beginning at 7:00 a.m. tomorrow. Jack laughed when he recalled his earlier phone conversation with Hannah; he thought she might be disappointed that the plant manager's job didn't work out.

After he told her the story, she said what she always said: "No problem, Jack, everything always works out for us. I'm certain there's something even better up the road."

What a rock she is, Jack thought. *Here she is expecting a baby, knowing we need the money the plant manager's position would bring, and yet there wasn't the slightest hesitation in her optimism.*

Then Jack's mood shifted, and his self-talk turned negative.

"Yeah, that all sounds good when I put a positive spin on it, but let's get down to reality here. Fred's back in the top job and I'm just his helper. No more

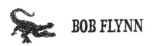 **BOB FLYNN**

money and no sign that there will be any in the short term. Did I do the right thing here? Should I have even taken this assignment in the first place? Will I ever really succeed?"

The Passage

The knock at the door interrupted Jack's thoughts. Opening the door, he was handed a small package. "What's this? I'm not expecting anything." Opening the package, he saw a small orange book. It was old and tattered. Thumbing through the pages he noticed a folded note that was addressed to his father Jim and dated March 17,1965. He immediately recognized the handwriting as his mother's. Continuing to thumb through the book, Jack found a sealed envelope with the following instructions:

Do Not Open This Envelope Until You Have Read Your Mother's Note.

Jack also recognized this handwriting. It was Hannah's.

Carefully unfolding the note, Jack began reading:

Dearest Jim, 3/17/65

You will no doubt be surprised to find this book when you unpack. I slipped it into your suitcase when you went upstairs to kiss little Jack goodbye. I put it there because I thought you might need a boost, a shot in the arm. You've been working so hard and I know you're faced with a lot of difficult decisions. Being out of town so much lately hasn't been easy for either of us, and I know you've had some doubts concerning your new job.

I just want you to know that we appreciate how hard you work and the fact that you're always trying to improve every aspect of your life. It troubled me when you called yourself a failure because it simply isn't true! You are a success, Jim, and you're going to be a bigger one, there is no doubt in my mind. What happened at Chadbourn wasn't your fault, so you just keep the faith and press on. You know Jim, everything always works out for us.

Read the passage on page 67-70.

All My Love,
Ann

AIN'T NO SUCH THANG AS
A PURDY GOOD ALLIGATOR RASSLER

Jack stared at the note and swallowed hard as he opened the envelope.

Dear Jack,

Back in 1965 your Dad lost his job at Chadbourn. It was a real tough time for him. You were only four and your mom was past due with Billy. The money was tight, and your dad was having big time self-doubts. He had just taken a new job and it wasn't going very well. He told me this letter from your mom and the passage she recommended was a major turning point for him. In fact, he said it saved him.

On our wedding day, your dad took me aside and told me there would come a time when you would need my total reassurance. He said I'd know when the time was right. He also gave me this book and your mom's note and said, "When you sense he needs it, make sure he gets it."

That time is now, Jack.

I know you're giving the job, our marriage, your responsibilities as a father, and your overall self-improvement everything you've got. You are exceptional, Jack, and I'm so proud to be your wife. You are a success, and you're going to be an even bigger one.

You're the man… you always were and always will be.

Now read that passage!

All My Love Always,

Hannah

THE SCROLL MARKED III

I will persist until I succeed.

In the Orient, young bulls are tested for the fight arena in a certain manner. Each is brought to the ring and allowed to attack a picador who pricks them with a lance. The bravery of each bull is then rated with care according to the number of times he demonstrates his willingness to charge in spite of the sting of the blade. Henceforth will I recognize that each day I am tested by life in like manner. If I persist, if I continue to try, if I continue to charge forward, I will succeed.

 **BOB FLYNN**

I will persist until I succeed.

I was not delivered unto this world in defeat, nor does failure course in my veins. I am not a sheep waiting to be prodded by my shepherd. I am a lion and I refuse to talk, to walk, or to act like sheep. I will hear not those who weep and complain, for their disease is contagious. Let them join the sheep. The slaughterhouse of failure is not my destiny.

I will persist until I succeed.

The prizes of life are at the end of each journey, not near the beginning; and it is not given to me to know how many steps are necessary in order to reach my goal. Failure I may encounter at the thousandth step, yet success hides behind the next bend in the road. Never will I know how close it lies unless I turn the corner.

Always will I take another step. If that is to no avail, I will take another, and yet another. In truth, one step at a time is not too difficult.

I will persist until I succeed.

Henceforth, I will consider each day's effort as but one blow of my blade against a mighty oak. The first blow may not cause a tremor in the wood, nor the second, nor the third. Each blow, of itself, may be trifling, and seem of no consequence. Yet from childlike swipes the oak will eventually tumble. So it will be with my efforts of today.

I will be likened to the raindrop which washes away the mountain; the ant who devours a tiger; the star which brightens the earth; the slave who builds a pyramid. I will build my castle one brick at a time, for I know that small attempts repeated will complete any undertaking.

I will persist until I succeed.

I will never consider defeat and I will remove from my vocabulary such words and phrases as quit, cannot, unable, impossible, out of the question, improbable, failure, unworkable, hopeless, and retreat. I will avoid despair, but if this disease of the mind should infect me, then I will work on in despair. I will toil and I will endure. I will ignore the obstacles at my feet and keep mine eyes on the goals above my head, for I know that where dry desert ends, green grass grows.

AIN'T NO SUCH THANG AS
A PURDY GOOD ALLIGATOR RASSLER

I will persist until I succeed.

I will remember the ancient law of averages and I will bend it to my good. I will persist with my knowledge that each setback will increase my chance for success at the next attempt. Each nay I hear will bring me closer to the sound of yea. Each frown I meet only prepares me for the smile to come. Each misfortune I encounter will carry in it the seed for tomorrow's good luck. I must have the night to appreciate the day. I must fail often to succeed once.

I will persist until I succeed.

I will try, and try, and try again. Each obstacle I will consider as a mere detour to my goal and a challenge to my profession. I will persist and develop my skills as the mariner develops his, by learning to ride out the wrath of each storm.

I will persist until I succeed.

Henceforth, I will learn and apply another secret of those who excel. When each day has ended, not regarding whether it has been a success or a failure, I will try one more time. When my thoughts beckon my tired body homeward, I will resist the temptation to depart. I will try again. I will make one more attempt to close with victory, and if that fails, I will make another. Never will I allow any day to end with a failure. Thus, will I plant the seed of tomorrow's success and gain an insurmountable advantage over those who cease their labor at a prescribed time. When others cease their struggle, then mine will begin, and my harvest will be full.

I will persist until I succeed.

Nor will I allow yesterday's success to lull me into today's complacency, for this is the great foundation of failure. I will forget the happenings of the day that is gone, whether they were good or bad, and greet the new sun with confidence that this will be the best day of my life. So long as there is breath in me, that long will I persist. For now, I know one of the greatest principles of success; if I persist long enough, I will win.

I will persist.

I will win.

OG MANDINO

 **BOB FLYNN**

The Commitments

Jack was almost overcome with emotion. His mind was racing, his heart pounding. *I never knew what Dad went through after he lost his job. He never discussed it; he just hid the pain and kept going. Now I know one thing for sure. He's been down the same road I'm on. He knows what it takes to move ahead, to persist until you succeed. And Hannah's timing, perfect as usual. How did she know I'd need that passage at the end of the day today?*

Jack reread the passage three more times as he let every word sink in. As he read, Jack began to realize just how profound this business of mind control really is. "We do in fact become what we think about. When I think about failure I attract it into my life as surely as a magnet attracts iron, and when I focus on success, the things I want to happen do happen." Jack felt the power in the passage, and right then and there he made a firm commitment to read the scroll marked III first thing in the morning and the last thing at night. He also committed to himself to never again focus on things he didn't want. He vowed to throw himself into his work and do the best he possibly could. He didn't take this job to whine and cry. He took it to succeed, and he would persist until he did just that.

And then he called his dad.

It was a great conversation, very fulfilling and especially encouraging. They talked for over an hour, and even though they covered several topics, one central theme surrounded his dad's admonishments:

Belief in limitation is the one and only thing that causes limitation!

"Don't allow yourself to get discouraged," Jack's dad had said right before they said their goodbyes. "It is astonishing how many people lack the power of holding on until they reach their goals. They can make a sudden dash, but they lack the grit. They give up easily. They do fine as long as everything moves smoothly, but when there is friction, disappointment, or pressure they lose heart. They look to stronger personalities for their spirit and strength. They lack the independence of originality. They only dare to do a little more than they've ever done. They do not step boldly from the crowd, face their fears, and persist."

"Well," Fred Rawlinson said addressing Mickey and Jack, "we're off to a great

new beginning. I think the team is starting to buy in. Our production numbers are trending in the right direction and morale has definitely improved. We've got some hurdles to jump, and jump'em we will. And listen, guys, thanks for a great week. I didn't know what to expect after you heard Pete's decision, but he told me you were both class acts, and he was right. You guys dove right in and started turning this thing around. Thanks again. I'm very encouraged. You guys have a super weekend and I'll see you first thing Monday morning. Oh, and by the way, I hope I get the opportunity to help you some day."

Jack could never have imagined just how soon that day would come.

Back at home, Hannah and the kids were great. Jack thanked her again for the letter and the passage. Hannah grinned and said, "You're on your way, big boy."

Jack finished up his preparation for tomorrow's *12 Absolutes* class, read the passage, and turned in for a few hours of sleep.

Absolute #4

THE QUESTIONS ARE THE ANSWERS

Undoubtedly there are no questions to us that are unanswerable.

ROBERT J. FLYNN

Dan Hardee welcomed the *12 Absolutes* participants on a beautiful Saturday morning. With a serious look and in a somber tone he began the lesson.

"Conditions were far beyond the worst imaginable, all hope was gone, escape impossible, and death certain. Every prisoner had accepted this as an unequivocal fact--every prisoner, that is, except one. He would have none of those thoughts; his focus was clear and absolute. He must escape! In the past weeks he had continually asked his fellow inmates at infamous Nazi death camp Auschwitz how they might escape. All their answers had been the same: 'There is no escape; accept your fate.' Alone with his thoughts, he finally realized that if he were to live, it was entirely up to him. Sensing that this was the time, he asked the same question he had asked hundreds of times before; the only

**BOB FLYNN**

difference was that this would probably be the last opportunity he would have to ask it. And so he reached deep within himself and asked:

❚ *"How can I escape from this living hell <u>today</u>?"*

"As he asked that simple question once again--How can I escape from this living hell <u>today</u> – the answer flashed through his mind. He thought of the mounds of bodies that had been piled into a truck only a few yards from where he was working. After all the agonizing and waiting, the answer had come in an instant. At the end of the workday he would strip and hide in the middle of the corpses and pretend to be one of them. His captors would eventually drive him to freedom. As the sun was receding and the workday ending, he took action on his plan, and before the guards missed him the truck pulled out of the hell on earth called Auschwitz. He was a free man.

"Perhaps you are familiar with the story," said Dan. "If you are, then you realize that the escapee was Victor Frankl, author of the classic book *Man's Search for Meaning*. Obviously, there are many factors relative to Mr. Frankl's escape; however, there is one major difference between him and the others at the camp. He refused to give in to his circumstances, to be a victim. And he persistently asked the right question instead of making negative statements to himself. He didn't allow himself to waste precious time bemoaning his perilous situation. He avoided statements to himself such as, 'This is awful.' 'Why has this happened to me?' 'I didn't do anything to deserve this.' Instead of making creativity-killing statements such as these, he asked himself, 'How can I escape from Auschwitz today?'

"Thankfully, it is highly unlikely that you and I will ever be faced with a problem as dire as Mr. Frankl's. We do, however, face a wide array of problems and difficulties every day. How we perceive and handle these inevitable 'obstacles' will determine the degree of our personal effectiveness and ultimate success.

"The truly effective person must learn to question everything and pay close attention to the answers. *To achieve the highest payoff, our questions must consistently focus on two primary areas: problems to be solved and opportunities to realize.* Your focus must remain on these critical areas: problems and opportunities. Get it? Problems and opportunities. Effective people train and discipline themselves to automatically link up the two. When faced with a problem, they immediately ask, where is the opportunity, or how can I convert this problem into an opportunity? These individuals are not blind optimists, they simply understand:

"The Natural Law of Balance, which states that there are equal and offsetting positives to every negative situation.

"Understanding this law, they immediately look for the opportunity when something goes wrong. Realizing there is an offsetting positive to every negative situation, highly effective people habitually maximize the positives that exist within every negative situation. They accomplish this by asking themselves questions.

"When marginally effective people encounter a problem, they do the intuitive thing and saturate their minds with immobilizing statements such as: 'This is terrible! This kind of stuff always happens to me. I knew something like this was going to take place.' These thoughts are intercepted by the subconscious mind, which believes everything it hears and swings into action to bring the negative thoughts into reality.

"This morning we are going to examine in depth Absolute #4, the tremendous power in strategic self-questioning. This absolute is so powerful because you already have the answers. You already know how to be happy, increase your income, get in shape, get promoted, become an expert, and so on. We search for answers, but that's the wrong end of the stick. The right end of the stick is the questions. Properly asked questions kick our brains into high gear. They force us to dig deep, thus tapping the unlimited resources of our subconscious minds that contain the right answers to all our questions.

"This afternoon we will cover Absolute #5, Embrace Change."

The Morning

"Okay, we've had a very productive morning," Dan continued. "Before we break for lunch, let's recap the key points. Who wants to lead off?"

Mary raised her hand. "Great, Mary, tell us what you consider the key points of the morning."

"I will start considering problems, obstacles, irritations, set-backs, disappointments, aggravations, and misfortunes as my teachers. By that I mean, whenever I encounter a problem, I will ask myself questions like:

BOB FLYNN

"• What are the causes of this situation?

"• How can I avoid similar problems in the future?

"• What can I learn from this so that it never happens again?

"• How can I turn this situation around?

"• What am I willing to do to change this from a bad situation to a good one?

"We have discussed several times that it's not the events that happen in our lives that determine how we feel and act, it's the way we interpret and evaluate them that really counts. I learned this morning that we evaluate situations by asking and answering our own questions. It's ironic, but we invest most of our day asking and answering questions to ourselves. Dan, it was like the light came on when you wrote on the chart:

> *"To improve the quality of our lives and thus become more effective we must change the quality of our questions, because it's our questions that direct our focus."*

Dan broke in, "Great job, Mary. Now, someone elaborate on Mary's last statement."

Tony immediately began speaking. "We all have habitual questions and statements that make up our internal dialogue. Typically, we just let these statements and questions take any course they choose and often it's the course of disempowerment. When faced with what we perceive as a bad situation, we usually ask ourselves questions like:

"• How did I get myself in this mess anyway?

"• What in the world will I do now?

"• Who would ever have imagined that it would fall apart like this?

"• Have you ever seen anything this bad?

"Questions of this nature magnify the problem and keep us in the victim role. Our focus is directed to and stays on our negative emotional state and not on seeking solutions. While it is important to clearly define the problem, we cannot allow ourselves to get stuck there. Mulling over the problem to the extreme solidifies the pattern and before long we're caught in the whirlpool of bemoaning the situation over and over. What we're responsible for doing is seeking the best solutions, and strategically positioned questions drive the process. They surface options that stop the 'ain't it awful stinkin' thinkin' syndrome. As we surface options, our mood improves, and soon we're in that 'resolve and solve' state you alluded to."

Again, Dan interrupted. "Someone else take it from there."

Up went William's hand. "I'll tell you what intrigued me," William began. "It was the PowerPoint statement you put up right before the morning break." William glanced at his notes, then began reading aloud:

"Effectively positioned questions are the catalyst for a ripple effect that has impact of such a magnitude that we cannot even imagine. When we question our limitations, the walls of disbelief come tumbling down. The fact of the matter is that:

"All improvements in personal effectiveness are preceded by questions we have never asked ourselves before."

The room was silent for several seconds, and then William continued.

"That was a blockbuster statement. I've pondered it all morning, and I believe it's going to bring me some long-sought-after answers."

Dan looked toward the back of the room and said, "James, you've been mighty quiet this morning. What's your take on the session?"

"I'm quiet because I'm in a state of shock. I've always considered myself a good problem-solver; and I've rated myself good to very good when it comes to identifying and capitalizing on opportunities. After completing Absolute #4, I clearly see where I can improve exponentially."

"How did you arrive at that conclusion?" Dan queried.

"Well, see, when I'm faced with problems, I automatically assume the blame and then I begin beating myself up by making statements and asking questions like:

"• How could you do such a stupid thing?

"• Why didn't you act sooner?

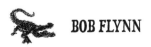 **BOB FLYNN**

"• This is a fine mess you've created.

"• When are you going to get it right?

"Even though I usually end up solving or at least improving the situation, I take the hard-disempowering road. My self-esteem takes an unnecessary hit and I make myself crazy. When we examined the Socratic method of asking ourselves questions it became obvious to me that:

"Questions are the primary way we learn."

Dan continued, "We have to ask ourselves not just any old questions, but questions aimed at solutions and not self-abasement. There's no doubt in my mind that:

"The main difference between people who are successful and those who are not is the fact that successful people ask better questions of themselves and as a result get better answers!"

Jack spoke up. "Dan, like the others, I'm excited about the power of strategically positioned questions. We got a taste of it when we began defining our vision and it proved very helpful to me, but I'm a little confused about one thing."

"What's that?"

"Well, you kept emphasizing the importance of specificity when asking questions. You said that general questions produce weak answers. How can we determine if our questions are specific enough?"

"That's a great question. Let's see if we can clear that up for you. I want you to think about a problem you're currently dealing with, one that you can share with the group."

"Okay, I've got it."

"Great, now tell us about it."

"It's a problem at work. I've just been appointed operations manager in a large manufacturing plant. One of our major concerns is the fact that morale in the plant is low—improving, but still sub par."

Dan threw it out to the class. "So, team, what do you think? What would be some good questions relative to Jack's morale issue?"

Back came a barrage of answers.

"What can we do to improve morale?"

"Where's the best place to start?"

"How can we get morale to an acceptable level?"

"What's causing our morale problems?"

"Which workers are demonstrating low morale?"

"How have we concluded that we have low morale?"

"Any more?" Dan asked. When the class offered no more questions, he continued, "These are pretty good questions, but they're not nearly specific enough to get our brains seeking definitive answers. So, let me ask you, how can we further clarify our questions? Hank, what do you think?"

"I don't know; these seem like really good questions to me."

"Clyde?"

"I think I'm catchin' holt to it, Dan. Here's a question I'd ask. 'As we use the term in this situation, what do we mean by morale?'"

"Excellent, Clyde. That's right on target. So, Jack, what's the answer?"

"Yeah, that is a great question. Let's see, as we use the term, what do we mean by morale? Okay, let me rephrase that to myself. Define what we mean by morale in this situation--in other words, what's the definition of morale as it pertains to our plant situation?"

Dan immediately broke in. "See what Jack's doing? He's processing, drilling down aloud. We're getting a look at what takes place in our minds as we seek to specify. Sorry, Jack, please continue."

"Okay, let me re-engage my brain. What is the definition of morale as it pertains to our situation at the plant?"

 **BOB FLYNN**

Before Jack could begin attempting an answer to his own question, Hank jumped in. "Tighten up the question, Jack. Ask what you mean by morale?"

"Thanks, Hank, that's even better. To me morale is a person's actions, his or her behavior."

Now it was Mary who responded. "Jack, if morale is behavior, here's the definitive question. What specific behaviors are causing the situation at the plant?"

"Good, Mary," Tony interjected. "I've got another question: What is the situation at the plant that's being caused by the low morale?"

Jack laughed and said, "Okay, okay, I've got the question now. What are the specific behaviors that are causing an 18% decline in productivity?"

Dan quickly spoke up. "Very good. So, Jack, what's the answer?"

"Absenteeism is up over 12%, people come in late and leave early, and there's a lot of milling around. Machinery down time has increased 8%, there's been increased turnover in supervisory personnel, and training in certain areas is ineffective. That's all I can think of right now."

"Very good Now who remembers the 'why-what-how-which analogy'?"

William raised his hand.

"Okay, William, tell us how it applies to Jack's circumstance."

"Let's start with the absenteeism issue. First, we would ask, why is absenteeism up over 12%? After we exhausted and captured the reasons, we would then ask…. What can we do about it? – Or – how can we fix it? We would apply one of those questions to each of the reasons that we generated. We would continue until we had thoroughly diagnosed every reason. Then we would ask which of these options offers us the best opportunity to improve the situation? Then, of course it becomes a matter of can do versus will do—right, Dan?"

"Right, William. If we don't take action on the options we've generated, then we're no better off than when we started. Now, Jack and class, does this clarify your understanding of the importance of asking specific questions and of how to identify those questions?" Dan paused, then continued, "Good. Our time is getting tight, so let me conclude the recap of Absolute #4. You may want to jot these down if you missed them the first time."

- Affirmations such as I'm happy, I can do it, never give up, and so on are not nearly as potent as questions. Example:

  - What can I do right now to make myself happy?

  - What specific actions can I take to get this done?

  - If I quit, what will I forfeit?

- We are continually asking ourselves questions, and by controlling those questions we significantly broaden our emotional range and increase the resources we have right at our disposal.

- If you're feeling good, it's because you're asking yourself questions that make you feel good. If you're feeling bad, it's because _____ _____.

- Our resources are limited only by the questions we ask ourselves.

- Thinking is nothing more than asking and answering questions, so to control our thoughts, we must control our questions.

- If you want to retrieve valuable information from a computer, you must give it proper commands. The same is true of your brain. Questions are the proper commands that release the power of your mind.

"All right, here's your homework for Absolute #4. I want each one of you to think of a problem or opportunity that you can share with the class. Take that problem or opportunity and develop questions that cause it to be clearly defined. Next develop questions that pinpoint potential solutions. Drill down until specificity is crystal clear. Prepare to share it next week.

"Any questions about questions? No? Then let's have lunch."

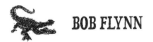

Absolute #5

EMBRACE CHANGE

You can't find your way around Georgia with a map of New Jersey

CLYDE

Hannah settled back on the family room sofa and said, "So Jack, tell me about Absolute #5. I'm all ears."

"Hannah, before I get into this very interesting but disturbing Absolute, I want to tell you how much I appreciate you giving up your Sunday afternoons to listen to my recaps. It really helps me gain a deeper understanding of the lesson."

"Don't be silly, Jack. I love learning with you, and what's even more important is that I can see how these Absolutes have helped both of us improve is so many ways. I can't think of anything I'd rather do."

"Well, the title of Absolute #5 is Embrace Change. Dan explained that in Russell James's study of countless numbers of effective and ineffective men and women, the way in which they dealt with change played a major role in their success or lack of it. The successful, highly effective individuals accepted that change is a constant and an opportunity for tremendous personal growth. These people realized that their personal effectiveness was dependent on their ability to recognize and capitalize on inevitable changing conditions. On the other hand, marginally effective and ineffective people denied and resisted change.

"They invested inordinate amounts of time and energy fighting against anything that took them out of the routine of their comfort zones. Dan said there was one of those change-fighters in his first class. He said the guy was hard- headed and stubborn but finally came around and saw the huge beneficial potential in getting on the right side of change. This fellow wrote a poem about his experience embracing change, and Dan gave us a copy."

AIN'T NO SUCH THANG AS
A PURDY GOOD ALLIGATOR RASSLER

The Wind of Change

We're not masters of the wind
It blows when and where it pleases
We can ride or we can fight
It's the latter that it teases
This wind can be known but never owned
Felt but not commanded
None can sail against its power
Lest they become stalled and stranded
I'm gonna ride, ride, ride, and ride
Ain't gonna fight no longer
Flew in the face of this wind so long
So long it proved the stronger
It may blow gentle, it may blow wild
No mortal can predict whom it favors
Yet it's for sure it will endure
To cripple or enable
I've rode it high and rode it down
Felt its warmth and fury
It's been my thorn and been my crown
Been my judge and jury
I'm gonna ride, ride, ride and ride
Ain't gonna fight no longer
Flew in the face of this wind so long
So long it proved the stronger
Finally, it's done, my lessons learned
The mystery's solved in time
The only real potentate
Is its direction, not mine
So where is it that you're taking me, wind
Which direction you blowin'?
Your answer don't matter no way
Cause it's your way I'm goin'
I'm gonna ride, ride, ride and ride
Ain't gonna fight no longer
Flew in your face so many times
Now I concede you're stronger

RJF

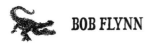 **BOB FLYNN**

"Wow, Jack! Sounds like this guy really struggled with change."

"Yeah, Hannah, as I mentioned, we learned that most of us do. Accepting change, much less embracing it, is much more of a struggle than most of us realize. It's so easy to get caught up in old habits and routines because even though they are not in our best interest, they are comfortable. I think the single most revealing lesson that I took out of this Absolute was that change offers us tremendous personal opportunity, and it really reveals ourselves to ourselves."

"What do you mean by that?"

"Change rocks our world. It calls for new decisions and new skills. It forces us to take a cold, hard look at our reality and determine what has to change."

"I don't quite get it. Give me an example, please."

"Okay, let's get up close and personal. Remember when Pete called me into his office and told me I was underperforming and that if I wanted to stay gainfully employed, I'd better make some changes?"

"Now, Jack, he didn't say it like that."

"Well, maybe not exactly, but that's what he meant. Anyway, it forced me out of my comfort zone. I had to take a look at myself, examine my reality, so to speak. When I did, I realized that I was complacent, satisfied with my conditions, playing far below my potential. From that point on I began determining what changes I needed to make, and then I set about making them. In between the stimulus [Pete's meeting], and the response (my decision to make changes), I fell into a highly predictable pattern."

"A predictable pattern?"

"Yes, there is a predictable pattern relative to change that most of us go through in route to either making changes or remaining where we are. This pattern is called:

THE DISCOVERY • DENIAL • DECISION • PATTERN

Discomfort: The feeling that something needs to change.

Examination: Taking a look at what's causing the aggravation.

Reality Check: The baseline analysis and where you are in your estimation.

Discovery: Pinpointing the changes that need to be made.

Denial: That changes really need to be made.

Discomfort: An increased feeling of uneasiness that returns with a vengeance.

Decision: To live with the uneasy feeling [continued denial] or change.

"When we scrutinize this pattern, we learn that it's discomfort that drives change. Unfortunately, it usually takes mega doses of pain before we're willing to make the changes necessary to elevate our situation. Often it takes a crisis.

"My man Clyde told an interesting and pertinent story relative to the pain-crisis-change connection. It seems Clyde's Uncle Rooster worked with a little traveling carnival. Rooster was a man of many talents, his main talent being that of a self-proclaimed animal trainer. His greatest accomplishment and the hit attraction of the carnival was an elephant that did tricks. Peanut, as he was called, would stand up on his hind legs and walk around, roll over, dance, and perform many other entertaining feats. Clyde was in a highly intellectual conversation with Uncle Rooster one day and asked him how he got old Peanut to change from an ordinary 'walk around in circles' elephant to the main attraction. Without batting an eye, Uncle Rooster inserted a chaw of Beechnut and told this story."

The Change

"Well now, Clyde, that's an interesting question. I got ol' Peanut when he was just a pup. Bought him from ol' 'Briar' Jenkins, you know, the guy who lives in Greelyville and has a house that's mobile and five cars that ain't. That's the same one that has to take his transmission out of the bathtub so's his wife Madge can take a bath. Anyhow, I acquired Peanut from Briar with great hopes of training him up to becoming a 'trick doing' elephant. He cost me a case of my finest moonshine whiskey and a broke-down Dodge pickup. Anyhow, Peanut didn't want no part of being no 'trick doing' elephant, in fact he didn't want no part of being in the carnival. That varmint kept runnin' off back to Briar's place. You know ol' Briar ain't never been just right. I remember when Sheriff Lyle Puckett arrested him in 'Mole Peterson's store for staring at the frozen orange juice cause it said, 'concentrate.'

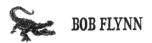

BOB FLYNN

"Anyhow, it got so bad that I finally had to chain ol' Peanut to a metal stake. Clyde, it near 'bout broke my heart to see that little critter just walk round and round all day long. Boy, I'm telling you I tried everything to git that elephant to change from bein' a 'walk around in circles' elephant to a 'trick doin'' one. I hollered at him, I whooped him, I brought over pretty elephants of the opposite sex to comfort him. I scratched him, I increased his vittles substantially, man I'm telling you I done everything I could conjure up. Ah, but to no avail. Peanut wouldn't change. Clyde, this went on for years and years. Ol' Peanut grew up and still he walked round and round, all pitiful like. There ain't no way that little stake and chain could hold him. He could snatch that sucker right out of the ground with just a flick of his foot, but he wouldn't do it because he liked things the way they were. He was satisfied, content and complacent, just like so many folks we have today.

"And then it happened. 'Speedy' Gimmerson, the cannonball catcher, and 'Stumpy' Lynch, the fireworks expert, got in a fight over Allie-Faye Redman, the snake charmer, and in the midst of their altercation Stumpy up and dropped a full bottle of moonshine in the campfire. KA BOOM! The whole thing exploded and there was fire everywhere. I cast down my copy of *Hick Is Chic* and commenced to gettin' the heck out of Dodge. Then I remembered ol' Peanut chained to the stake and I figured he was goin' round and round pretty fast by now. Anyhow, I run through them blazes like a scalded dog and when I arrived at his stake, I couldn't believe my eyes. Ol' Peanut had done jerked that stake plum out of the ground. He was rearing up on his hind legs and rollin' around tryin' to put out that fire. I'm telling you boy, he was doin' all the things I had been trying to git him to do but he wouldn't. Well, I can tell you this, when he breathed that fire up his trunk, he changed...quick.

Clyde, I don't know why, but it's like that with most people. They know they could do so much better and that change is the ticket. They also know what changes need to be made, but they just refuse to make 'em until ..."

"Until what, Uncle Rooster?"

"Until their tent catches fire, and then they'll git out from under the porch and make it happen.

That is..."

"That is, Uncle Rooster?"

"That is, unlessen hits too late!"

AIN'T NO SUCH THANG AS
A PURDY GOOD ALLIGATOR RASSLER

Jack chuckled to himself as he thought, *Seems like I've heard a slightly different version of this story before.*

"After Clyde told the story, Dan explained that many individuals and organizations are like Peanut and it takes huge pain, perhaps even the motivation of a crisis, before they change, and even then, it's often too late. By the time they hit bottom, they're too far gone to recover. This is very unfortunate, because usually the changes that are required are easy to discern. We know what we should do, but we don't do it. Dan recommended a book for all of us involved in change management called *The Knowing-Doing Gap: How Smart Companies Turn Knowledge into Action.* I'm going to get it, Hannah. I think it will help me turn things around at the plant. See, we know what to do, and I've got to find out why we're not doing it.

"Next, Dan gave us the 'don'ts of personal change management'. He said these were the knee-jerk reactions to change that we should be keenly aware of so that we could avoid them."

The Don'ts

"Embracing personal change requires strategy. Understanding and avoiding the most common pitfalls can simplify development of our personal change strategy. Dan called the most common change inhibitors don'ts." Jack thumbed to a marked page in his workbook and began reading:

- **Deciding Not to Change:**

  It takes far more emotional energy to desperately hang on to the old ways than it does to embrace change. Get real. Do you really think you can stop or even slow down change? It's going to happen, and it doesn't matter whether you like it or agree with it. Change is here to stay.

- **Acting Like a Victim:**

  Self-victimization is very disempowering. Change goes right on in the midst of our whining and crying. It's totally impersonal; it could not care less that we're behaving like a child that didn't get his way.

- ## Trying to Play the New Game by the Old Rules:

  You're playing baseball and the game changes to hockey. Better play hockey, or you're going to look foolish. We need to respect that our rapidly changing circumstances require actual changes--big actual changes. Changes in our condition can take on totally new dimensions that demand new skills and habits. Perhaps you think adapting is tough, but just try not adapting and see how tough things get.

- ## Easing into Change:

  Easing into the change is a good strategy, right? Wrong! The evidence is conclusive. Slow-changing companies and slow-changing individuals are headed for the most trouble. Slowing down and taking change easy may give a little temporary relief, but it's just that, temporary. This strategy just postpones tough times for tougher ones.

- ## Trying to Control Change:

  Go ahead, knock yourself out trying to resist the inevitable. Feel free to attempt to undo something that can't be undone. Be my guest in trying to push change back into the bottle. Good luck when you try to insert the cork! Rather than scratch and claw in a futile attempt to control the uncontrollable, we should salute reality and get on with the needed changes.

- ## Remaining Neutral to Change:

  Remaining neutral in the midst of change is like getting half pregnant; it's not possible. If we're not changing as fast as the world around us, we're losing ground. There is no neutral when it comes to change; you're either moving forward or moving backward. Change knows no status quo.

- ## Failing to Abandon the Expendable:

  There are limits to the workload that we can carry. Trying harder can only take us so far. Inherent with change is new duties, and unless we dump some of the old baggage, we simply won't be able to handle the increased demands that change requires. We must abandon the expendables because that creates valuable space and makes room for the new skills that are needed to effectively facilitate change.

AIN'T NO SUCH THANG AS
A PURDY GOOD ALLIGATOR RASSLER

- **Failing to Speed Up:**

  Change is picking up speed, and the natural response of people is to slow down their efforts in an attempt to cope. On the surface this seems to make sense, but a more in-depth analysis reveals that there's no chance of change slowing down. So, when we do, change overtakes us, and in no time, we're left behind.

- **Expecting Others to Protect Us from Change:**

  Change does not operate within anyone's comfort zone. It's challenging to everybody. Change cannot be avoided. Like the lava of an erupting volcano, it is no respecter of persons and no one can protect you from it. The ones who attempt to are only false protectors. Sooner or later they, as well as you, will have to deal with change. Trying to keep people comfortable in rapidly changing times is the most non-caring act of all.

Jack put down the book. "Dan concluded the lesson on change by telling us that all the futurists agree that we are only at the beginning of the greatest changes in human history. The changes we have seen in the recent past are portents of more change to come, and it is essential, if we want to truly be effective, that we embrace changing conditions. He admonished us to do the following."

The Do's

"Identify the Changes You Need to Make... Then Make Them."

Jack and Hannah chatted awhile longer and then turned in. Before going to sleep, Jack contemplated the upcoming week. Certainly, it was fraught with uncertainty, but he was much less interested in security and more interested in opportunity these days. Jack had changed. He was much more resilient, less anxious, and downright mentally tough. It was a good thing, because he would need these and more to face the challenges and opportunities that lay ahead.

Absolute #4

THE QUESTIONS ARE THE ANSWERS

The great end of life is not knowledge but action.

THOMAS HENRY HUXLEY

KEY POINT ————————————————————

To improve the quality of our lives and thus become increasingly effective, we must change the quality of our questions, because it's our self-questions that direct our focus... And, all improvement in personal effectiveness is preceded by questions we have never asked ourselves before.

❑ Obey the Law of Balance.

❑ Our questions should focus on problems and opportunities.

❑ When we question our "limitations," the walls of disbelief come down.

❑ Questions are the primary way we learn.

❑ Successful people ask better questions of themselves than do the marginal.

❑ Problems, disappointments, setbacks, etc. will teach us if we ask.

❑ Questions surface options and improve our mood.

❑ Questions tap into the unlimited resources of our subconscious.

❑ Strategically positioned questions surface the best solutions.

❑ Don't say "It stinks in here." Ask, "Where's the pony?"

MAJOR POINT

We all have habitual questions and statements that make up our internal dialogue. Typically, we just let these questions and statements take any course they choose, and often it's the course of disempowerment. Uncontrolled statements and questions magnify the problem, lessen the opportunity, and keep us in the victim role. When we develop strategic questions, we get unstuck; we develop options that combined with action set us free.

WHAT SPECIFIC ACTION WILL YOU TAKE TODAY TO IMPROVE YOUR INTERNAL DIALOGUE?

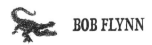

BOB FLYNN

ABSOLUTE #4

EXERCISE

Develop a question around each of your top five priorities. Record your answers.

PRIORITY #1: _____

QUESTION: _____

ANSWERS: _____

PRIORITY #2: _____

QUESTION: _____

ANSWERS: _____

PRIORITY #3: _____

QUESTION: _____

ANSWERS: _____

PRIORITY #4: _____

QUESTION: _____

ANSWERS: _____

PRIORITY #5: _____

QUESTION: _____

ANSWERS: _____

AIN'T NO SUCH THANG AS
A PURDY GOOD ALLIGATOR RASSLER

Absolute #5

EMBRACE CHANGE

You can't find your way around Georgia with a map of New Jersey.

CLYDE

KEY POINT

The manner in which you deal with change will play a major role in your success or lack of it. Successful, highly effective individuals accept change as a constant, a fact of life. They view it as an opportunity for tremendous personal growth. These people realize that their personal effectiveness is dependent on their ability to recognize and capitalize on inevitable changing conditions. On the other hand, marginally effective people deny and resist change.

- ❏ Change reveals ourselves to ourselves.

- ❏ Change requires new decisions and new skills.

- ❏ Change requires we take a cold hard look at reality.

- ❏ Becoming satisfied with existing conditions is folly.

- ❏ For many it takes massive doses of pain to initiate change.

- ❏ The future has an annoying habit of arriving whether you're ready or not.

- ❏ Hanging on to the old takes more effort than embracing change.

- ❏ Change is impersonal, whining and crying has no effect.

- ❏ If you're not changing as fast as the world around you, you're losing ground.

- ❏ If you think adapting is tough, try not adapting.

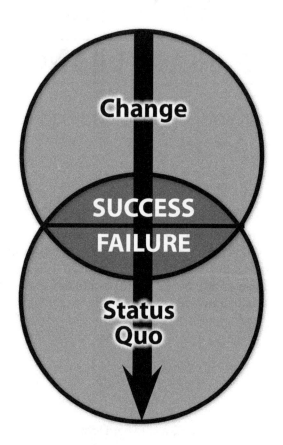

MAJOR POINT ————————————————————

There are limits to the workload we can carry. Trying harder only takes us so far. Inherent with change is new duties, and unless we dump some of the old baggage, we simply won't be able to handle the increased demands that change requires. We must abandon the expendable because it takes up valuable time. We must make room for the requirements of change.

THERE IS NO NEUTRAL
WHEN IT COMES TO CHANGE.

AIN'T NO SUCH THANG AS
A PURDY GOOD ALLIGATOR RASSLER

ABSOLUTE #5

EXERCISE

Identify one major change you need to make to become more successful in each of your top five priorities.

Commit to a date that you will begin making the change.

PRIORITY #1: _____

CHANGE: _____

_____

_____

_____

_____

_____

DATE: _____

PRIORITY #2: _____

CHANGE: _____

_____

_____

_____

_____

_____

DATE: _____

BOB FLYNN

PRIORITY #3: _____

CHANGE: _____

_____

_____

_____

_____

_____

DATE: _____

PRIORITY #4: _____

CHANGE: _____

_____

_____

_____

_____

_____

DATE: _____

PRIORITY #5: _____

CHANGE: _____

_____

_____

_____

_____

_____

DATE: _____

AIN'T NO SUCH THANG AS
A PURDY GOOD ALLIGATOR RASSLER

CHAPTER SEVEN

Ain't No Such Thang AS A PURDY GOOD Alligator Rassler

The Walk

ABSOLUTE #6

Build Rapport

As one makes an impartial study of the prophets, philosophers, miracle workers, and religious leaders, one is drawn to the inevitable conclusion that persistence, concentration of effort, and definiteness of purpose, were the major sources of their achievements.

NAPOLEON HILL

The Walk

Except for one major aggravation, the week was going well. Production at the plant was inching up, and morale was showing a slight improvement. There was, however, this one burning question that kept nagging Jack. "What can I do to fast cycle increased production and morale improvement? Yes, there is progress, but it's so painfully slow; how can I get these people to take their responsibilities more seriously and pick up the pace?" He had learned the importance of self- imposed questions, but he just couldn't seem to get the definitive answers to come.

Then it happened.

Wednesday had been a particularly difficult day. Many unforeseen problems had arisen. Two machines had malfunctioned, a major customer had cancelled a large order, and a safety inspection had revealed "conditions" that must be corrected by noon the next day or an entire line would have to be shut down.

"Can't be done," the shop foreman had advised in a condescending tone. "It'll take three days minimum."

"We don't have three days!" Jack responded. "We simply can't afford that much down time. It's gotta happen by noon tomorrow."

"Then you better get on it, Jack, because it ain't my problem. I got three jobs ahead of you."

Jack fought back his anger, mumbled something underneath his breath, and reluctantly walked away. Sitting in his office, he began to gather his thoughts. He decided to skip lunch and go for a walk in a nearby park, since walking always seemed to clear his head and calm him down.

The walk was working. Jack felt his anger subside. The tightness in his neck was gone, and as the warm sun beamed down on his face, he felt quite relaxed. Approaching a large pond in the middle of the park, he noticed a light fog beginning to roll in off the water. A mist to begin with, it thickened rapidly and was now engulfing Jack's entire surroundings. Barely able to see his hand in front of his face, he bumped harmlessly into a large table. *I must have strayed off the path*, he thought. Rubbing his eyes, he was surprised to see what

 **BOB FLYNN**

appeared to be people sitting around the table chatting. Glancing up at Jack, a distinguished-looking man in his mid-sixties said, "Hello, Jack, pull up a chair and join us. We've been expecting you."

Jack squinted, attempting to see through the fog. Then, just as suddenly as it had appeared, the fog was gone. He was startled to see five people sitting around the table, none of whom he recognized.

"You've been expecting me?"

"Oh yes, Jack, we've been expecting you since you made the decision."

"The decision!" What decision?"

"The decision to take full responsibility for yourself and your circumstances. You see, my boy, anytime a person is wise enough to make that decision, we know they are going to need us, and so we get them on our calendar, and we make it happen."

"You make what happen?"

"A one-time-only meeting with us, your mastermind alliance."

"My mastermind alliance! What's that?"

"Well, a mastermind alliance is a group of people possessing a body of knowledge that pertains to you and your situation. These people can advise you with complete objectivity and certainty. They're people of great wisdom and insight, people of significant achievement."

"Sir, with all due respect, I don't recognize you or any of the others. I would expect to see Churchill, Lincoln, Martin Luther King Jr., Henry Ford, Coach Lombardi, Deming, people of that ilk."

"Yes, of course you would, and these and many others could be of immeasurable value to you; however, you may find us of even more value because… we are their teachers."

"Their teachers?"

"Yes, we have taught all these people and many other famous and not-so-famous high achievers. Our instruction and influence got them aimed in the right direction."

"So, who are you?"

"My name is Dr. Alfred Adler. I have counseled many high-achieving dignitaries as well as everyday individuals, many of whom are quite effective and others who have fallen far short of their God-given potentials. I've studied their lives and I've drawn insightful conclusions as to why some people make it and some don't. I wrote a book in 1927 called *Understanding Human Nature*. I was blessed by the fact that this book served as a mastermind alliance to countless thousands."

"What can you teach me, Dr. Adler?"

"Based on your current situation at the plant, I believe I can teach you a great deal. You see, Jack, you have fallen into a very predictable mindset, and as a result you are taking a very predictable approach to your problem. Unfortunately, your approach will not produce the results you desire."

"Okay, I'm ready to learn, Dr. Adler."

"Very well, my boy; let's get started."

The Lecture

"Jack, you have a strong tendency, as do most people, to expect others to behave as you would have them behave. When they don't, which is usually the case, you become quite anxious and attempt to control them. Human nature dictates that people will do almost anything to escape from control, and so your controlling efforts accomplish the exact opposite of your intent." Dr. Adler ticked off points on his finger:

"• Attempting to over control is a strong indicator that you believe that you cannot meet the demands of the situation.

" You must develop full trust of your own inherent capabilities. Then, and only then, will you break your dependence on controlling others.

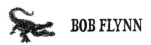 **BOB FLYNN**

" Unhappiness, loneliness, and neurotic symptoms arise directly from your unresolved habit of trying to control others.

"You see, Jack, attempting to control people further indicates that you have a dependent nature."

"Now wait a minute, Dr. Adler, are you referring to my encounter with the shop foreman?"

"Why, yes, but that is just one of many similar situations where a person didn't behave as you wished, and you went immediately into control mode. When it didn't work, you fled the scene and began pouting, same as always."

"That is so childish!"

"That it is, Jack my boy."

"So how should I have handled it?"

"Simple, by taking full responsibility."

"Dr. Adler, that's crazy. I can't fix the safety problem, that's far beyond my capabilities, and besides it simply isn't my responsibility. It's the responsibility of Tim, the shop foreman."

"You're right on point one, confused on point two. It's true that you can't physically fix the safety problem; however, it is your responsibility to make certain it is fixed. Let me ask you a question. Who are Pete, Fred, and Mickey depending on to improve morale and productivity?"

"Me."

"If it doesn't happen and you tell them that Tim didn't cooperate, will they accept that?"

"No way! I don't even want to think about what Pete would say."

"What would he say?"

Jack pondered the question for what seemed like an eternity. Then he answered: "Well, Pete would say something like this. 'Jack, it's your responsibility to improve productivity and morale, and you've accomplished neither.

Furthermore, you have attempted to shift the responsibility to an overworked teammate. I had hoped that you had matured as a manager to the point of realizing that simply telling someone what to do almost never gets the job done. You must collaborate with people, strive to understand where they are coming from, gain their perspective, and then guide them from their point of view. You must check in with them periodically to see how they are doing, provide coaching, feedback, and encouragement.'"

"See, you knew exactly what to do, but you simply didn't do it. And you know what else? You also know why you didn't take the correct action."

"I do?"

"Sure. Think back to the big E."

"Oh yeah, expedience. I took the expedient route, the route to disaster."

"Correct. Now think not so far back to the other big E."

"Ego," said Jack. "My ego took over and kicked my butt."

"Jack, you have heard all this before, and until you get it, you will continue to turn in a sub-par performance, especially as it pertains to effectiveness with people. Until you master the two big E's, your performance will disappoint you and others."

"Thank you, Dr. Adler. What else should I know?"

Glancing toward an olive-skinned man who appeared to be of Lebanese decent, Dr. Adler said, "Gib, why don't you speak to our friend?"

The Prophet

"Al, it would indeed be my pleasure."

Rising to his feet and looking Jack squarely in the eye, the olive-skinned gentleman began speaking in a heavy Arabic accent.

"Mr. Williams, permit me to indulge in a brief personal introduction. My name is Kahlil Gibran from Lebanon. Some people greatly honor me by saying

that I'm a poet, philosopher, and artist. I, however, consider myself to be a teacher, because to my mind this is the highest honor and privilege that can be bestowed on a person. But even more important than being an honor and a privilege, teaching is my passion and my love."

"What would you teach me, Mr. Gibran?"

"Ah, Mr. Williams, we have observed your struggles with your work, and for that reason I would teach you about work."

Mr. Gibran picked up a book lying open in front of him, and Jack squinted to see the title. It was *The Prophet*.

Mr. Gibran began reading:

"When you work, you are a flute through whose heart the whispering of the hours turns to music. Which of you would be a reed, dumb and silent, when all else sings together in unison?

"Always you have been told that work is a curse and labor a misfortune. But I say to you that when you work you fulfill a part of earth's furthest dream, assigned to you when that dream was born, and in keeping yourself with labor you are in truth loving life. And to love life through labor is to be intimate with life's inmost secret.

"But if you in your pain call birth an affliction and the support of the flesh a curse written upon your brow, then I answer that naught but the sweat of your brow shall wash away that which is written.

"You have been told also that life is darkness, and in your weariness, you echo what was said by the weary. And I say that life is indeed darkness save when there is urge, and all urge is blind save where there is knowledge, and all knowledge is vain save when there is work, and all work is empty save when there is love; and when you work with love you bind yourself to yourself, and to one another, and to God.

"And what is it to work with love? It is to weave the cloth with threads drawn from your heart, even as if your beloved were to wear that cloth. It is to build a house with affection, even as if your beloved were to dwell in that house.

"It is to sow seeds with tenderness and reap the harvest with joy, even as if your beloved were to eat the fruit.

AIN'T NO SUCH THANG AS
A PURDY GOOD ALLIGATOR RASSLER

"It is to charge all things you fashion with a breath of your own spirit, and to know that all the blessed dead are standing about you watching.

"Often, I have heard it said as if speaking in sleep, he who works in marble, and finds the shape of his own soul in the stone, is nobler than he who ploughs the soil. And he who seizes the rainbow to lay it on a cloth in the likeness of man, is more than he who makes sandals for our feet.

"But I say, not in sleep but in the over-wakefulness of noontide, that the wind blows not more sweetly to the giant oaks than to the least of all the blades of grass; and he alone is great who turns the voice of the wind into a song made sweeter by his own loving.

"Work is love made visible.

"And if you cannot work with love but only with distaste, it is better that you should leave your work and sit at the gate of the temple and take the alms of those who work with joy.

"For if you bake bread with indifference, you bake a bitter bread that feeds but half a man's hunger. And if you grudge the crushing of the grapes, your grudge distils a poison in the wine. And if you sing though as angels, and love not singing, you muffle man's ears to the voices of the day and the voices of the night."

Jack sat in respectful silence. *What a magnificent description of work,* he thought. "This man is a prophet. I will never look at work the same… NEVER."

"Teach me more, Mr. Gibran."

"I truly regret that our time together is over, Mr. Williams. You are such an apt student, but I must go now, as there are so many to instruct. Before I depart, permit me to introduce you to your next teacher."

The Influencer

Rising from the table was a bespectacled man, gray at the temples and around fifty years of age. He smiled warmly and extended his right hand toward Jack.

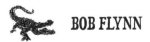

Gibran said, "Mr. Williams, it is my pleasure to introduce Dale Carnegie."

Dale Carnegie? I've heard of him, Jack thought. He said, "I'm glad to meet you, Mr. Carnegie."

"Call me Dale, and the pleasure is mine as well."

"What will you teach me, Dale?"

"Mr. Williams--"

"Please, call me Jack."

"Very well, Jack it is. Jack, back in the early 1930s The University of Chicago, The American Association for Adult Education, and The United YMCA conducted an extensive survey that covered two years. This survey clearly revealed that next to improving their health, adults of that era were most interested in developing their skills in human relationships; they wanted to learn the technique of getting along with and influencing other people. Interestingly, nothing has changed since that survey was taken so long ago. A recent study conducted by the American Psychological Association revealed exactly the same interest; people of today want to know how to improve their interpersonal relationships so that they can enhance their ability to influence. Jack, I'm going to give you a crash course in influencing. By learning and practicing the art of influencing, you will no longer need to control others. I'll be using a book I wrote titled *How to Win Friends and Influence People* as the text. What I'm going to do is give you the most important lessons in bullet point fashion. Then I'm going to give you a copy of the book in hopes that you will read and study it. Okay?"

"Okay."

THE IMPORTANCE OF BEING EFFECTIVE WITH PEOPLE

- If one aspires to success in life, the ability to effectively express oneself combined with a pleasing personality are more important than any other factors.

- Leadership gravitates toward people who can express themselves effectively.

- 15% of one's success is due to technical knowledge, and 85% is due to skill in human engineering.

- John D. Rockefeller said: "I will pay more for the ability to deal effectively with people than I will for any other skill."

- Your happiness and income have a great dependence on your skill in dealing with people.

CRITICISM DOESN'T WORK

- Don't criticize people. It's very dangerous; it wounds their pride, hurts their sense of importance, and arouses resentment.

- Criticisms are like homing pigeons. They always return home.

- Even God does not propose to judge a person until the end of their days, so why should we?

THE SECRET OF DEALING WITH PEOPLE

- There is only one way to get people to do what you want… make them feel important.

- The deepest urge in human nature is the desire to feel important.

- The second deepest urge in human nature is to be appreciated.

- Learn the things a person treasures most and talk about those things.

- A person's name is to them the most important sound in any language.

HOW TO INFLUENCE

- Learn what the other person wants, talk about it, and show them how to get it.

- The only way to really influence someone is to focus on what *they* want.

- Learn the other person's perspective then guide them from that perspective.

- You can influence more people in two months by becoming sincerely interested in them than in a lifetime of trying to get them interested in you.

BOB FLYNN

- You can win the attention and time of even the most sought-after people by becoming genuinely interested in them.

- Talk to people as you would a friend to whom you are conveying very important information.

- Do things for people that require time, energy, unselfishness, and thoughtfulness.

HOW TO BECOME AN EXCELLENT CONVERSATIONALIST

- Exclusive attention to the person who is speaking to you is very important. Nothing else is so flattering as that.

- Listening is the most valuable communication tool.

- Listening is more prized than any other interpersonal relationship skill.

- If you aspire to be an excellent conversationalist, become an excellent listener.

GETTING PEOPLE TO SEE THINGS YOUR WAY

- Show understanding and respect for their opinions.

- If you are wrong, admit it quickly and emphatically.

- Begin in a friendly, understanding way, especially when you don't want to.

- Let the other person do most of the talking.

- Throw down a friendly challenge.

MOTIVATING CHANGE IN OTHERS

- Begin with praise and honest appreciation.

- Call attention to people's mistakes indirectly.

- Talk about your own mistakes before talking about theirs.

AIN'T NO SUCH THANG AS
A PURDY GOOD ALLIGATOR RASSLER

- Use questions instead of direct statements.

- Always allow them to save face.

- Praise the slightest improvement.

- Praise every improvement.

- Treat the person as the person you want them to become.

- Encourage... make the change you desire seem easy.

"These items seem mundane, I know; however, they are commonly overlooked, and as a result, the overlookers have trouble winning friends and influencing people. Don't be put off by their simplicity, Jack. When mastered, they will greatly assist your personal effectiveness."

"Thanks, Dale."

"You're welcome, Jack. Now let me introduce you to Mr. Lester Levenson."

The Healer

Shaking Jack's hand, Lester Levenson smiled and began speaking in a rapid, excited tone. "Well, you may have heard of Dale Carnegie, but without a doubt, you've never heard of me, correct?"

"That's correct," Jack answered as he surveyed the small, athletically built man he estimated to be in his seventies.

Without hesitation, Levenson continued. "Made a lot of money in my day, Jack. By the time I was forty-two years old, I was a very rich man. Then I had my second coronary and the doctors sent me home to my ritzy Penthouse in New York City... to die.

"I've always been the type of guy that loved challenges, so I decided to beat the odds and prove the doctors wrong, and that's precisely what I did. I went deep inside myself and came up with some conclusions, applied them, and lived in complete health and happiness another forty-two years. So many people asked me how I did it that I began to teach my methods. I created a

course of study called the Sedona Method that's still a very popular course even today. If you're interested, I'll give you the key point right now."

"I'm interested, Mr. Levenson."

"Then back to my story. I was at the end of my rope, you see. I was told not to take another step unless I absolutely had to, because there was a strong possibility that I could drop dead at any moment. This was a terribly shocking thing, to be told I couldn't be active any more. An intense fear of dying overwhelmed me. After three days, I realized that I'm still alive and as long as I am, there's still hope. I began to ask myself a simple question. Do you know that questions are the answer, Jack?"

"Yes, Mr. Levenson, I've recently learned that."

"Good, very good. Never forget it. The question I kept asking was: what do I want from life? Happiness kept coming back as the answer, so I asked another question. What is happiness? The answer that kept returning was being loved. I pondered that answer for quite a long while. I finally concluded that while it was close, it was not correct. See, I surmised that I was already loved by a lot of people. In fact, I had much more love than the vast majority. I had all this love and still I was not happy; I was sick and miserable. No, more love for me was not the answer.

"I kept sensing that the closest thing relating to happiness was love, and after days of further introspection, I realized that my happiness did not equate to how much love I received, but to how much love I gave. The truth I came to realize was … I could increase my happiness in direct proportion to the amount of love I gave! Immediately I began reviewing incidents from my past, and where I saw that I did not love, I began to see that as a source of unhappiness. I learned, that instead of trying to get people to love me and do things for me, the key was loving and doing things for other people. This revelation began to free me, and any bit of freedom when you're plagued feels mighty good. I knew that I was going in the right direction. I had gotten hold of a 'secret' to health and happiness.

"Finally, I saw that everything that had happened to me and put me on my death bed was the result of my thinking. I can control my thinking if I so desire, and as a result control my health and happiness. And above all, I saw that I was responsible for everything that had happened to me. It wasn't the world that was abusing me, it was me that was abusing me.

"Discovering that my happiness equated to my loving others and discovering that my thinking was the cause of things happening to me in my life, gave me more and more freedom. It will do the same for you."

"Thank you, Mr. Levenson."

"You're quite welcome, my young friend. I wish you health and happiness. Now, I would like for you to meet one of Spain's greatest writers, Mr. Baltasar Gracian. Over 300 years ago Mr. Gracian wrote a classic titled *The Art of Worldly Wisdom*. A Jesuit scholar, Baltasar had the rare opportunity to observe many in positions of power. He carefully observed and documented the actions and inactions of both the effective and ineffective statesmen and potentates of his era. There's no doubt that he can offer you valuable insights on the art of living and the practice of achieving."

Wow, Jack thought, *this is some heavy stuff!*

"Glad to meet you, Mr. Gracian. What will you teach me?"

The Admonition

Gracian began in a gruff, almost sarcastic tone that seemed to suggest that Jack would not even pay attention, much less apply the words that would follow.

"I will teach you nothing, Mr. Williams. Even assuming a person can be taught anything is but human folly, and I have an undying disdain for that oh-so-common malady. I will, however, offer you some observations in hopes that you will instruct yourself. For you see, Mr. Williams, in the final analysis we are always our own teachers. People like Mr. Adler, Mr. Gibran, Mr. Carnegie, Mr. Levenson, and myself are but conveyers of the wisdom of the ages. Speaking for myself, I take no responsibility for your education. If you choose not to be a lamp unto your own feet, then ignorance remains your lot. It has been a matter of honor for me to make myself obscure to self-induced ignorance, for precious pearls should never be cast before swine."

"I understand, Mr. Gracian, that it's up to me."

"Very well then, I shall proceed. I have been observing you, Mr. Williams, especially your thinking and your dealings with others. You have ample room for improvement. I advise you to consider the following:

 **BOB FLYNN**

"• Know your best quality, your outstanding gift. Cultivate it and nurture all the rest. All people could have achieved eminence in something if only they had sought to discover what they excelled at. Identify your king of attributes and apply it in double strength.

"• Never lose your composure. Prudence seeks to never lose self-control. The person with a true heart for magnanimity is slow to give in to emotion. Your difficulties, especially with people, must bring out the best in you. You must discipline yourself to change yourself, not others.

"• It is an insufferable fool that measures all things by his/her opinion.

"• Do not seek praise, seek criticism. It is quite easy to get approval if we ask enough people, or if we ask those who are likely to tell us what we want to hear. The likelihood is that they will say nice things rather than be too critical. We tend to edit out the bad so that we hear only what we want to hear. So, if you have produced an acceptable piece of work, you will have proved to yourself that it is good simply because others have said so. It's probably all right, but not great. Instead of seeking approval ask yourself, 'What's wrong with it? How can I make it better?' You are still in a position to reject criticism if you think it is wrong.

"• It is wrong to be right. Being right is based upon knowledge and experience and is often provable. Knowledge comes from the past, so it's safe. It is also out of date. It's the opposite of originality. Experience is built from solutions to old situations and problems. The old situations are usually different from the present ones, so that old solutions will have to be bent to fit new problems and usually they fit badly. Also, the likelihood is that, if you've got the experience, you'll probably use it. THIS IS LAZY! Experience is the opposite of being creative. If you can prove you're right, your mind is set. You'll not be able to move with the times or with other people. It's wrong to be right, because people who are right are chained to the past, rigid-minded, dull and smug. There's no getting through to them.

"• It is right to be wrong. Start out wrong, and suddenly anything is possible. You're no longer trying to be infallible. You are in the unknown. There's no way of knowing what can happen, but there's more chance of it being amazing than if you try to be right. People are afraid of being wrong because of what others might think. The dull dare not take such a risk. Ah, but risks are a measure of people. People who won't take them are merely trying to preserve what they have. Being right is like walking backwards, proving

AIN'T NO SUCH THANG AS
A PURDY GOOD ALLIGATOR RASSLER

where you've been. Being wrong isn't in the future or the past. Being wrong isn't anywhere but being here, which is the best and only place you can be.

"• You can achieve the unachievable. To do so, you must aim beyond what you're capable of. You must develop a complete disregard for where your abilities end.

"• Rebel against mediocrity, even though there's great demand for it. The nature of the creative person is rebellion. All creative people need something to rebel against, but often they choose the wrong thing and so alienate others as to render themselves impotent. When the object of their rebellion is mediocrity by default, they choose excellence.

"Heed these admonitions, Mr. Williams. Learn the actions of the resourceful, then go ye and do likewise."

"Thank you, Mr. Gracian."

"With your words you have thanked us all, Mr. Williams. Words are easy; words alone are the tools of the uninitiated. Thank us with your discipline and your actions, your commitment and resolve, your love and passion. Thank us with a determined dedicated life lived with the purpose of excellence."

Just as Jack began to respond to Mr. Gracian's parting remarks, he disappeared, as did the table and all the rest of the teachers.

Startled, Jack sat up straight and rubbed his eyes. Looking around, he realized he wasn't in a park at all but in his hotel room. The illuminated clock immediately informed him that it wasn't early afternoon but 3:18 a.m. "I've been dreaming," Jack announced out loud. "Man, that was some kind of vivid dream." Confused, Jack began to reconstruct the week. He quickly surmised there had been no confrontation with the shop foreman. And there was no safety problem. What was real, however, was his continued concern for the lack of responsibility accepted by the majority of the plant personnel. Thinking deeper now, Jack concluded that it was this concern that precipitated the dream. The messages delivered by the "teachers" were to remind him of the critical importance of controlling himself, not others. As long as he focused his attention "out there," the focus was off the only thing he really could control… HIMSELF. It was at that moment that Jack officially decided to no longer bring about self-victimization by giving his power to circumstances or other people. Having made that decision, he fell into a deep, peaceful sleep.

 **BOB FLYNN**

Absolute #6

BUILD RAPPORT

One who is too insistent on his own views, finds few to agree with him

LAO TSU

Thursday and Friday were seemingly uneventful and passed rapidly. Arriving home Friday evening, Jack discussed the week with Hannah. She was her usual upbeat, curious self and had many questions, especially about the dream. Other than Dale Carnegie, she was not familiar with the other teachers. She vowed to research them, and there was no doubt in Jack's mind that she would do just that.

"I'll tell you all about these guys when you get back," she announced as Jack hit the road to learn about Absolutes # 6 and 7.

Jack was delighted to be back in class. As he surveyed the room, he couldn't help but be aware that William, Tony, James, Mary, Hank, and Clyde were as eager as he was to continue their learning experience.

"People are your greatest resource," Dan Hardee began. "Personal effectiveness is dependent on a person's ability to build rapport with all types of people and to rally them to their cause. Absolute #6 is Build Rapport, and that's what we'll be studying this morning. We'll be learning that the ability to establish and build bonding rapport is invaluable in your quest for enhanced personal effectiveness. You see, no matter what your goals, rapport is the ultimate skill set for producing the results you seek. Whatever you want in life you can have if you get support from the right people. Rapport with others makes any task simpler, easier, and considerably more enjoyable, because rapport is the foundational quality of synergy. And like anything else, rapport-building is a process that can be mastered with focus, practice, and… the suppression of your ego.

"Rapport-building, like all the other Absolutes, is counterintuitive. Since we intuitively think about ourselves over 90% of the time, that's where we naturally place our focus. We see the world through our lens, so to speak. This works fine when we encounter people whose lens is focused similarly to ours. Problems arise, however, when we come into contact with people who view things from a perspective that is not aligned with ours. This degree of perspective differentiation will determine the degree of difficulty relative to rapport-building. No doubt you're familiar with the well-worn cliché that opposites attract. While this might be true from an initial romantic perspective, it doesn't last long. The harsh truth is… OPPOSITES ATTACK.

The Process

"Effective rapport-building starts with first discovering and then building on similarities. Again, this is counterintuitive. Our natural tendency is to quickly recognize and then get hung up on the *differences* between others and us. Once this occurs, the ego takes over, and discord results. So how do we go about determining similarities between other people and ourselves? Most people attempt to discover or establish similarities by seeking things they have in common with others. Usually they do this by talking about themselves, where they grew up, their interests, profession, hobbies, and so on. They are searching for common denominators, a connection and a link. This approach is marginally effective because it contains two major flaws:

"• Flaw number one… when talking you are learning nothing and revealing everything. The danger is that you will reveal major differences in your perspectives and the perspectives of the other party.

"• Flaw number two…you are revealing information through the use of words.

"Studies reveal that:

"• 7% of communication occurs through the use of words.

"• 38% through voice tone.

"• 55% through physiology or body language.

"By attempting to create rapport through words alone, we miss a major opportunity to communicate more effectively. Voice tone, facial expressions, gestures, the quality and type of movements we make, all express much more than words. Similarly, when the other person is talking, they are revealing significantly more through their voice tone and physiology than they are through their words.

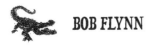 **BOB FLYNN**

"The key to rapport-building is to suppress your natural inclination to talk about yourself. Your objective must be to cause people to talk about themselves. By taking this counterintuitive approach you surface the information you need to form and execute your rapport-building strategy.

"Adhering to these three simple steps will prevent you from over talking, will build trust and credibility with the other party, and will provide you with critical information, allowing you to 'read' the other person.

"• Step #1: Ask questions that cannot be answered with 'yes' or 'no' 90% of the time. These questions should be prefaced by: What, When, Why, Which, Who, Where, and How.

"• Step #2: Listen, and observe the other party's physiology.

"• Step #3: Inform [talk] 10% of the time with the majority of your commentary focused on the other party.

"• When you are asking and listening, you are building trust.

"• When you are commenting positively about the other person, you are building credibility.

"• Trust and credibility are the cornerstones of rapport."

Absolute #6

BUILD RAPPORT

One who is too insistent on his own views, finds few to agree with him

LAO TSU

KEY POINT

No matter what your goals and priorities, rapport is the ultimate skill for producing the results you seek. Whatever you want in life, you can have if you get support from the right people. Rapport with others makes any task simpler, easier, and considerably more enjoyable, because rapport is the foundational quality of synergy. Rapport-building is a process that can be mastered with focus, practice, and... **THE SUPPRESSION OF YOUR EGO.**

❏ Rapport-building is counterintuitive. Our focus is intuitively self centered.

❏ Rapport is built on agreement, not disagreement.

❏ Take a sincere interest in the other person; obey The Law of Indirect Effort.

❏ Behavioral styles are underpinned by values and beliefs.

❏ 55% of communication occurs non-verbally.

❏ It's your responsibility to build rapport, not the other person's.

❏ You must master the two E's Ego and Emotion and the three C's to Criticism, Condemnation, and Complaining.

❏ Make the other person feel important and appreciated.

❏ Learn what the other person wants, and focus on that.

❏ Seek first to understand... then to be understood.

❏ Use questions, not direct statements.

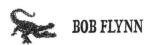 **BOB FLYNN**

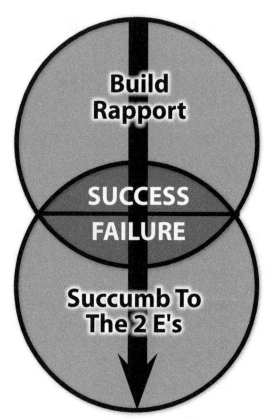

Build
Rapport

SUCCESS
FAILURE

Succumb To
The 2 E's

MAJOR POINT——————————————————————

The ineffective give in to their Egos and therefore rebel against building rapport, (especially with those who are "different" from them). Cease rebelling against those who have perspectives that don't align with yours. Rebel against mediocrity even though there is a great demand for it. The nature of the highly effective person is rebellion. All creative people need something to rebel against, but often they choose the wrong thing, like the person with a contrary perspective. As a result they alienate and render themselves ineffective.

MAKE MEDIOCRITY THE
OBJECT OF YOUR REBELLION

AIN'T NO SUCH THANG AS
A PURDY GOOD ALLIGATOR RASSLER

ABSOLUTE #6

EXERCISE

As it relates to your top five priorities, identify one person per priority that you will establish and build rapport with. State your rapport-building plan and the date you will initiate it.

PRIORITY #1:_____

PERSON: _____

PLAN: _____

_____

_____

_____

_____

DATE: _____

PRIORITY #2:_____

PERSON: _____

PLAN: _____

_____

_____

_____

_____

DATE: _____

 **BOB FLYNN**

PRIORITY #3:_____

PERSON: _____

PLAN: _____

_____

_____

_____

_____

DATE: _____

PRIORITY #4:_____

PERSON: _____

PLAN: _____

_____

_____

_____

_____

DATE: _____

PRIORITY #5:_____

PERSON: _____

PLAN: _____

_____

_____

_____

_____

DATE: _____

AIN'T NO SUCH THANG AS
A PURDY GOOD ALLIGATOR RASSLER

CHAPTER EIGHT

Ain't No Such Thang AS A PURDY GOOD Alligator Rassler

The Personalities

ABSOLUTE #7

Master Fear

NOTES

AIN'T NO SUCH THANG AS
A PURDY GOOD ALLIGATOR RASSLER

The Personalities

After a question-and-answer session, Dan continued with the next aspect of rapport-building.

"A major factor in effective rapport-building is the development of an understanding of the four basic personality types. Knowledge and strategic action in this area are essential because:

"A person's personality is underpinned by their values and beliefs.

"People behave as they do in large part because of what they value and believe in. And a person's personality is intrinsically linked to his or her behavior. Now think about it: does it get any more emotional than that? Values and beliefs are not only emotional, they are also highly personal. So, doesn't it stand to reason that the more we know about a person's personality, the more we will know about their values and beliefs? And knowing those values and beliefs will make our rapport-building strategies more effective. An understanding of a person's basic personality provides us with the information we need to *modify our behavior accordingly.* So, let's take a look at this crucial component of rapport-building.

"As I mentioned, we will be studying the four basic personality types. Before we examine each one individually, we need to understand two major components of behavioral styles: responsiveness and assertiveness. Here's what I mean by these two terms."

Dan touched the advance arrow on his computer and up on the screen flashed…

 **BOB FLYNN**

RESPONSIVENESS

LOW	HIGH
Logical	Less logical
Thoughts	Feelings
Facts	People
Controls emotions	Emotional
Precise	General
Formal, stiff, serious	Casual, playful
Task-oriented	Relationship-oriented
Few facial expressions	Animated, smiling
Independent	Dependent
Disciplined	Less disciplined

ASSERTIVENESS

LOW	HIGH
Asks, listens	Tells
Unassuming	Forceful
Non-aggressive	Aggressive
Quiet	Talkative
Goes along	Takes Charge
Avoids confrontation	Confronts
Low-risk	Risk
Little eye contact	More eye contact
Slower decisions	Faster decisions
Qualifies statements	Definite statements

"You can see at a glance," Dan continued, "that if a person low in responsiveness came in contact with a person high in responsiveness and neither was willing to modify their behavior, the chances of rapport happening would be highly improbable. In reality, what usually occurs when conflicting styles encounter each other is that only a minimum of behavioral modification takes place, and it is typically too little too late to establish a foundation for building rapport. We want to avoid that all-too-common occurrence by engaging in keen observation and personal flexibility. So, let's take a look at how you can become an expert rapport-builder by determining a person's dominant style, the specific actions to take, and the behaviors to avoid. From personal experience, I can assure you that by following this process you will significantly enhance your effectiveness with people. We're going to start by identifying the behavioral characteristics of each of the four personality types."

Dan asked the class to turn to page 37 in their *12 Absolutes* workbook.

The Driver

Behavior: High assertiveness / low responsiveness

Emphasis: Dominance of environment and of people

Pace: Fast

Priority: The task

Focus: Results, not the details leading to the results

Irritation: Wasting time. "Touchy-feely" behavior

For Decisions: Give several options, let them make the decision

They Question: What will be done? When will it be done?

Specialty: Being in control

For Personal Security: They gain and maintain control

For Acceptance: They depend on their competitiveness and leadership skills

Measures Personal Worth By: Their results and their track record

Greatest Fear: Loss of control

Theme: Notice my accomplishments

Behavioral Characteristics: Independent, strong-willed, high ego strength, needs maximum freedom to manage himself/herself and others, expects immediate results, decisive, goal-oriented, cool and competitive, accepts and embraces challenge and authority, dislikes inaction, works quickly and impressively alone, good administrative skills, initiates action, fast-paced, questions status quo, quite impatient, solves problems rapidly.

Probable Strengths: Decisive, initiating, forceful, assertive, competitive, goal-oriented, authoritative, independent, organized.

Possible Weaknesses: Overbearing, abrasive, impatient, blunt, demanding, hasty, dictatorial, belligerent, controlling.

Environmental Clues: Desk will appear busy, lots of projects and papers. Walls may contain achievement awards, planning calendars. Environment will be decorated to express power, authority, and control. Likes big black cars. Dresses for success, businesslike.

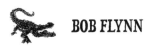 **BOB FLYNN**

Dan covered each of the points relating to the Driver, then continued the discussion.

"So, this should give you a solid overview of the behavioral characteristics of the Driver. Before we continue on to the other three personality types, I want you to understand a few other facts about behavioral styles. First of all, you're going to recognize bits and pieces of all the styles in everyone you meet. You'll also see aspects of all the styles in yourself as well. That's because almost no one will fit exactly into any of the profiles, because the profiles represent the very essence of the style. With keen observation and a little practice, you should be able to discern a person's dominant behavioral style and that's what you're looking for. Remember, a person's personality or behavioral style is underpinned by their values and beliefs, so when you accurately identify their style, you have the information necessary to determine what modifications you need to make in your own behavior in order to lay the groundwork for rapport-building. Yes, Clyde?"

"Dan, I been thinking about this Driver personality style, and I have determined that I know one. It's an ole boy from down home, name of Jasper Dupree."

"Is that right, Clyde? Well, tell us about him."

"Well, ole Jasper's got more determination than a Kamikaze pilot what just got a 'Dear John' letter. Now Jasper, he's competitive just like that Driver feller you just described. I run into him last time I was home and he told me he'd been working six days a week fourteen hours per day. I told him, 'Jasper, you need to stop and smell the roses.' I ran into him the next day and he said, 'I smelled 124 roses, how many did you get?' And see, Jasper doesn't have ulcers. No sir, he's an ulcer carrier. He's so demanding that he causes other people to get ulcers."

"Clyde, you pretty well have the Driver pegged."

Dan continued.

"Before we move on to the Amiable behavioral style, you should be aware that most people have a dominant and a secondary behavioral style. The secondary style is the style closest to the dominant style. Most people move in and out of either their dominant or secondary style depending on the situation. Also, some people are quite different depending on the situation. As an example, some people may be high assertive/low responsive on the job and low assertive/ high responsive at home."

AIN'T NO SUCH THANG AS
A PURDY GOOD ALLIGATOR RASSLER

"Yeah, that's me!" Clyde chimed in. "See, when I get home after bein' on the road all week, I want to hug mamma, if you know what I mean. The sap still rises in an old tree. But see, if I behave at home the way I do on the road, frost begins to appear on the inside of my windows, and there ain't gonna be no huggin'."

"That's well said, Clyde. My point exactly. Okay, let's get familiar with the Amiable. Turn to page 38, please."

The Amiable

Behavior: Low assertiveness / high responsiveness

Emphasis: Steadiness, cooperating with others to carry out the task

Pace: Slow and easy, and relaxed

Priority: Relationships

Focus: Building trust and getting acquainted

Irritation: Pushy, aggressive behavior

For Decisions: Give guarantees and personal reassurance

They Question: How it will affect personal circumstances and the circumstances of others

Specialty: Support

For Personal Security: Relies on close personal relationships

For Acceptance: Depends on conformity, loyalty, and helpful nature

Measures Personal Worth By: Attention from and relationships with close associates

Greatest Fear: Confrontation

Theme: Notice how well liked I am

Behavioral Characteristics: Slow and reluctant to change, close personal relationships very important, supports and actively listens, warm and accepting, works slowly and cohesively with others, agreeable, steady and calm, supportive, empathic listener, shares personal feelings and emotions, approaches risk cautiously, good counseling skills, slow to take action and make decisions, dislikes interpersonal conflict, excellent ability to gain support, patient and considerate, loyal and dependable, warm and friendly, prefers informality, asks many questions, relationship- oriented, consistent, respectful.

 **BOB FLYNN**

Probable Strengths: Self-controlled, accommodating, persistent, patient, good listener, easygoing, calm, sympathetic, warm, dependable, high value for relationships.

Probable Weaknesses: Complacent, says yes when they want to say no, lenient, smug, indifferent, non-demonstrative, confrontation-averse, apathetic, plodding, passive, possessive, indecisive.

Environmental Clues: Family pictures, personal items, serene pictures, memoirs, décor will be open, airy, friendly, soothing. Open seating arrangement, informal and conducive to building relationships.

Dan covered the key points relating to the Amiable and then asked if someone would describe an Amiable they knew. Tony raised his hand.

"Yes, Tony?"

"I can sure describe one--Lucy, my wife. She's all the things you described in the text; relationship-oriented, warm, supportive, good listener, patient, slow to change, curious, agreeable, steady, calm, all those things. But there are a few behavioral characteristics about her that I didn't hear described, and I was wondering if they are consistent with the Amiable behavioral style."

"Give us some examples."

"Well, for example, while Lucy is certainly non-confrontational, she has other ways of fighting back. When I want her to speed up, she seems to slow down. If I'm pressing for an answer, she seems to stall me out. She disagrees without being disagreeable. Does that make sense?"

"It makes complete sense," Dan laughed as he continued responding to Tony's question. "There are several important characteristics of Amiables that you should be aware of. First, they tend to be passive-aggressive. Instead of fighting openly, remember that their greatest fear is confrontation, so they fight in different, much more subtle ways. Tony, your example is perfect. When you try to get Lucy to speed up, she slows down. I'll bet the harder you push, the slower she goes, right?"

"That's exactly right."

"And when you press for an answer or commitment you don't get a yes or no, you simply get put on hold--stalled out, as you put it."

Clyde interjected. "Down home we call that givin' someone a firm maybe."

"Thanks, Clyde." Dan continued. "When pressed, Amiables will hedge, put you on hold, stall you out, and give you firm maybes. The bottom line is," and Dan headed for the board.

> **"Putting the Amiable under pressure or attempting to control them doesn't work. The rule Is…The more you're out of control, the more you're in control.**

"Here's something else you should know about Amiables. They do what behavioral psychologists term gunny sacking. This means that if you frighten, insult, interrupt, embarrass, or display anger or annoyance, the Amiable will probably appear to agree and not be disturbed by your behavior. They very well may smile and nod their head in what seems like agreement. Again, they will do almost anything to avoid confrontation. The truth is, they are more than likely throwing your perceived caustic behavior in an invisible gunnysack. Since Amiables tend to be patient and forgiving, it will usually take considerable time, but one of these days their gunnysack will fill up and then look out! Amiables rarely get angry, but when they do, there's no holding back. All the garbage that has accumulated in their gunnysacks gets emptied on the head of the perceived perpetrator.

"All right, let's go over to page 39."

The Analytical

Behavior: Low assertiveness / low responsiveness

Emphasis: Compliance, working with existing circumstances to promote quality

Pace: Slow, steady, methodical

Priority: The task

Focus: The details, the process

Irritation: Surprises, unpredictability

For Decisions: Give facts, details, and documentation

They Question: How it works, how you reached your conclusions

 **BOB FLYNN**

Specialty: Processes, systems

For Personal Security: Relies on preparation

For Acceptance: They depend on being correct

Measures Personal Worth By: Precision, accuracy, and progress

Greatest Fear: Being wrong

Theme: Notice my efficiency

Behavioral Characteristics: Serious, persistent, orderly, perfectionist, seeks facts and data, "show me" attitude, structured and organized, asks specific questions about specific details, over relies on data collection, good problem-solving skills, concentrates on the details, diplomatic with others, critical of performance, complies with authority, cautious actions and decisions, likes organization and structure, dislikes too much involvement, moves at cautious pace, time-disciplined, precise, likes problem-solving activities, prefers objective, task-oriented, intellectual environment, works well alone, works slowly and precisely, follows directions and standards, works well under controlled circumstances, checks for accuracy.

Probable Strengths: Precise, adaptable, thorough, systematic, cautious, conscientious, orderly, well prepared, accurate, disciplined.

Probable Weaknesses: Too careful, obsessive/compulsive, nitpicky, analysis paralysis, suspicious, finicky, detached, sensitive, indecisive, quiet.

Environmental Clues: Décor will be functional, organized. Seating will suggest formality and non-contact. Walls may contain charts, graphs, exhibits. Will probably put desk between you and them.

After covering the information on page 39, Dan asked if any class members would like to describe an Analytical they know. Mary jumped right in.

"Yes, I know one; it's me. I'm an Analytical, no doubt. Dan, remember when you said these profiles were the essence of the personality style and that almost no one would fit precisely into them?" Not waiting for a response, Mary continued. "I'm the exception; I seem to fit into every category. Is that possible?"

"Yes," Dan responded. "Most people have a dominant behavioral style with a secondary mode. There are, however, some people whose dominant style is so pronounced that there is no secondary mode. That could very well be the case with you."

"So, what does that mean? Is it a blessing or a curse?"

AIN'T NO SUCH THANG AS
A PURDY GOOD ALLIGATOR RASSLER

Smiling at her, Dan answered: "Honestly, Mary, it's neither. Perhaps this is a good time to discuss each of our personal behavioral styles."

"No doubt as we've been discussing the first three basic styles each of you has determined whether or not you fit the category, correct?"

Everyone nodded in agreement.

"So, by a show of hands, let me see how many of you think you have identified your dominant style?"

With the exception of Clyde, every hand went up.

"Just as I thought," said Dan. "Now let me see if my assessment is correct. William I've got you pegged as a mid-level Analytical with an Amiable secondary mode. Tony, high Driver, mid-level Analytical secondary. James high Analytical, low Driver secondary. Hank, mid-level Amiable, I don't have your secondary yet, but my guess is that it's Expressive. Clyde, high Expressive, but I haven't determined if you have a secondary. I can't seem to get you out of Expressive mode, but I think there's at least a low-level Driver in there somewhere. Jack, low Driver, low Expressive secondary. Mary, you see yourself as an off-the-charts Analytical with no secondary, and I think you're right on target.

"Clyde, I think you'll agree with my assessment after we complete the Expressive style. We're going to get right into that after the break. When we complete our study of the Expressive style, we'll continue our discussion of your individual style with special emphasis on specific changes we'll need to make to increase our effectiveness with styles different from ours."

"Dan, I'd like to tell an Analytical story before we break, okay?

"Sure, Clyde."

"Well, see, there was two old boys from down home, Homer and Skeeter, and even though they was best buddies they as opposite as beans and collards. Now Skeeter, he's more of the Amiable type, nice guy, easy goin', a basic good ole boy. Homer, now he's a different story. He's a total Analytical, and I do mean Analytical. See, Homer is the most skeptical critter on planet earth. He just don't believe nothing. I mean Homer's philosophy is… if yo momma tells you she loves you…

"CHECK IT OUT!

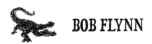

BOB FLYNN

"About a year ago, I ran into Skeeter at the chicken fight. We chatted a while and then I asked how ole Homer was doin'. Skeeter said he was doin' fine, just as skeptical as ever, but fine. Well, I said, 'Skeeter, do you think ole Homer is ever going to change? I mean, do you think he'll ever start taking a more positive view of things, become more of a believer, so to speak?'

And Skeeter, he said, 'Well now, Clyde, it's funny you should ask cause I'm gonna break ole Homer from his disbelieving ways tomorrow. Yeah Clyde, forty years of skepticism is goin' out the window tomorrow.'

"Skeeter," I said, 'how you gonna do that?'

" Why don't you come and see for yourself, Clyde. I'm gonna carry Homer duck huntin'.'

"So, I did. I went duck huntin' with Skeeter and Homer. Now before I tell you the rest of the story, let me give you a little background. In my home state, North Carolina--not South Carolina, Jack, North Carolina--anyhow in my home state we love to go duck huntin'. And we take great pride in our duck-huntin' dogs, our favorite being the Black Lab Retriever.

"So here we are, Skeeter, Homer (the skeptic), me, and a Black Lab Retriever a-sittin' in Skeeter's duck huntin' boat when all of a sudden over flies two nice ducks. Skeeter raises up his double barrel Parker shot gun and fires. BOOM! BOOM! Bein' a crack shot, Skeeter got' em both. Those ole ducks fell about 150 yards from Skeeter's boat. Skeeter looks at me and he winks. Then he looks at that Black Lab and hollers FETCH! That dog leaps a good 20 feet into the Catawba River, but when he lands, he don't sink down into the water like no ordinary duck-huntin' dog. No sirree, he runs on top of that water 150 yards, gathers up both them ducks, turns around and runs 150 yards back to the boat, and drops both them ducks right in ole Homer's lap. Skeeter looks at Homer with a sly grin and says; 'What you got to say about that, Homer?'

"To that Homer replies, 'HE CAN'T SWIM, CAN HE?'"

"Now let's take a fifteen-minute break."

Returning from break, Dan directed the class to page 40.

AIN'T NO SUCH THANG AS
A PURDY GOOD ALLIGATOR RASSLER

The Expressive

Behavior: High assertiveness / high responsiveness

Emphasis: Influencing others into an alliance to accomplish results

Pace: Fast

Priority: Relationships

Focus: Interaction, dynamics of the relationship

Irritation: Boring tasks and being alone

For Decisions: Give incentives and testimonials

They Question: Who else uses it

Specialty: Socializing

For Personal Security: Relies on flexibility

For Acceptance: They depend on their playfulness

Measures Personal Worth By: Acknowledgement, recognition, applause

Greatest Fear: Loss of spotlight

Theme: Notice me

Behavioral Characteristics: Spontaneous actions and decisions, stimulating, talkative, quick pace, gregarious, spontaneous, dramatic actions and opinions, jumps from one activity to another, works quickly and excitedly with others, operates on intuition, likes involvement, exaggerates and generalizes, dreams and gets others caught up in their dreams, undisciplined about time, risk-taker, enthusiastic, optimistic, good persuasive skills, emotional, friendly.

Probable Strengths: Charismatic, confident, gregarious, persuasive, participative, optimistic, stimulating, enthusiastic, communicative, visionary.

Possible Weaknesses: Impulsive, superficial, unrealistic, glib, over-confident, poor listener, self-centered, too trusting, emotional, dislikes detail.

Environmental Clues: Fashionable, latest style dresser, workspace disorganized (but they'll know if something is missing), walls may contain awards, motivational slogans, stimulating posters and notes, open décor, friendly seating arrangement indicates openness, contact, and activity.

After covering the basic information relative to the Expressive, Dan began the in-class discussion.

"Expressives tend to be the most creative of the behavioral styles. They seek and often find unique ways in which to solve problems and capitalize on opportunities. Rallying people to a cause or pulling people into alliance is a hallmark of this style. Quite entertaining, Expressives are not only the life of the party, they are usually the ones that get it started. They can frustrate Analyticals with their 'Let's skip the details and get on with it' attitude. Action is their byword, calling attention to themselves is their goal, and influencing others is their gift. Who knows someone that fits into the Expressive category?"

Hank's hand went up.

"Okay, Hank, tell us about it."

"Now Clyde, don't be disappointed, I know you're Expressive, boy are you Expressive, but the person that comes to mind is my former college roommate and still good friend Bill. This guy is off the wall. I mean, he can have fun getting a root canal. Bill's really smart, but he gets a kick out of acting stupid. He loves to put people on, kinda like Clyde with his 'I'm just a dumb country boy, lost as a varicose vein in a wooden leg' routine. I'm telling you, Bill can read the phone book and make it sound interesting. Bill's mostly upbeat and positive, but at times he can be moody and pretty emotional. He fires up pretty easily and will argue with you about things he knows nothing about, and win, or at least never concede defeat. Dan, that part of him doesn't seem to fit the expressive profile."

"Oh, but it does," Dan responded. "It fits the Expressive profile perfectly. Ever heard of the mongoose? They are cute and personable, action-oriented, fun-loving, and deadly. They are the only jungle creatures that can kill the king cobra. They can go from being these frisky seemingly harmless little varmints, scurrying around having a ball, to vicious attackers. Expressives can be like that, especially when challenged. They can also be subject to mood swings and a fascination for varying intensities of arguments."

AIN'T NO SUCH THANG AS
A PURDY GOOD ALLIGATOR RASSLER

The Actions

Dan concluded the discussion on Expressives and then provided further insight into behavioral styles.

"Every one of you has asked me in one way or another if one behavioral style is more effective than another. The answer is, it depends. It depends on the situation. Behavioral psychologists tell us that the more we can incorporate all the styles into our persona, the more effective we'll be. This is the personal flexibility component of effective relationship strategies."

"Wait a minute, Dan," James interrupted. "This sounds like you are suggesting that we become chameleon-like, take the manipulative approach, pretend we agree when we don't, act interested when we're not. Frankly, I want no part of it."

Dan quickly surveyed the room with his eyes. He immediately recognized that all of the participants agreed with James.

"James, as usual you make a great point, but let me clarify my statement. What we are talking about here are minor modifications in your behavior, slight nuances that make huge differences in whether we connect with styles different from ours. I'm not suggesting in any way that you abandon the essence of who you are. You see, we don't trust wishy-washy people, people who are chameleon-like, as you put it. No, we trust people who are genuine and consistent. So, I'm not recommending in any way that you try to be exactly like another person. What I am suggesting is that we make minor behavioral modifications to establish a foundation for mutual opportunity. Let's take an example. What if a Driver and an Amiable tried to form an association and neither was willing to modify their behavior?"

William answered. "The association wouldn't work, or at least it wouldn't work to its optimum potential. Take my ex and me. She's the Driver, I'm Analytical/Amiable, and neither of us was willing to modify our behavior, so we ended up in divorce."

Now James jumped back in. "That's all well and good, and I agree, but that's not the way it happens in the real world. In my world one person might be willing to modify their style to accommodate the other, but it's highly unlikely that the other party is going to simultaneously reciprocate."

 **BOB FLYNN**

"That's right," Dan answered. "The key word is simultaneously. You see, we don't know the time lapse between stimulus, our behavioral modification, and the other person's response, reciprocation. What we do know is that by taking this approach we significantly improve our odds of connecting with the other person. Conversely, when we are unwilling to modify our behavior in accordance with the style of the other person, we severely hamper our opportunity to establish rapport because . . .

▌ *"We Do Not Trust People Who Are Inflexible.*

"James, there are two sides to this coin. On the one side we have the person who is in fact chameleon-like, wishy-washy. We don't trust these types, because they are not genuine, and we don't know who they are. On the other side, we have the types who say: 'This is just the way I am, what you see is what you get, take it or leave it.' Now if that person has a style that is similar to ours, we may very well take it. However, if our styles are dissimilar, we will be put off by that person's inflexibility and the establishment of rapport is highly unlikely.

"There's another point I'd like to make, and then we'll discuss the specific behaviors to apply to each personality type. Actions and behaviors that are effective for one style may be marginally or even totally ineffective for another. An obvious conclusion, perhaps, but it's very easy to get caught in the trap of thinking that simply because certain actions are not appealing to you and your style, then they won't be appealing to anyone else. It's so easy to fall into the trap of myopic thinking, especially as it pertains to behavioral styles. As an example, Expressives are significantly influenced by incentives and testimonials. This approach would be totally ineffective with Analyticals, who require facts, details and documentation."

Dan then broke the group up into teams. Each team was assigned a behavioral type and asked to create a list of behaviors and actions that would be effective with their assigned type. Clyde and William took the Driver. Tony and James the Amiable. Mary and Hank the Analytical. And Jack and Dan the Expressive. After thirty minutes had elapsed, Dan asked each team to present their behaviors and actions list. Dan also asked the class members to circle any behaviors they felt would be difficult for them to execute.

AIN'T NO SUCH THANG AS
A PURDY GOOD ALLIGATOR RASSLER

Effective Actions and Behaviors for the Driver

- Recognize and respond to their personal need for esteem and independence.
- Don't reason or argue with their negative emotions.
- Expect early and multiple objections.
- Show appropriate firmness and conviction.
- Maintain a business orientation.
- Focus on the process without personal blame or challenge.
- Offer choices in problem-solving.
- Concentrate on the task.
- Don't share personal feelings.
- Speak directly and formally.
- Avoid expressing your opinions.
- Focus on results.
- No warm-ups; get right to the point.
- Show how you will improve present results.
- When the meeting has peaked, move on.
- Tell them what you are going to do and by when.
- Speak rapidly.
- Communicate with intensity.
- Offer several alternatives.
- Use businesslike language.

Effective Actions and Behaviors for the Amiable

- Recognize and respond to their personal need for social esteem and security.
- Allow for some meandering without losing direction.
- Probe for concerns. (Amiables are uncomfortable sharing negatives.)
- Guide the conversation toward problem-solving.
- Focus on establishing and maintaining a positive relationship.
- Talk in a relaxed manner.

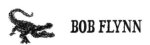 **BOB FLYNN**

- Do not attempt to control.
- Share your feelings; let your emotions show.
- Respond to the expression of the Amiable's feelings.
- Pay personal compliments.
- Show them how it will strengthen their position with others.
- Use friendly – less intense – voice tone.
- Be willing to leave the agenda and go with the flow.
- Listen more – talk less.
- Slow down the pace – talk slower.
- Seek their opinions.
- Share decision-making with them.
- Allow them to assume leadership
- Demonstrate less drive and energy.
- Don't interrupt. Pause – allow them to speak.
- Don't criticize or challenge.
- Disagree mildly and carefully; state opinions moderately.
- Don't push. Compromise; negotiate.
- Don't position anything as big change or risk.

Effective Action and Behaviors for the Analytical

- Recognize and respond to their personal need for security.
- Get them involved and willing to share ideas.
- Build trust.
- Probe for hidden concerns, agendas, and doubts.
- Support with timely data and facts.
- Use a logical approach to solving problems.
- Control more – relax less.
- Get right to the agenda at hand.
- Maintain logical, factual orientation.
- Stay on the agenda.

AIN'T NO SUCH THANG AS
A PURDY GOOD ALLIGATOR RASSLER

- Limit enthusiasm.
- Use businesslike language.
- Make objective decisions.
- Speak forcefully – authoritatively.
- Use direct statements.
- Provide documentation, substantiation, facts, and details.
- Use intense voice tone.
- Be totally organized and prepared.
- Be serious and businesslike.

Effective Actions and Behaviors for the Expressive

- Recognize and respond to their personal need for esteem and independence.
- Listen with empathy.
- Be prepared for irrational behavior with strong emotion.
- Maintaining their self-esteem is critical.
- They must feel like they won.
- Pick up the pace – speak faster.
- Initiate decisions.
- Give recommendations.
- Use direct statements.
- Communicate with intensity.
- Take risks.
- Challenge – disagree when appropriate.
- Face conflict openly.
- Relax.
- Display emotions.
- Show interest in their feelings.
- Develop the relationship.
- Avoid detail and boring conversation.
- Be willing to get off the subject.

 **BOB FLYNN**

Dan concluded the discussion on behavioral types by saying, "Your behavioral or personality type is your comfort zone. You're comfortable and secure there. The problem is, it's limiting.

> *"The more you can force yourself out of the comfort zone restriction of your behavioral type, the more effective at rapport-building you will become.*

"With discipline and practice, you'll be able to recognize behavioral differences between yourself and others. With continued study of the behavioral types, you'll increase your skill and accuracy in selecting and executing optimal strategic behaviors.

"Also, take a close look at the probable strengths and weaknesses as they relate to your dominant behavioral style. Develop strategies to enhance your strengths and eliminate or at least mitigate your weaknesses. And finally, continually suppress your ego by focusing on the other person. Stay on the right side of The Law of Indirect Effort by becoming sincerely interested in the other party, especially if their perspectives are 'different' from yours. Keep in mind that the biggest error you can make in rapport-building is attempting to change the other person, trying to get them to see things through your lens. Stay on the right side of The Law of Reciprocity by keeping the focus on them, their problems, perspectives, hopes, dreams, and opportunities. Be impressed by them, and as if by magic, they will become impressed by you. Do this and you will be well on your way to building bonding rapport.

"Now we're going to discuss non-verbal communication, sometimes referred to as body language."

The Signals

"Reading a person's non-verbal communication or body language is essential to rapport-building for this simple reason… the body never lies. In other words, you can tell what a person really means by asking, listening, and then observing the changes in their facial expressions (physiognomy), and their physiology or body positioning before, during, or after they respond to your question. Effectively building rapport requires that you accurately read situations and people so that you can recognize and eliminate potential problems and initiate the optimum strategy. By combining your knowledge of behavioral types with non-verbal communication, you have a formidable duo for building rapport.

"It is important to understand that body *language is meaningful only in the context of the situation,* and you should test most signals with either a request for more information or a question.

"Example: A person's neck may itch and they scratch it. This gesture has no useable meaning out of context. However, if you were to ask the person. 'What do you think of my suggestion?' and they answered that they like it while simultaneously scratching their neck under their collar, the probable meaning is that not only do they not like your suggestion, but also it has in fact irritated them.

"The action you should take is to seek their 'real' perspective by saying, 'Linda, you won't hurt my feelings if you disagree with my idea, so come on, tell me how you really feel.'"

Dan then provided each participant with a partial list of the most often used body language 'signals,' and their probable ___**in-context**___ meaning. Dan also provided examples and the actions they should take.

Signals and Probable "In-Context" Meaning

SIGNAL: Person Touches Nose, Mouth or Forehead Before Speaking or While Answering a Question.

Probable Meaning: Lying, being partially truthful, does not believe what they are saying, is not sure of what they are saying.

Action: Request additional information, ask for proof.

Example: "Tom, I'm not comfortable with that statement, and I'd like more information."-or-"That sure sounds good, how can you substantiate it?"-or- "What proof can you offer?"

SIGNAL: Person Answers Question or Makes Statements and Spreads Arms with Hands Open and Palms Up.

Probable Meaning: Being truthful, revealing all they know, full and honest disclosure.

Action: If the information provided seems complete, accept it and take no further action. If the information seems incomplete, probe further and be alert for additional signals.

Example: "Thank you for the information, Mary, it's much appreciated. There is one area that's still a little unclear to me. I'd like to learn more about _____."

SIGNAL: Person Sits Erect, <u>Holds Head Straight</u>, and Makes Good Eye Contact.

Probable Meaning: Pseudo listening, pretending to listen while their mind is engaged elsewhere.

Action: Ask question, change topic.

Example: "Bill, what's your opinion of that suggestion?" -or- "I think we've gone about as far as we can on that topic, Bill what's on the front burner with you?"

SIGNAL: Person Sits with <u>Head Slightly Tilted</u>, Makes Good Eye Contact.

Probable Meaning: Person is paying attention.

Action: No action required unless you want to "test" the signal. If so, ask a question.

Example: "Brenda, how are you feeling about this discussion?"

SIGNAL: Stroking Chin, Looking Up, or Chews on Glasses or Pen While Looking Up.

Probable Meaning: Positive contemplation.

Action: No action required, best not to interrupt.

Example: "Alan, how do you suggest that we proceed?"

AIN'T NO SUCH THANG AS
A PURDY GOOD ALLIGATOR RASSLER

SIGNAL: Stroking Chin – Looking Down, or Chews on Glasses or Pen While Looking Down.

Probable Meaning: Negative contemplation.
Action: Get the other party's perspective out in the open.
Example: "Susan, I sense some concern on your part. Where do you think we should take this?"

SIGNAL: Following Your Comment, Glasses Are Taken Off Quickly and Put Down on Table.

Probable Meaning: Blatant disagreement.
Action: Immediately solicit the other party's opinion.
Example: "Gerald, I don't think you agree, so what's your take on this matter?"

SIGNAL: Person Makes Good Eye Contact with Index Finger Over Mouth.

Probable Meaning: They have something to say but are reluctant to say it. If eyes are up, they are withholding something positive. Eyes down they are withholding something negative.
Action: If finger remains over mouth, draw them out with an open question.
Example: "Jenny, what course of action do you suggest?"

SIGNAL: One or Both Hands on Hips.

Probable Meaning: I'm taking charge, or I'm in charge. If hands are open, the approach will more than likely be diplomatic. If hands are closed in a fist, the approach will more than likely be hostile.
Action: Proceed immediately but carefully. Draw the person out with a "soft" open probe; continue drawing the person out until the hands are off the hips.
Example: "Larry, I sense you have a strong opinion on this matter. I'm interested in exploring it."

SIGNAL: Person Crosses Legs, Grabs Knee or Ankle with Both Hands.

Probable Meaning: I've made my decision. If eyes are up, the decision is favorable. If eyes are down, they are in disagreement.
Action: Test the signal by immediately seeking their opinion.
Example: "Patty, if you had to decide today, what would you do?"

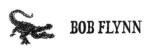 **BOB FLYNN**

"Dan?"

"Yes, Tony?"

"As part of our business development training, my company has provided us with extensive training in both behavioral types and non-verbal communication, and I've found it not only interesting but also very practical."

"I'm glad to hear that. Give us an example of how your training has proved helpful."

"Okay, here's an example that took place less than a month ago. I was making a proposal for a large piece of business to a gentleman named Joe. I had several telephone conversations with him and had met with him twice prior to my proposal presentation. I assessed his behavioral type as Amiable. After an exchange of pleasantries, I handed Joe his copy of the proposal and began my presentation. Within the first thirty seconds of my presentation Joe began looking down and rubbing his neck at the same time. I tested the signal by asking, 'Joe, what's your opinion of the venue?' (I was suggesting that we hold the training in a remote area far away from the distraction of the big city. Frankly, I considered it a great idea and was sure he would agree).

"Joe responded by answering; 'Yeah, well, sure it sounds okay.' I noticed that while he was answering that he touched his nose twice. Then I knew I was in trouble. See, with my training in behavioral types, I had learned that the Amiable's greatest fear is confrontation. Joe was uncomfortable with the location, but because he didn't want to debate it, he just let it ride.

"Here's what I did next. 'Joe,' I said, 'it's fine if you don't agree with the location. Actually, it's a minor consideration and if you feel it's not appropriate, no problem. I'm sure you'll have a better recommendation.'

"With that he responded…

"'Yeah Tony, I think it would be better to have the training in a hotel. I think our people would get considerably more out of the session.'

"I simply agreed and continued on with my presentation—which, by the way, was accepted."

"Tony," James asked, "what do you think would have happened if you did not catch the signals and respond according to Joe's behavioral type?"

"James, there's no doubt in my mind that Joe would have listened to the rest of my presentation, thanked me for my time, then hired one of my competitors. Oh, and Dan, you may be interested to know that we had a really good textbook for the non-verbal communication course."

"Let me guess," Dan said. "It was *Signals* by Allan Pease."

"That's it, Dan."

"I'm not surprised. We consider it the definitive work on the subject."

"It's very good, and I would certainly recommend it to the class."

"Well, Tony, that was certainly a good example because it demonstrated the practical application of behavioral types in combination with non-verbal's."

> **Dan went on to explain that with a little practice and the application of the magic words, <u>KEEN OBSERVATION</u> and <u>PERSONAL FLEXIBILITY</u>, everyone would be well on the way to mastering the rapport-building process.**

Absolute #7

MASTER FEAR

There is a tide in the affairs of men,
Which taken at the flood, leads on to fortune;
Omitted, all voyage of their life
Is bound in shallows and miseries.
On such a full sea are we now afloat;
And we must take the current when it serves,
Or lose our ventures.

JULIUS CAESAR, ACT IV. SCENE III.

 **BOB FLYNN**

Flight 2122 DELAYED…

Great, Jack thought, as he glanced at the flight monitor, *this is all I need. I was hoping to get in early and get a good night's sleep so I would be well prepared for work in the morning, but it looks like that's not going to happen.* Attempting to work through his disappointment, Jack began to think of ways to pass the time. *Absolute #7,* he thought. *Yeah, I'll review the Saturday afternoon session, maybe get into my homework.* Turning to the title page, Jack's mind returned to Saturday afternoon.

"Fear is the dream killer," he recalled Dan saying. "Fear saps our drive and energy, it impedes our initiative, weakens our resolve, and lowers our expectations. Fear is the greatest enemy of personal effectiveness. If we don't have a workable strategy for identifying and dealing with our fears, they will forever hold us in check."

Jack laughed as he recalled saying to himself, "I'm not a fearful person. Sure, a few things frighten me, but fear is not a big issue in my life. I don't see it impeding my personal effectiveness."

That all changed when Dan made the statement…

FEAR OF FAILURE
IS THE GREATEST IMPEDIMENT
TO PERSONAL EFFECTIVENESS…

And then he asked the question…

WHAT WOULD YOU ATTEMPT
IF YOU KNEW
YOU COULD NOT FAIL?

After the statement and the question, the class was up in arms. He recalled William, of all people, saying, "Dan, what if I said that I would attempt becoming a defenseman in the NHL?"

James chimed in, saying, "Dan, that's a very dangerous question. We might all go running off into areas that are ridiculous and impossible!"

Next, Mary had her say. "I have to agree that becoming wild-eyed risk-takers not only seems illogical, it seems insane."

No doubt Dan had heard these types of responses before, because what he did next quieted the uproar. Dan offered no rebuttal, but simply handed out an exercise form and asked the class to answer the questions in fifteen minutes.

The Fear of Failure Exercise

What is the first thing I would attempt if I knew I could not fail?
_____
_____

The second thing:
_____
_____

The third thing:
_____
_____

The fourth thing:
_____
_____

The fifth thing:
_____
_____

The sixth thing:
_____
_____

The seventh thing:
_____
_____

The eighth thing:
_____
_____

The ninth thing:
_____
_____

The tenth thing:
_____
_____

 **BOB FLYNN**

When fifteen minutes had passed, Dan asked William, James, and Mary to read their list. It was quite interesting. As each person read their list it was obvious that as they descended down their lists, the things that they would attempt if they knew they could not fail became more realistic.

Dan continued. "Let me explain something. When you challenge your mind with the question; what would you attempt if you knew you could not fail? your initial answers will be pretty silly. Clyde, what was your first "thing?"

"Play banjo at the Grand Ol' Opry."

"Your third thing?"

"Build my family a large house in the nicest part of town."

"Jack," he remembered Dan asking. "What was your first thing?"

Jack laughed out loud when he recalled his answer, and the waiting passengers all turned and looked curiously at him.

"Pitch for the Yankees, of course."

"And your fifth thing?"

"Break the all-time productivity records at my plant."

Dan asked, "Does everyone understand what I'm saying? The questions are the answers and you have them. All you have to do is get through fantasy, and a simple exercise like this is all you need.

"Now we're going to do the exercise for real. Remember back in Absolute #1 when you prepared your Key Categories list? I want you to take each one of those categories and list the ten actions you would take if you knew you could not fail. Each action must have the potential to cause significant improvement in each category. Complete this exercise as homework for next week."

Jack thumbed through his *12 Absolutes* workbook to his Key Categories section, perusing each one carefully. He decided the homework exercise would be most beneficial, and he looked forward to completing each list.

As he continued thinking about the "Master Fear" session, another key take-away surfaced. Closing his eyes, he pictured Dan saying…

AIN'T NO SUCH THANG AS
A PURDY GOOD ALLIGATOR RASSLER

"There's another insidious fear that dilutes our personal effectiveness. It's a first cousin to the fear of failure, and it's called fear of underqualification. The studies conclusively show that fear of failure, combined with fear of underqualification, represents the greatest impediment to enhancing personal effectiveness. Fear of underqualification, simply defined, means fear of trying new things, or fear of trying things we feel we'll not be good at. Like behavioral types, it's fear of leaving a comfort zone, because we're afraid that we might look foolish or fail entirely. As you complete the Fear of Failure Exercise, you should be able to also identify your fear of underqualification items. Examine each one closely and assess just how much the fear of trying something new or attempting something you feel you'll not be very good at is holding you back. When you identify your fear of failure and fear of underqualification areas, your next step is to determine your strategies for overcoming them. Typically, all it takes are some good old-fashioned guts. In other words, take action, and as Mark Twain said, 'Do the things you fear, and the death of fear is certain.'"

The Unknown

Uncertainty was the final fear area that Dan covered. Jack recalled that this fear factor really hit home with him. He didn't handle the unknown very well. He liked things nice and orderly, as predictable as possible. It was interesting to learn that it's usually our early training that tends to encourage over caution at the expense of trial-and-error exploration. Most people equate the unknown with danger. The purpose of life, they think, is to cling to certainty, and to always know where they're headed. "The truth," Dan explained, "is that we can't grow if we already know the answers before the questions have been asked. Think about the times you remember most fondly. The odds are that you were spontaneously alive, doing whatever you wanted, and delightfully anticipating the unknown. Cultural messages of certainty abound--don't get lost, be prepared, and have the right answers. Certainly, these messages have their time and place, but when overdone, they sap creativity, stifle the imagination, and create fear."

Jack pondered these words, assessing the part they played in his life. He was especially drawn to what Dan called the importance of trial-and-error exploration and to the words of Wayne Dyer: Nothing fails like success because you don't learn anything from it, and…

> **The only thing we learn from is failure. Success only confirms our speculation.**

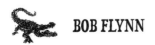

To double our success rate, we must double our failure rate, which means we have to explore the unknown and not fear failing. Jack recalled Clyde's comment to that admonition…

"Try lots of stuff, keep what works."

Unfamiliar ground is going to become more familiar, Jack promised himself.

Dan's explanation of the security trap also registered with Jack.

"Chasing after security means limiting your excitement; being risk averse offers no challenge. It means no growth, and if we are not growing, we're in the first stages of death. Ironically, external security is a myth; we live in a dangerous and uncertain time. There is, however, a security worth perusing, and this is the internal security of trusting yourself and a higher power to handle anything that this insecure life has to offer. Security can be redefined as: The knowledge that you can handle anything, including having no external security."

Next, Jack recalled the statement that hit him right where he lived.

▍ *Embracing security paves the way to complacency.*

My complacency is the very reason I'm involved in the 12 Absolutes *program, Jack thought. I reached a level of security, and then I became complacent. There's a paradox here. The more secure we become, the more complacent we become, which leads to insecurity.*

Jack glanced at the notes he took following Dan's statement.

- Make selective efforts to try new things.

- Listen carefully and without interruption to people who have points of views different from yours.

- Give up having to have a reason for everything that you do.

- Begin to take some risks that will get you out of your routine.

- Remind yourself that…

The fear of failure, the fear of underqualification, and the fear of the unknown are very often grounded in the fear of someone else's disapproval or ridicule.

Reading his notes triggered another thought. It was a statement that Hannah had made when Jack was discussing the Master Fear Absolute. He thought her comment was quite profound: In order to eliminate the fear of the unknown, uncertainty or however you label the future, you must have a rock, something you're absolutely certain of; uncertainty requires certainty.

"Flight 2122 is now ready for boarding."

The announcement abruptly ended Jack's recap of the 7th Absolute. It was a good thing that he was learning how to deal with the unknown, because what would happen in less than twelve hours would ROCK HIS WORLD!

 **BOB FLYNN**

Absolute #6

MASTER FEAR

There is a tide in the affairs of men, which taken at the flood, leads on to fortune; omitted, all voyage of their life is bound in shallows and miseries. On such a full sea are you now afloat; and you must take the current when it serves or lose your ventures.

JULIUS CAESAR, ACT IV. SCENE III.

KEY POINT

Fear is the killer of your dreams and ambitions. It leads to permanent potential and a sub-par life. Fear saps your drive and energy, it impedes your initiative, and lowers your expectations. Fear is the greatest enemy of personal effectiveness. If you don't have a workable strategy for identifying and mitigating your fears, they will forever defeat you.

❑ Fear of Failure is the greatest impediment to your personal effectiveness.

❑ Fear of Under Qualification is the second-greatest fear holding you back.

❑ Fear of Uncertainty is the third-greatest fear holding you back.

❑ Do the things you fear, and the death of fear is certain.

❑ You can't grow if you already know the answers.

❑ To double your success rate, you must double your failure rate.

❑ Promise yourself unfamiliar ground is going to become more familiar.

❑ Embracing security paves the road to complacency.

❑ Trial-and-error exploration is the key.

❑ The only thing we learn from is failure.

❑ Try lots of "stuff," keep what works.

❑ Your "comfort zone" is temporary.

AIN'T NO SUCH THANG AS
A PURDY GOOD ALLIGATOR RASSLER

MAJORPOINT

Chasing after security means severely limiting your potential. Remaining risk adverse means no excitement, offers no challenge, and assures no growth. When you're not growing, you are in the first stages of death. Ironically, external security is a myth; we live in perilous and uncertain times. There is, however, a security worth pursuing, and this is the internal security of trusting yourself to handle anything this life has to offer, including huge responsibility and success.

THE FEAR OF FAILURE, THE FEAR OF UNDERQUALIFICATION, AND THE FEAR OF UNCERTAINTY ARE VERY OFTEN GROUNDED IN THE FEAR OF SOMEONE ELSE'S DISAPPROVAL OR RIDICULE...

 BOB FLYNN

Absolute #7

EXERCISE A

In each of your top five priorities, identify any fears that might be hindering your potential. Commit to the actions you will take to deal with the fears. Commit to a date you will begin taking the actions.

PRIORITY #1:_____
FEAR: _____

ACTION:_____ DATE:_____

PRIORITY #2:_____
FEAR: _____

ACTION:_____ DATE:_____

PRIORITY #3:_____
FEAR: _____

ACTION:_____ DATE:_____

PRIORITY #4:_____
FEAR: _____

ACTION:_____ DATE:_____

PRIORITY #5:_____
FEAR: _____

ACTION:_____ DATE:_____

AIN'T NO SUCH THANG AS
A PURDY GOOD ALLIGATOR RASSLER

EXERCISE B

- Identify any persons that may have caused or are causing you to be fearful.
- Identify the nature of the fear.
- Develop action plans to mitigate the fear.
- Commit to a date to initiate the actions.

PERSON #1:_____

FEAR: _____

ACTION: _____

_____

_____

_____DATE: _____

PERSON #2:_____

FEAR: _____

ACTION: _____

_____

_____

_____DATE: _____

PERSON #3:_____

FEAR: _____

ACTION: _____

_____

_____

_____DATE: _____

 **BOB FLYNN**

PERSON #4:_____

FEAR: _____

ACTION: _____

_____

_____

_____**DATE:** _____

PERSON #5:_____

FEAR: _____

ACTION: _____

_____

_____

_____**DATE:** _____

AIN'T NO SUCH THANG AS
A PURDY GOOD ALLIGATOR RASSLER

CHAPTER NINE

The Questions

ABSOLUTE #8

Create Happiness

*The greatest impediment
to learning is what we think
we already know.*

RUSSELL JAMES

AIN'T NO SUCH THANG AS
A PURDY GOOD ALLIGATOR RASSLER

The Questions

The questions screamed for resolution; they simply would not go away:

How can I get maximum productivity out of others?

How can I get maximum productivity out of myself?

Jack had learned a lot from his mastermind alliance. He felt that he understood and could execute the "soft skill" side of maximizing personal results and maximizing results through people. Still, the analytical side of him needed something more solid, more of a system, a process based on sound, proven principle. "Touchy-feely" was great, but it wasn't the complete answer. Or was it?

Little did he know that the answer would come as the result of a very surprising turn of events.

Even though he was tired from his delayed flight, Jack wanted to get the week off to a fast start, so he arrived at the plant at six in the morning. Knowing that questions are the answer, he had been constantly asking himself the same question: how could he get plant productivity to an acceptable level and beyond? In other words, how could he maximize results through effectiveness with people?

He was grateful for the incremental improvements, but he knew there were miles to go before Fred and Pete would utter the magic words "well done." The plant had so much potential, and Jack was more than anxious to realize it. He figured he could clear his desk by 10 a.m. and spend the rest of the day on the floor; perhaps the answer was there.

"Morning, Jack," Mickey proclaimed as he walked into Jack's office unannounced. "What are you in such deep thought over?"

"Productivity, Mickey. I know it's only been a short time, but we seem stuck. Of all the plants we're still dead last. I'm ready to get this thing humming."

"You know, our crew has been through a lot. It takes time to build trust and credibility and you're off to a good start, but just a word of caution. If you start pushing too hard too soon, you can easily undo the foundation you're building.

 **BOB FLYNN**

Keep in mind that we're trending in the right direction."

"Yeah, you're right, Mickey. I'm glad you admonished me before I ran out on the floor and shot myself in the foot. But you know, there has to be an answer, a process, something that causes people to consistently take personal responsibility and give their best effort."

"Why don't you call your *12 Absolutes* guy? I'll bet he can give you some guidance."

"You know what? That's a good suggestion. I'll call Dan later this morning."

"Good. Hey, don't forget Fred is meeting with us at 8 o'clock."

Fred's meeting only solidified Jack's determination to find the answer to the productivity deficiency. As he ran through the numbers, it all pointed to that one issue: PRODUCTIVITY. As Operations Manager, Jack knew that this issue was his number one responsibility. The same question burned: How, how do you get people to give their best effort?

"Dan, this is Jack. Say, I hate to bother you first thing Monday morning, but I need a little advice."

"No bother, Jack. I'm glad to hear from you. What's going on?"

Jack explained the productivity situation to Dan, including Fred's decision to leave and then return. He also told Dan about Mickey's warning.

Dan asked a few clarification questions and then said, "Mickey gave you some good advice. You saw the power of rapport in last Saturday's class. You're beginning to build that with the crew at work, and undermining them now would be disastrous. Jack, I'm going to send you my notes from a book written by Russell James titled *Maximizing Results with People*. This is the methodology all *12 Absolutes* instructors are trained in. I've found it totally applicable whether you're conducting a class, working with your children, or trying to enhance productivity. If you have any questions, just give me a call."

"Email it, will you Dan?"

"It's on its way. Oh, and Jack?"

"Yes?"

AIN'T NO SUCH THANG AS
A PURDY GOOD ALLIGATOR RASSLER

"This is also the way you inspire and motivate yourself, so when you're studying it, think of it in two dimensions: maximizing results with others and maximizing results with yourself."

"Will do."

Jack turned down lunch with Mickey so he could take a first pass at the material Dan sent. Lunch at the desk wouldn't be so bad if this stuff could help speed up productivity.

The Resolution

MOTIVATING DESIRED ACTION. The heading immediately caught Jack's attention, and he read on with great anticipation.

In a *Public Agenda Report on Restoring North America's Competitive Vitality*, it is revealed that fewer than one out of four employees – 23% – said they were performing anywhere near their full potential. The majority agreed that they could easily increase their effectiveness significantly. Nearly half the work force, about 48%, revealed that they did only what was required to keep their jobs, and held back any additional effort.

As managers and leaders, the question we must continually ask ourselves is: "How do we motivate people to do their best because they want to, not because they have to?" To answer that question, we must understand the concept of discretionary effort.

Discretionary effort is defined as *that level of effort people could give if they wanted to, but which is beyond what is required.*

- Discretionary effort is what is possible.
- Discretionary effort is within the power of every individual to give or withhold.
- Discretionary effort is the "bridge" between good and great.

Setting the Stage for Maximizing Discretionary Effort

There are two ways to motivate and sustain discretionary effort:

1. Do something that will motivate the desired behavior. This is called an antecedent.

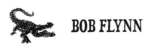 **BOB FLYNN**

2. Do something that will reinforce the desired behavior. This is called a consequence.

- Antecedents set the occasion for the desired behavior to occur.

- Consequences alter the probability that the behavior will occur again.

To optimize motivation and create an organization that consistently achieves discretionary effort, it is essential that you understand and employ antecedents and consequences correctly.

Antecedents / Setting Events

- Set the stage for a behavior to occur; they do not cause the behavior to occur.

- Inform people of what you want to happen.

- Have very limited effect on behavior.

- May cause behavior to occur once, or at best, a few times.

- Business invests inordinately in antecedent activity such as: training, policies, mission/vision statements, slogans, memos and directives, conference calls, meetings, posters and buttons.

- For antecedents to have any lasting effect on behavior, they must be continually repeated. (Very inefficient and costly.)

- Antecedents have sustaining behavioral influence only when they are paired with consequences.

- People must experience the antecedent/consequence pairing a minimum of five times before behavior is affected.

- No matter how attractive or frightening an antecedent is, it will have a sustaining effect only when paired with a consequence.

- The search for more effective antecedents leads managers to use threats as motivators.

Consequences

- Behavior is how things get done, and behavior is a function of its consequences.

AIN'T NO SUCH THANG AS
A PURDY GOOD ALLIGATOR RASSLER

- Consequences follow the behavior and causes it to occur more or less often in the future.

- The role of consequences is to sustain a desired behavior.

- Consequence is reinforcement; without reinforcement, no behavior (either desired or undesired) will last long.

- Antecedents *get* people going. Consequences (reinforcement) keep people going.

- The effective use of consequences is often misunderstood and violated in managing organizational performance.

Taking the Mystery Out of Motivation

Motivation is not hit or miss guesswork, and it's not best accomplished through trial and error, though that's the way it's usually approached.

<u>*Precise laws*</u> that govern human behavior determine effective motivation.

Understanding this is critical because:

The behavior of people is the only way anything gets accomplished!

Understanding and applying these precise laws is critical to motivating desired behaviors and achieving optimal discretionary effort.

So . . .

Whenever an organization strives to improve, it must cause people to change their behavior through effective motivation.

Unfortunately, . . .

Most managers are not effective motivators. Why? Because their motivational approaches are usually not rooted in anything more than personal experience and limited observation. Emotion, perception,

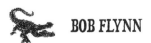

and THE WAY <u>THEY</u> PREFER TO BE MOTIVATED typically underpin their methods.

These typical managers who attempt to motivate from personal experience and the thoughts and feelings that accompany that personal experience, are subject to *very unpredictable results.*

Wow, Jack thought, *that's just like everything else I've been learning. This business of effective management is counterintuitive. I've been taking the actions that I would consider motivational simply because I assumed everybody would be motivated by the same methods that were motivational to me. Now I understand why a few of the people are responding with a good degree of discretionary effort, while most of the others continue to withhold their best efforts. This explains why I'm getting very unpredictable results.*

He read on.

The Problem with Individual Management "Styles"

Personal experience, feelings, and beliefs produce what's commonly called the management "style." Most organizations have as many management styles as they have managers. This is a very dangerous phenomenon, because an organization cannot optimize performance if its managers have their own individual styles. How does the company know that each of the management styles is going to support its values and mission? Different management styles yield confusion and inefficiency. Attaining maximum discretionary effort requires that managers know that what they are doing will produce the desired performance with great predictability.

"Okay, okay," Jack said, talking to the screen. "So what style should the manager use?"

Management Dimensions and Styles
The Three Dimensions

Dimension #1 reflects how managers prefer to motivate. There are two approaches to this dimension: *directive* and *nondirective.*

AIN'T NO SUCH THANG AS
A PURDY GOOD ALLIGATOR RASSLER

Directive Management

- Gives advice.
- Gives instructions.
- Tells what to do.
- Teaches.
- Shows or models.
- Lectures.
- Directive manager is presumed to be older, more experienced.
- Has perspective the person[s] being managed does not have.
- Most favor directive management because it's what we grew up with.
- We know what directive management looks like and sounds like. It's familiar.
- Few can resist the impulse to manage others from the directive perspective.
- Directive management is very effective under the right circumstances.

When Directive Management Is Most Effective

- When you have little time.
- When there is only one right way to do something.
- When you have a lot more knowledge and experience.
- When the risk of nonperformance is a safety issue.
- When the person being managed is unaware of the need.
- When the person being managed wants to be told what to do.

Non-Directive Management

- When the person being managed is already highly skilled.
- When the person being managed wants to be self-reliant.
- When your goal is to help the person being managed to learn to manage themselves.
- When the commitment to the solution of the person being managed is critical.
- When the directive approach would be inappropriate because of role or power differences.

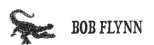

NOTE: Directive and nondirective styles are very different. It's not possible to use them simultaneously. However, you can begin with one and switch to the other in the same management encounter.

Dimension #2 reflects *when* managers prefer to manage. There are two sides to this dimension: the *programmatic* approach or managing on an ongoing basis, and the circumstantial approach, which involves managing only in response to a specific need.

Dimension #3 reflects *what* a manager's focus is on during management encounters—tasks, skills, behaviors (specific)—or the overall growth and development of the person being managed.

The key is for the manager to learn his/her management style preference and the style of management best responded to by the person being managed. If the manager and the person being managed take an assessment test called The Motivational Style Assessment, they can get an accurate reading of their preferred styles. When the "style gap" is determined, both parties can determine and commit to the actions each should take to maximize discretionary effort.

For a copy of the Motivational Styles Assessment email peopleworks@aol.com.

The Two Most Powerful Motivational Tools

1. Feedback

Feedback Facts...

- Feedback is information about performance that allows an individual to adjust his performance.
- Feedback deficiencies are a major contributor to virtually all problems of low performance.
- Most people do not get the feedback they need to perform optimally.
- Typical performance data alone does not tell people what to do to improve performance.
- Sharing sales, production, quality, and financial information is NOT providing feedback; it's sharing information. This type of information gives employees only a vague idea of how they are doing. It has minimal impact on job performance.
- With effective feedback, improvements of 20% to 600% aren't unusual.

- Graphed feedback has many advantages over charts, text, or data presented verbally. Graphs demonstrate at a glance where a person is in relation to where she's been and where she's going. Graphed data allows a person to see performance trends earlier, permitting a more timely response to potential problems.

- Immediate feedback on performance is preferred. With immediate and frequent feedback, people learn more quickly, because they are provided more opportunities for reinforcement than less frequent feedback would permit.

- Feedback delivered less often than weekly is better than nothing, but not much better.

- Monthly feedback, the most common, is much too delayed to have any significant impact on performance. Monthly feedback provides only eleven opportunities a year to correct performance.

- Without feedback, there is no learning!

2. Reinforcement/Consequences

Reinforcement/Consequences Facts

- Feedback is an antecedent; it will get the right behavior started, but it will not sustain it.

- How people choose to respond to antecedents depends on the consequences they experience, have experienced, or expect to experience.

- The rate of performance improvement is directly related to the number of reinforcements/consequences received.

- The ability to shape behavior is the essence of effective managing, teaching, coaching, and supervising. Shaping behavior is at the heart of achieving discretionary effort.

- In environments where management is not making a conscious attempt to reinforce, the extinction of best efforts is assured.

- If management is getting desired behavior, it's because they are reinforcing it.

- If management is getting undesired behavior, it's because they are reinforcing it.

Jack carefully pondered what he had just read. "Let me get this straight," he said to himself. "I think I'm on to something. I want to make sure I understand this process." Bringing up a blank screen on his computer, Jack typed the following:

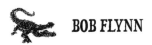 **BOB FLYNN**

Collaborate with the Persons I'm Managing Throughout the Process, and

1. Determine my preferred management style.

2. Determine the management style most effective for the person I'm attempting to motivate.

3. Pinpoint the specific results I'm seeking.

4. Identify the behaviors required to achieve the results I'm seeking.

5. Assess the gap between the desired and actual behaviors required for results.

6. Determine the antecedents to jump start the desired behaviors.

7. Determine the most effective reinforcement required to sustain the desired behavior.

8. Measure and report results using timely graphed data.

9. Set higher goals when initial goals are achieved in order to maintain the process.

Jack laughed in mock delight. "No wonder productivity is suffering. My process is flawed because it's strictly based on my perspective." Another revelation filtered through. "This is the process Pete uses; no wonder he's such an effective manager. Everybody busts it for him. He's the best discretionary-effort-getter I know!"

Jack still had several questions regarding sustained motivation, but he was satisfied he had enough meaningful information to get started. He vowed to begin the process that very day. Ironically, he would never get the opportunity....

The Unexpected

Jack's thoughts were interrupted by the familiar sound of his telephone ringing.

"Jack Williams."

"Jack, it's Pete. How's the battle going?"

"Pete, I was just thinking about you."

"Hope it was good."

"Yeah, it was. I think I've discovered your motivational secret, or at least some of it anyway."

"You've been talking to Dan."

"How'd you know?"

"Actually, I just got off the phone with him."

"So, you been checking up on me?"

"As a matter of fact, I have. I wanted to see how you were doing with the *12 Absolutes*."

"Well, that's your prerogative. After all, you're picking up the tab. What kind of a report did I get?"

"I'm proud to say you got an excellent report and that's not easy with Dan. He's a hard grader. Jack, I'll come to my point. I need you to come to Dallas right away. I've already booked you on the 6:30 flight this evening. I'll pick you up at baggage claim, we'll have a late dinner and I'll tell you what's on my mind. And no, I can't tell you anything now. I'll explain everything at dinner."

"Sure, okay. How long should I expect to be in Dallas?"

"The rest of the week. I'll have a hotel set up for you in Big D."

It was almost midnight when Jack finally made it to his room. The day had seemed like a blur. Lack of sleep combined with the unexpected turn of events had Jack's world turned upside down. It was exciting, though; a real opportunity, and the money was very good.

He hated to do it, it was so late, but he felt compelled to call Hannah. He hadn't told her about the impromptu trip.

"Jack, I've been a little concerned. I called your hotel and they said you'd checked out. Where are you? What's going on?"

 **BOB FLYNN**

"Sorry, Hannah, everything happened so fast I really couldn't take time to call you earlier. I thought I'd be in before now, but my meeting with Pete took longer than expected."

"Your meeting with Pete?"

"Let me start from the beginning."

Jack told her about Pete's call and the hastily arranged trip to Dallas.

"So, here's what this is all about, dear. As you know, the company has made several acquisitions, and one of them is a major plant in Dallas. It's where Pete's been spending most of his time in recent weeks. The bottom line is he released the plant manager and offered me the job."

"Jack, that's wonderful!"

"It is exciting, Hannah, but I'm going to have my hands full. Pete was totally up-front, as usual. From an experience standpoint, he doesn't feel I'm ready for an assignment of this magnitude. He's confident, however, that I can make up for my lack of experience with hustle and the application of my *12 Absolutes* training. He's going to provide me with some initial technical assistance and personally hold my hand as best he can, so that should help. Beyond that, you now know as much as I do. Oh, the money is good; and there are some bonus opportunities and a few other minor perks, so all in all it's a nice package.

"So, Hannah, are you ready for this, for saying goodbye to your friends, leaving the garden club, our church, selling the house, giving birth in a new city?"

"You bet, as long as I don't have to become a Texas Rangers fan. When does Pete want your decision?"

"The sooner the better, obviously, but he said by next Monday at the latest."

"I say buy his breakfast in the morning and do the deal, my man."

"Hannah, you're a doll, one in a million—no, one in ten million."

"Keep talking, big boy; you're on the right track."

"Let's sleep on it. I'm not meeting with Pete until 10 a.m., so we'll have time to make sure we're on the same page regarding this very big decision. I'll call you around eight, okay?"

"Good idea, Jack. I love you. Good night."

"Pete, I want to thank you for this opportunity, and I pledge my total commitment. I know there are other more experienced people you could have selected, and I'm deeply appreciative of your confidence in me."

"Jack, I take it you've discussed this with Hannah."

"She supports the decision 100%."

"Well, I appreciate your decisiveness. This will help speed things up considerably. We can now spend the rest of the week bringing you up to speed. There's one other thing."

"What's that?"

"Prior to making this decision I had lengthy discussions with several people, one of whom was Fred. I gotta tell you, this guy insisted that I offer you this position. He was totally impressed by the way you pushed your ego aside, quickly forgave him, and threw yourself into the operation. He said he learned a lot about attitudinal quality from you. Make sure you give him a call."

"Thanks for telling me that. I'll call him before the sun sets. You know I never would have been able to adjust to the disappointment of not getting the plant manager's job and to Fred's behavior prior to taking the *12 Absolutes*. I would still have been brooding, even today. After learning about the tremendous downside of clutter and ego, I fought through my funk and look what's happened. It's so true what Dan taught us:

❚ *"At the Feast of the Ego, Everyone Leaves Hungry...."*

As Jack expected, Pete had an aggressive, well-thought-out plan. For the remainder of the week, Jack would be meeting with his staff and the rest of the plant team. They would be reviewing the production figures, determining priorities, and solidifying their plan of action. Jack liked what he saw, but he wanted to know more about achieving discretionary effort.

"Pete, I appreciate all the planning, and no doubt if I execute well, we'll get off to a good start. There is one more item I'd like to include in the plan."

"Of course. What is it?"

"Monday morning, I called Dan to get some advice about how to get productivity back on track. He sent me some information that was quite compelling. Frankly, I can't get it off my mind. Looking at the challenges and opportunities of my new assignment, I truly believe the key to effectively executing our plan and putting this plant on the map is maximizing the discretionary effort of the entire plant team and myself. I've learned enough about it to know it's potentially quite powerful, and there's no doubt it's the methodology you employ. As another component of our strategy, I want you to help me learn and master it, and the sooner the better."

Pete flashed a wide, engaging smile, chuckled, and then responded. "Well, this is really ironic. I was going to suggest that we block out Thursday and invest the entire day in working on how you can maximize the discretionary effort of your people and yourself. We'll work in the hotel so we won't be disturbed."

"Yeah, that's great. I've got lots of questions."

Thursday morning came fast. After Jack briefed Pete on what he'd learned about motivating action and attaining maximum discretionary effort, Pete began the session.

"Okay, you've got a good fundamental conception of how this business of motivating discretionary effort works.

"• First you determine the goal to be achieved.

"• Then you access the behaviors required to attain the goal.

"• Next you access the behaviors that need to cease in order to reach the desired goal.

"• Now you devise the antecedents that will get the desired behaviors started and the undesired ones stopped.

"• Then you devise the reinforcement that will sustain or cease the desired behaviors.

AIN'T NO SUCH THANG AS
A PURDY GOOD ALLIGATOR RASSLER

"Now keep in mind what Dan told you," said Pete. "This is also the process you apply to yourself. Right?"

"I got it, Pete."

"Good. Now, based on what you've learned so far, let's discuss the two types of reinforcement and how they are best applied to sustain the desirable behaviors and stop the undesirable ones. This will be a little redundant based on what Dan sent you, but it's well worth reviewing because if you don't get this--and most managers, parents, etc., don't--the rest is just an exercise in futility.

"Now, did Dan explain to you that reinforcement and consequences mean the same thing?"

"Yeah, he did, but why use both words? It's a little confusing, so why not just use one or the other?"

"That's a great question. We found that when we just used the term consequences, people seemed to automatically associate it with some form of punishment. It just had a negative connotation. Now that I'm going to explain the two types of consequences. We can use either reinforcement or consequences. Which would you prefer?"

"Reinforcement works best for me."

"Reinforcement it is. Okay, Jack let's quickly review." Pete went over the key points.

Reinforcement

- Follows the behavior.
- Causes the behavior to occur more or less often in the future.
- The role of reinforcement is to sustain desired behavior.
- Behavior both desired and undesired is a function of its reinforcement.
- Without reinforcement, desired behavior will stop.
- Without reinforcement, undesired behavior will not stop.
- The misunderstanding of applied and misapplied reinforcement is the major impediment to gaining and sustaining discretionary effort.

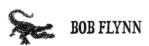 **BOB FLYNN**

To fully comprehend the tremendous power of reinforcement we must understand that…

People do what they do because of what happens to them when they do it.

"All right, now we're going to move into new territory. There are two types of reinforcement that increase behavior: positive and negative reinforcement. And there are two types of reinforcement that decrease behavior: punishment and extinction. Let's look at these four types of reinforcement this way."

Reinforcements That Increase Behavior

1. Get something you want…*positive reinforcement*.

2. Escape or avoid something you don't want…*negative reinforcement*.

Reinforcements That Decrease Behavior

1. Get something you don't want…*punishment*.

2. Don't get what you want…*extinction*.

"See Jack, your job as a manager is to make sure the 'right' reinforcement is occurring for the 'right' behaviors. And that you are withholding reinforcement for the 'wrong' behaviors."

Pete outlined the process.

1. Identify the Specific Desired Outcome (SDO).

2. Clearly communicate the SDO.

3. Determine the behaviors required to produce the SDO.

4. Determine the behaviors that must cease to achieve the SDO.

5. Deliver the reinforcement that supports the desired behaviors and facilitates the SDO.

6. Withhold the reinforcement that motivates the undesired behavior and prevents the SDO.

Pete continued. "It's so vital that you understand the essence of human behavior, which is…

WHEN PERFORMANCE IS NOT IMPROVING REINFORCEMENT FOR THE RIGHT BEHAVIORS IS NOT OCCURRING REINFORCEMENT FOR THE WRONG BEHAVIORS IS!"

"Pete, that's profound."

"Yeah, Jack, I'm telling you it's the hard, cold essence of motivation, and most people never get it, or if they do, they don't apply it."

"Why is that?"

"Because it takes analysis, planning, and it's counterintuitive. The fact is, it's just easier to shoot from the hip and assume that everyone will respond to the same reinforcement.

"Now let's get a little deeper into this business of reinforcement. There are two types of reinforcement, negative and positive. Both negative and positive reinforcement get results. Negative reinforcement, however, rarely motivates discretionary effort. And, it has the potential to cause a lot of trouble. To bring this into a clearer focus, let's draw a contrast between positive and negative reinforcement."

- Positive reinforcement causes both desired and undesired behavior to increase because a positive meaningful consequence follows the behavior.

- Negative reinforcement causes both desired and undesired behavior to increase in order to avoid or escape some unpleasant circumstance.

"It's critical that you understand the difference, because …"

| *The characteristics of the performance motivated by each are VERY different.*

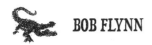

The Skinny

"Here's the bottom line, Jack. Negative reinforcement works and it can cause short-term performance to improve, but it's a good news/bad news scenario. It's so popular because it requires minimal planning, it's relatively easy to execute, and it can often help to achieve the weekly production goal, the monthly sales quota and the like, BUT…

> **"The long-term use of negative reinforcement can never _sustain_ high levels of performance.**

"In the long term, the continual pushing and prodding that negative reinforcement requires is far too intense and punishing for the performers and their management.

Pete went on to explain the down sides of negative reinforcement.

- Working to avoid negative consequences will never come close to maximizing discretionary effort.
- Negative reinforcement gets a level of performance that is just enough to get by.
- If you are getting results primarily with negative reinforcement, you will miss the substantially greater results you could be getting if positive reinforcement was the predominant reinforcer.
- Performance motivated by negative reinforcement will tend to increase at the last minute, and then only to the 'just enough to get by' level.
- The short-term "victories" of negative reinforcement often produce the seeds of future defeat.
- Negative reinforcement is effective only when all that is required is minimal compliance or performance.
- Without the addition of positive reinforcement for improved performance, the improvements you get through negative reinforcement will soon disappear. The past problems will resurface and probably be worse.
- If goal attainment is negatively reinforced, people will fall back into the old behaviors when they reach it.
- Deadlines are typically negative reinforcement and cause people to wait until the last minute and then sprint to the finish line. Deadlines also

AIN'T NO SUCH THANG AS
A PURDY GOOD ALLIGATOR RASSLER

cause people to fear reaching the goal too early because they surmise management will only raise the ante.

- It's work only if people would rather be somewhere else…negative reinforcement motivates them to want to be somewhere else.

"You know, Pete, up until now I've been having a difficult time seeing how well thoughts and goals, plus antecedents combined with positive reinforcement and timely feedback applies to motivating myself. But it's getting clearer now."

"How so, Jack?"

"To make myself do some things I surmise are necessary, I set deadlines and quotas. I give myself a 'pump up' by focusing on the bad things that are going to happen if I don't get off my butt and get going. I tell myself things like: I'd better, I have to, I must, I can't, I'm lazy, I'm undisciplined, and on and on. Just like you explained, the negative reinforcement works for a while. When I just can't take it anymore, I fall back into old habits and I'm right back where I started. But I'm often worse off, because now I've let myself down by not following through. Inevitably, the problem I set out to correct reoccurs, and I start the process over again, expecting a different outcome. It's a frustrating and exhausting roller coaster ride."

"It's good that you're seeing how this process applies to your personal motivation as well as to those you love, manage, and lead. I think it will get even clearer as we go deeper into positive reinforcement."

The Revelation

"Jack, positive reinforcement is the most misunderstood, misused, and under-utilized motivational tool available today."

"Why do you say positive reinforcement is misunderstood, misused, and under-utilized?"

"Well, when most people hear the term positive reinforcement they immediately think of such things as, 'atta-boys,' pats on the back, service plaques, a round of applause or some kind of public recognition like Employee of the Month. This is a totally shallow understanding of positive reinforcement, and it's

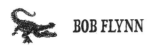
BOB FLYNN

this understanding that prevents most managers from effectively motivating performance.

"So, let's do a quick simple review.

"Remember, positive reinforcement is any consequence that follows a behavior and increases its frequency in the future."

Pete gave several examples of positive reinforcement.

• We flip the switch and the light comes on.

• You pull on your desk drawer and it opens.

• You press your pen on a piece of paper and it makes a mark.

• You call someone's name and they respond.

• You press a letter on your computer and the letter appears on the screen.

"When you understand positive reinforcement in this context, you see how frequently it occurs in everyday functioning, and…

"If positive reinforcement were not built into these performances…

"THE BEHAVIOR WOULD STOP!

"Keep in mind that positive reinforcement occurs every time a behavior produces a favorable change in the environment. And as managers and leaders, it's our responsibility to design work so that positive reinforcement occurs as a natural part of the process."

"So, Pete, if I'm hearing you correctly, positive reinforcement does not have to be huge 'blockbuster' items. Little things count too."

"That's right. The fact is that most of what motivates people on a day-to-day basis are the *seemingly* small things. When these 'little' positive reinforcers are withheld, desired as well as undesired behaviors cease."

The Twins

Pete continued. "Now Jack, there are two ways for positive reinforcement to occur: *naturally* and *created*. Natural reinforcement occurs when the behavior automatically produces it. Pushing the button on the water fountain automatically produces positive reinforcement in the form of flowing water.

"Created reinforcement does not occur automatically but must be added by a person. A congratulatory note, praise, public acknowledgment, money, plaques, or trophies are all forms of created reinforcement.

"*Social* and *tangible* are the two most common forms of created reinforcement.

"Social reinforcement involves doing or saying something to another. This symbolic reinforcer has value only to the person receiving it. The examples I just cited are all social reinforcers.

"Tangible reinforcement is a positive reinforcer that has salvage value. A bonus, an appliance or a piece of furniture are examples of tangible reinforcers.

"The most available form of created reinforcement is social reinforcement. You do not have to have a budget for it; you don't need permission to give it; and when administered correctly, it has tremendous power to motivate desired behavior.

"Are you tracking with me, Jack?"

"Yeah, Pete, I am. Not only tracking, but I'm recalling how effective both social and tangible reinforcement have been in motivating yours truly to enter into positive behaviors."

"So, what were the personal incidences you recalled relative to social and tangible reinforcement?"

"When you defined them, the first thing that popped into my mind was something you did."

"Oh?"

"Over three years ago, you called me at home several days before Christmas and you thanked me for my good work and loyalty during a most difficult

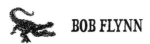 **BOB FLYNN**

year. You cited a particular project I assisted you with, you reminded me how successful it had turned out and how integral my contribution was. It epitomized the tremendous power of social reinforcement. You had no way of knowing this, but a competitor was recruiting me, and I was seriously contemplating a change. After receiving your call, I phoned them immediately and said thanks but no thanks.

"You followed up the phone call with a bonus check. The combination of the phone call and the money formed a powerful and memorable motivational experience. You know, over the years I've received both social and tangible reinforcement--I may be the exception, but I swear the social reinforcers seemed to have had the most impact."

"No, you're not the exception. True to form, social reinforcement has significantly more influence on behavior than does the tangible variety. As a matter of fact, …

"Tangible reinforcement should serve as a <u>backup</u> to social reinforcement – not a substitute for it.

"You see, tangible reinforcers that are not paired with social reinforcers are almost powerless. Social reinforcers can stand alone, but tangible reinforcers cannot."

"Yes, I do see. I also see that with just a little thought and strategy, I can initiate these reinforcers in every aspect of my life."

"That's true, and here's just a word of warning…reinforcers that are not backed by <u>sincerity</u> are perceived for what they are, manipulative devices to get people to do our bidding. When this occurs, their intent backfires and trust and credibility go out the window."

The Converse

"Now Jack, so far we've been talking about the application of positive reinforcers for the purpose of motivating the initiation and continuation of desired behavior. Let's examine the converse, withholding positive reinforcement from undesired behavior. Conceptually, it's quite simple; when behaviors, *desired* or *undesired* do not receive reinforcement, they stop."

AIN'T NO SUCH THANG AS
A PURDY GOOD ALLIGATOR RASSLER

"Yeah, Pete, take a look at Dan's notes. That point really impacted him because he wrote the principle in big bold letters."

> *In work (and family) environments where management and parents __are not__ making conscious attempts to positively reinforce, the extinction of best behaviors (discretionary effort) is absolutely assured!*
> *-And-*
> *If management (and parents) __are__ experiencing undesired behavior, it's because they are positively reinforcing it.*

"Okay, let's bring Dan's thoughts down to a common real-world example. A new employee arrives on the scene believing that her best efforts are required and that those best efforts will be appreciated, acknowledged, and rewarded."

"That's what we tell them at orientation, right?"

"Sure is. Now after a few weeks on the job our highly motivated, 'go the extra mile, give 100%' employee begins to realize that nobody is noticing her above-average efforts. As a matter of fact, some of the other employees have asked her to slow it down a bit. Guess what happens?"

Jack smiled as he responded, "She succumbs to the peer pressure and gets in lockstep with her environment. It happens every day."

"Right. Now let's take it a step further. This same, formerly motivated person observes that the employees who whine, complain, and are disruptive and obstinate are getting most of management's attention. Guess what happens?"

"She either quits or emulates their behavior."

"Right again. So, based on what we've discussed, what have you learned?"

"I've got it down right here in my notes."

Jack handed his notes to Pete, who nodded in agreement as he read:

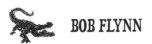

BOB FLYNN

Promoting Desired Behaviors

- Determine specific desirable outcomes and the behaviors required for achievement.

- Determine and administer antecedents that will get the behaviors started.

- Determine and continually administer positive reinforcers that will sustain the desired behaviors.

Eliminating Undesired Behaviors

- Determine behaviors that are hindering the specific desirable outcomes.

- Determine the reinforcers that are sustaining the undesirable behaviors.

- Remove the reinforcers.

"Good; you've been listening carefully. It shows in the succinctness and accuracy of your notes. Keep up the good work, and it will pay off handsomely."

"Thanks for the positive social reinforcement, Pete."

"My pleasure. The positive tangible reinforcement will come when you apply what you're learning."

"I have no doubt."

The Burst

"Jack, I want to make one more point relative to eliminating undesirable behaviors."

"Sure."

"'Ignore it and it will go away' is an old saying that is true but incomplete. By ignoring or withholding reinforcement for counterproductive behavior it will go away, but it won't happen immediately."

"So how long will it take?"

AIN'T NO SUCH THANG AS
A PURDY GOOD ALLIGATOR RASSLER

"That depends on how long the bad behavior has been occurring and how much reinforcement the perpetrator's been receiving. The rule is:

> *"The length of time the undesired behavior has been occurring combined with the amount of reinforcement the person has been receiving will determine the length of time for the behavior to be eradicated.*

"And there's something else you should know, otherwise you could lose faith in the process."

"What's that?"

"When you begin ignoring and failing to reinforce undesired behavior you can expect…

"AN <u>INCREASE</u> IN THE BAD BEHAVIOR!

"Let's take a common occurrence. You push the button for the elevator, and it is slow to arrive. What do you do?"

"I push it harder and faster."

"What if it still doesn't arrive?"

"I push it even harder and faster."

"What if that doesn't work?"

"If no one was looking, the child in me would probably kick the door."

"What if that didn't work?"

"I'd forget it and walk away."

"Now let's rewind. What if by pushing the button harder and faster and kicking the door the elevator showed up? What would you do the next time you encountered a balky elevator?"

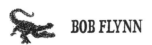

"Why, I'd push the button fast and hard and kick the door at the same time, of course."

"Why would you do that?"

"Because it got the results I wanted the last time I did it."

"Well Jack, you now understand the process called 'extinction burst.' When you stop reinforcing undesirable behavior, expect the volume and frequency to increase. That's a good sign, because it's the first step in the extinction burst process. Write this down Jack:

> *"The reason many managers and parents cannot eliminate undesired behavior is because they cannot emotionally handle the extinction burst process. They cave in to the exacerbated bad behavior and continue to solidify its effectiveness in the mind of the perpetrator.*

"Another probability to be aware of is termed *erratic* behavior. That simply means that when you withhold reinforcement for bad behavior for a period of time, the undesirable behavior may cease. Unfortunately, this does not mean that it's permanently eliminated. You must now be on the lookout for erratic behavior, which is the final stage of extinction burst. See, when the negative emotional behavior runs its course, it may rear its ugly head at various intervals until it stops altogether. Make sure you don't reinforce it in any way.

"Also be aware that the undesired behaviors will sometimes be replaced by other undesired behaviors. Again, make sure you recognize them and in no way reinforce their continuance.

"When you follow the process, the desired behaviors you're after will emerge. Recognize and reinforce, or they will cease and then you're right back where you started."

The Rebuttal

"Pete, I'm enthused about the reinforcement process, but I have a major concern."

"Oh, what's that?"

"Time. You are always touting a keen sense of urgency, and this seems very time- consuming."

"So, how would you speed it up?"

"I'd kick a little butt, Pete. You know, my way or the highway."

"Sure, that type of stuff can speed up the process temporarily. I mean, if you've got a situation where people are behaving in an unsafe or illegal manner, you might offer up threats and punishment as an antecedent, but I gotta tell you, they are quite difficult to use effectively."

"Why's that?"

"Threats and punishment may decrease or even stop a behavior, but you can't predict what behavior will replace the one you stopped. To have any chance at all with threats and punishment, you must clearly identify the behaviors you expect and be prepared to substantiate them with positive reinforcement.

"You see, punishment and threats don't tell people what you want them to do. They only tell them what you don't want them to do. It is quite common to stop one behavior and have it replaced with one that's worse. Then when you confront the person about the new bad behavior, they'll infer in one way or another that 'You told me to stop doing that or I get canned. I stopped it and you're still not satisfied. You don't know what you want and no matter what I do it isn't acceptable. You just can't win in this place!'

"If you're going to threaten and punish, you'd better clearly identify the behaviors you want to replace the bad ones, and you'd better have a strategy for reinforcing them as soon as they occur."

"Okay, I see your point. Looking back over the times I used threats and punishment, I can't think of one instance where they got me where I wanted to go and kept me there. The instant gratification and ego satisfaction I got was

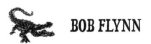

BOB FLYNN

short lived. So, I've got it. Threats and punishment only work when I've got an emergency situation."

Jack listed the process for Pete.

• Clearly define and relate the behaviors I want stopped.

• Clearly identify and relate the replacement behaviors.

• Immediately reinforce the new better behaviors.

• Watch out for the "eliminated" behaviors to be replaced with even worse ones, and…

• Make sure I'm not reinforcing any behaviors I don't want.

"Yeah, Jack, sounds like you've got the concept. Now let's discuss…

The Errors

"If positive reinforcement is so effective, why do managers, parents, and other leaders rarely use it, or if they do, use it incorrectly? Why do they prefer punishment, threats, and negative reinforcement? These are questions I often hear, and they are usually accompanied by this statement…

"I've tried that pat them on the back stuff, but this positive reinforcement stuff, it doesn't work."

"How do you respond to that?"

"I usually explain that more than likely they were managed or parented with a combination of punishment and negative reinforcement. Most of us were, and that's what we're used to; that's what we understand. Additionally, I tell them that punishment and negative reinforcement are tricky, because they appear to get fast results with minimum effort, and they provide much faster feedback than does positive reinforcement."

"The trap of expedience, Pete?"

AIN'T NO SUCH THANG AS
A PURDY GOOD ALLIGATOR RASSLER

"The trap of expedience, Jack."

"I then go on to explain that when managers complain that positive reinforcement doesn't work, I suspect that they have made one or more of the four fatal errors, which include:

"1. Perception

"2. Contingency

"3. Immediacy

"4. Frequency."

"Explain those, will you?"

"Sure."

Perception

"Managers typically choose reinforcers they like, rather than finding out what appeals to the person being managed. They make the common mistake of thinking people will like the reinforcers they like. In other words, they should like what we give them because we like it. When managers apply their self-proclaimed reinforcers, they don't work because they are unattractive to the recipient."

Contingency

"Take good notes, Jack, because the contingency error represents the most common flaw in attempts to positively reinforce.

"Companies often give up on positive reinforcement as a viable motivator because the reinforcers they use are not contingent on anything. For example, improved benefit packages carry great expectations as performance-improvers. The fact is they rarely improve performance because everyone gets it, including the chronic complainers and poor performers. Profit-sharing and gain- sharing programs are other examples of the contingency error. In most organizations, there is only an indirect contingency between profit and the performance of any given individual. The same could be said for most bonus programs.

"The bottom line is that for reinforcers to be most effective, they must be contingent on something that the recipient can control or at least influence."

 **BOB FLYNN**

Immediacy

"Delayed reinforcement is only marginally effective. The longer the time lapse between the desired behavior and the reinforcer, the weaker the effect. It is imperative that organizations examine their process and tie positive feedback to positive behavior in the shortest time interval possible, keeping always in mind that immediate feedback is best."

Frequency

"Studies indicate that a 4 to 1 frequency ratio of positive reinforcers as compared to negative reinforcers is usually adequate to influence desired behaviors. Unfortunately, the way most organizations perceive frequency may be seen in annual performance appraisals, annual recognition dinners, quarterly bonuses, and monthly reports.

"Jack, just to give you a perspective on frequency, listen to this. It takes approximately 50,000 reinforcers to teach competence in basic math. Many of the managers I've counseled over the years claimed to have provided positive feedback frequently, but when I ask them to define frequently they'll say something like…'At least twice last month.'"

As he boarded the plane for the trip home, Jack began to reconstruct the past week in his mind. What a week it had been! It started out in one city as operations manager and ended up in another as plant manager. He thought, *I began my week searching for a way to maximize productivity and came away with an answer that far exceeded anything I could have possibly imagined. I wanted an answer, a process, and boy did I ever get one!*

Jack recalled Pete's concluding comments as he finished Thursday's session…

"Jack, it is currently beyond the scope of the *12 Absolutes* program to instruct motivating others, and I think that's the only oversight of the program. My experience has been that, no matter what I'm engaged in – my work, raising kids, church activities, you name it…

"The ability to inspire and motivate others is invaluable to personal effectiveness.

AIN'T NO SUCH THANG AS
A PURDY GOOD ALLIGATOR RASSLER

"I hope you will consider our discussion today as a bonus module in the 12 Absolutes program. I'm going to do my best to get Russell James to include it in future curriculums."

Pete's right, as usual, Jack concluded. *Motivating others is a critical ingredient in the recipe of maximizing personal effectiveness.*

Then he recalled Pete's parting challenge…

"Now it's a matter of studying and executing what you've learned. No matter how you slice it my friend, it always boils down to learning and executing, and I know you're up to the challenge."

That I am, Jack thought, as the big bird lifted off and headed for home.

Dan smiled and began speaking. "Before we get started on Absolute #8, I've got an announcement for the class. Mr. Jack Williams has just received a major promotion. He'll be moving his family to Dallas, where he will be assuming the duties and responsibilities of plant manager."

After the applause, every class member walked over and shook Jack's hand. Clyde gave him a big bear hug and said, "I love ya, man."

"So, Jack," Tony asked, "when will you be moving?"

"Soon as Hannah finds her house. Her mom's coming to keep the kids' week after next and she'll be joining me in Dallas to begin the search."

"Well, best wishes from all of us. We know you'll be quite successful."

"Thanks, William. I really appreciate your confidence in me."

Once again Dan spoke. "Okay, gang, let's get started."

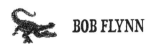 **BOB FLYNN**

Absolute #8

CREATE HAPPINESS

There is no duty we so much underrate as the duty of being happy. By being happy we sow anonymous benefits upon ourselves and the world.

ROBERT LOUIS STEVENSON

"Twenty-three hundred years ago, Aristotle concluded that, more than anything else, men and women seek happiness. While happiness itself is sought for its own sake, every other goal–health, beauty, money, knowledge, or power – is valued only because we expect it will make us happy. The secret to happiness has and is being continually sought. Many argue that mankind has made little if any progress toward being happy. How can this be? Today we are healthier and grow to be much older; we are surrounded by material luxuries and stupendous scientific knowledge undreamed of even a few short years ago. Yet, the surveys reveal that the majority of people we pass on the street are anxious and bored. They see happiness as fleeting, elusive, or nonexistent.

"Today we will devote the entire session on happiness--specifically, your happiness. We will determine how you can create and embellish a lifestyle that has the realistic potential to maximize a feeling of well-being, and as a result keep you in a state that will greatly enhance your personal effectiveness. That state is called flow. Flow, for our purposes, is defined as *the state in which people are so involved in an activity that nothing else seems to matter; the experience itself is so enjoyable that people will do it even at great cost, for the sheer sake of doing it.* Happiness results from flow. To put that statement in perspective, let's examine the facts of happiness."

Dan went to the board and wrote…

Happiness Facts

- Happiness is not something that just happens.

- It does not depend on outside events.

- It does not result from good fortune or random chance.

- It cannot be achieved by consciously searching for it.

- Happiness occurs through the interpretation of our experiences.

- People who learn to control their inner experiences achieve a high degree of happiness.

- Total Involvement in every detail of our lives is where we find happiness.

- Happiness is a side effect of one's personal dedication to a course greater than oneself.

"Contrary to what most people believe, happiness is not found in passive, receptive, relaxing times unless we have worked hard to earn them."

Our best moments occur when our bodies or minds are stretched to their limits of voluntary effort to accomplish something challenging and worthwhile. Such experiences are usually not pleasant at the time they occur.

Dan continued. "Each of us has a picture, however vague, of what we would like to accomplish here on earth. How close we get to attaining this goal becomes the measure for the quality of our lives. If it remains beyond reach, we grow resentful or resigned; if it is at least partially achieved, we experience a proportionate degree of happiness and satisfaction. For the few that actually set and achieve worthy goals, there is an automatic and continuing cycle of setting higher and higher goals. There's nothing wrong with this cycle, providing the goal-seeker derives pleasure and satisfaction from present moment experiences. This will not occur if the goal seeker has chosen the wrong goals. The obvious key then is to choose goals that are consistent with our authentic selves.

"Perhaps now you can even better understand why we place so much emphasis on determining your own personal goals.

"See, gang…

BOB FLYNN

> *"When we choose the correct goals and invest ourselves in them to the limits of our concentration, whatever we do brings happiness. Once we have experienced this degree of happiness, we will redouble our efforts to experience it again. This is the way we grow into becoming a truly effective individual."*

The Strategies

"There are two main strategies we can adopt to achieve happiness. The first is to mold external conditions so that they match our goals. The second is to change how we experience external conditions to make them fit our goals better. Now a word of clarification…*neither of these strategies is effective when used alone.*"

"Dan, give us an example."

"Sure, James. Most people concur that feeling secure is an important component of happiness. Let's say you live in an area that's had several recent break-ins. What are some things you could do to make you feel more secure? i.e.: mold external conditions?"

"Git a mean dawg."

"Good, Clyde."

"Buy a gun."

"Good, William."

"Install stronger locks."

"Sure, Mary."

"Move to another neighborhood."

"Right, Hank."

"Put political pressure on city hall for more police protection."

AIN'T NO SUCH THANG AS
A PURDY GOOD ALLIGATOR RASSLER

"Well said, Tony. Those were all excellent examples of how we mold external conditions by bringing conditions in the environment in line with our goal of feeling secure. Now, give me an example of how we could change how we are experiencing the external condition of increased break-ins so that it better fits our goal of feeling secure."

"Well, we could modify our personal definition of security."

"Okay, Jack, that's a good start. Now how would we go about that modification?"

Mary's hand went up. "All right, Mary, give it a shot."

"We could stop expecting perfect safety and accept that break-ins and other crimes happen everywhere. We could face the reality that risks are inevitable and that we live in an unpredictable world. By taking on that mindset, the threat of insecurity will have less impact on our happiness."

"Yes, Mary, that's precisely what we could do."

Dan continued. "I want you to keep these two strategies in mind and practice them beginning immediately. Why? Because they are so potent. But always keep in mind that they rapidly become marginally effective when used alone."

"Why is that, Dan?"

"Well, Hank, changing external conditions might seem to work at first, but if you are not in control of your consciousness, the old fears or desires will soon return, reviving the previous anxieties."

The Elements

Dan continued the discussion. "When people reflect on when they experience happiness, they mention at least one and often all of the following elements.

"First, the happiness experience usually occurs when they confront tasks they have a chance of completing. By far, the overwhelming proportion of optimal experiences is reported to occur within sequences of activities that are goal-directed and receive immediate feedback.

 **BOB FLYNN**

"Unless a person learns to set goals and to recognize and gauge feedback in any activity, the activity will not be enjoyed.

"Second, they must be able to concentrate on what they are doing. This element of the happiness experience is one of the most frequently mentioned. This feature of the happiness experience is an important byproduct of the fact that enjoyable, happiness-producing experiences require complete focusing of attention on the task at hand, thus leaving no room in the mind for irrelevant information.

"Third and fourth, the concentration is possible because the task they have undertaken has clear goals and provides positive feedback.

"Fifth, one acts with a deep but effortless involvement that removes from awareness the worries and frustrations of everyday life.

"Sixth, happiness experiences allow people to exercise a sense of control over their actions.

"Seventh, concern for the self disappears, yet paradoxically, the sense of self emerges stronger after the experience is over. Hundreds of times every day, we are reminded of the vulnerability of the self. And every time this happens, psychic energy is lost trying to restore order to consciousness. Happiness-producing experiences have no room for self-scrutiny. They have clear goals, stable rules, and challenges well matched to skills, so there is little room for the self to be threatened. When not preoccupied with ourselves, we actually have a great opportunity to expand the perception of our self-imposed limitations.

"Finally, the sense of the duration of time is altered; hours pass by in minutes, and minutes can stretch out to seem like hours. One of the most common descriptions of the happiness experience is that time no longer seems to pass the way it ordinarily does."

The Conditions

"In his studies, Russell James found that every happiness-producing activity, whether it involved competition, chance, opportunity, or any other dimension of experience, had this in common: It provided a sense of discovery, a creative feeling of transporting the person into a new reality. It pushed the person to

AIN'T NO SUCH THANG AS
A PURDY GOOD ALLIGATOR RASSLER

higher levels of performance and led them to previously undreamed—of states of consciousness. In short, it transformed the self by making it more complex."

Dan went to the board and wrote…

IT IS THE GROWTH OF SELF THAT IS THE OPTIMAL HAPPINESS EXPERIENCE…

"You see, guys, we simply do not enjoy doing the same thing at the same level for long. We grow either bored or frustrated, and then the desire to again achieve happiness pushes us to stretch our skills, or to discover new opportunities for using them."

Again, Dan went to the board…

WHEN WE STOP GROWING, WE STOP BEING HAPPY…

"One of the most ironic paradoxes of our time is that we have the greatest abundance of leisure time in human history. Compared to people living only a few generations ago, we have enormously greater opportunities to enjoy leisure time activities, yet there is strong evidence that our overall happiness is declining."

Tony spoke up. "Dan, are you suggesting that leisure is a bad thing? I mean I truly love golf. I play a lot of it. I'm telling you that I'm a happy guy when I'm on the golf course."

"Tony, that's a great question and an astute observation. There's nothing wrong with leisure time activities as long as they are not interfering with our responsibilities or serving as a diversion. Activities like golf, skiing, playing chess, traveling, and the like meet the happiness criteria. They are goal-oriented, challenging, and provide constant feedback. We can most certainly get lost in them from a time perspective; so far, so good. It's when they divert us from other more important activities that they become problematic. For example, if playing golf is interfering with your family responsibilities or diverting you from cleaning up the 'clutter, in your life, it is diversionary and potentially harmful. This is another reason why prioritization is so critical."

"Okay, Dan, I'm feeling better."

 **BOB FLYNN**

269

"Glad to hear it, Tony. Now let's discuss the second condition relative to happiness."

The Ability

"There is a second condition that affects whether or not a happiness experience will occur. This developed ability is called transmutation. Simply stated, transmutation is an individual's ability to restructure consciousness so that the happiness experience occurs of his or her own volition. This ability is of tremendous importance. Many experts consider it the essence of happiness. Some people have developed this ability to such a high degree that they can be truly happy no matter what the circumstances or conditions."

"Like Paul of Tarsus?"

"Yes Mary, like Paul of Tarsus. There are some people who create happiness wherever they are, while others stay bored and marginally happy even when confronted with the most exciting of possibilities. So, in addition to considering the *external* conditions, or the structure of external happiness-producing activities, we also need to take into account the internal conditions that make happiness possible. What I'm advocating here is a developed ability to immediately begin expanding your focus on the task at hand and create happiness in an ever-widening sphere of circumstances.

"With a little observation, you'll discover that…

"The most effective persons on planet earth have developed the ability to transform ordinary, even unpleasant experiences into experiences of happiness…."

"That's Hannah!"

"Hannah?"

"Oh, sorry for the interruption, Dan."

"No apology necessary, Jack. Tell us about Hannah."

"Hannah, as you all know, is my wife. Everything we have been discussing

AIN'T NO SUCH THANG AS
A PURDY GOOD ALLIGATOR RASSLER

about transmutation, she does. When Hannah washes dishes, vacuums the floor, handles issues with the kids, goes grocery shopping, whatever the mundane task or whatever happens, she throws herself into the experience and stays happy. Even when unexpected problems arise, she quickly disciplines her mind to look for the opportunity, the solution, the positive, the pony in the manure pile, as Clyde says. She's never had the *12 Absolutes* training, yet she perfectly fits the criteria you just described."

"Has she always been like that?"

"Ever since I've known her she has, but she tells me she was quite different in her childhood and young adult years. She claims she was negative, skeptical, and angry. I'm telling you that's close to impossible for me to believe, because this woman's attitudinal quality and capacity for happiness are truly remarkable."

"So what happened? How did Hannah learn to restructure her perceptions?"

"First you have to understand that Hannah was raised in a very dysfunctional environment. There were six kids in her family, they were poor, and her parents had alcohol and other serious behavioral problems. The bottom line is that she was abused and neglected. It breaks my heart to even think about it. She left home at age fifteen. Through a series of disastrous decisions over the course of several years, Hannah managed to create some serious problems for herself. Given her upbringing, her problem-solving skills were marginal at best. Finally, Hannah hit bottom, and I mean bottom. It was at that point that she surrendered her will and lifestyle to a Higher Power. She began digging out. Over the course of the next several years she completely and dramatically turned her life around. Today Hannah is the most positive, happy, and caring person I've ever known, and I have the privilege of being married to her."

"Jack, is Hannah okay with you revealing such a private side of her life?"

"Absolutely, Mary. Hannah's not only okay with it, she uses it as a means to reach others. See, Mary, Hannah is very positive about her past. She tells people all the time how grateful she is for all that happened to her. She says it prepared her for the marvelous life she has today, and without it she wouldn't appreciate everything that comes her way."

"So, Jack, could you say that Hannah learned to be positive, to make almost any circumstance a happy one, to restructure out of necessity?"

"Stronger than that, Dan, much stronger. How about life or death?"

"That's what it took?"

"Yes, that's what it took."

Tears streamed down Jack's face. The classroom remained silent for what seemed like an eternity. Finally, Dan broke the silence.

"Let's take a break."

Returning from break Dan continued. "Hannah's story brings to bear an extremely important point as it relates to achieving happiness…

> *"It usually takes tremendous emotional pain for a person to begin examining their thought processes, behavior, general well-being, and overall happiness. It often takes the continuation and amplification of that pain to cause any appreciable change in its causes.*

"Pain will take a person one of three ways:

1. It will break them to the point that they give up on ever having a happy, productive life. They simply give in to the push and pull of circumstances.

2. They deny the pain and live in fleeting moments of happiness, never coming close to their full potential.

3. They fight back with everything they've got, learn to restructure all circumstances, and enjoy escalating degrees of happiness and productivity.

"What Hannah and many others have developed is what's called the Autotelic Personality. This is the person who has trained himself or herself to automatically transform ordinary, even negative experiences into positive happy events. The traits that mark an autotelic personality are most clearly revealed by people who seem to enjoy situations that ordinary persons may find distasteful, even unbearable.

"Bertrand Russell, one of the greatest philosophers of our century, described how he achieved personal happiness. He said, 'Gradually I learned to be indifferent to myself and my deficiencies; I came to center my attention increasingly upon external objects: the state of the world, various branches of knowledge, individuals for whom I felt affection.' In my estimation there could be no better short description of how to build for oneself an autotelic personality."

"So Dan, how do we go about cultivating the autotelic personality?"

"Well, James, as Clyde says, I'm fixin' to tell ya."

The Cultivation

"Let's examine some pertinent facts, conditions, and misconceptions surrounding the achievement of happiness. This will help us to better understand the four master skills required for cultivating the autotelic personality."

- A major obstacle hindering the cultivation of the autotelic personality is excessive self-consciousness. A person who is constantly concerned about how others will perceive them, who is afraid of creating the wrong impression, or of doing something inappropriate, is also condemned to permanent exclusion from happiness.

- Self-centered individuals do not tap into their "autotelic self." These people evaluate all circumstances only in terms of how they relate to his or her desires. For such a person, everything is valueless in itself. A flower is not worth a second look unless it can be used; a man or a woman who cannot advance one's interest does not deserve further attention. Consciousness is structured entirely in terms of its own ends, and nothing is allowed to exist in it that does not conform to those ends.

- People pursuing leisure activities that are expensive in terms of resources required are significantly less happy than when involved in inexpensive leisure. People are happiest when they are talking to one another, when they garden, knit, or are involved in an inexpensive hobby; all of these activities require few material resources, but they demand a relatively high investment of psychic energy. Autotelic personalities understand that expensive toys do not equate to happiness.

- Contrary to what most people assume, the normal state of the mind is chaos. Without training, and without a compelling goal in the external world that incites attention, people are unable to focus their thoughts for more than a few minutes at a time. When left alone, with no pre-

determined goals and destinations, the mind begins to follow random patterns, usually focusing on something painful and disturbing. Unless a person knows how to give order to his or her thoughts, attention will be attracted to whatever is most problematic at the moment; the mind will focus on some real or imaginary pain, on recent grudges or long-term frustrations. Autotelic personalities consciously direct their thought processes toward predetermined destinations. They filter out any interference.

Dan went on to explain that cultivating the autotelic self requires strict adherence to these four master skills:

Goal-Setting.

To be able to develop the autotelic personality, one must have clear and continual goals to strive for. These goals range in magnitude from lifelong commitments to what to do while waiting to see the doctor. When confronted with unexpected adversity, the autotelic personality rapidly begins establishing goals for solving or ameliorating the problem. They don't spend much time fretting and hand-wringing. They spend zero time in the victim role. As soon as they define a system of action, they get on with it.

The major difference between a person with an autotelic personality and one without it is the former knows that it is she that has chosen whatever goal she is pursuing. What she does is not random or determined by outside forces. When a person takes ownership of their decisions, that person is more strongly dedicated to her goals. Her actions are reliable and internally controlled. Knowing them to be her own, she can easily modify her goals whenever the reasons for pursuing them are no longer prudent. In this respect, an autotelic person's behavior is both more consistent and more flexible.

Become Immersed in the Activity.

After choosing a system of action, a person with an autotelic personality grows deeply involved with whatever he is doing. He invests total attention in the task at hand, pays close attention to the feedback resulting from his actions, and makes modifications according to the results his actions are producing. Total involvement is critical. One just does not allow secondary thoughts to interfere with concentration on the goal at hand. People who do not master their thoughts are at the mercy of whatever stray stimulus happens to flash by.

Pay Attention to What Is Happening.

Having an autotelic personality implies the ability to sustain involvement. Self-consciousness, which is the most common source of distraction, is not a problem for such a person. Instead of worrying about how he is doing, how he looks from the outside, he is wholeheartedly committed to the goal at hand. In most cases, it is the depth of involvement that pushes self-consciousness out of awareness. With the non-autotelic personality, it is the other way around. It is the very lack of self-consciousness that makes deep involvement possible.

Learn to Enjoy the Experience.

Being in control of the mind means that literally anything that happens can be a source of happiness. To be able to transform all experiences into happiness, one must become much more than one is. Pursuit of happiness drives individuals to creativity and outstanding achievement. The necessity to develop increasingly refined skills to sustain happiness is what lies behind the evolution of culture. Converting all experience into happiness isn't easy, but when mastered, the payoff is a tremendously effective life!

The Meaning

"Before we move on to the next section, I've got something that's really bothering me, and I've got to get it off my chest."

"Sure, James, tell us about it."

"This autotelic personality concept is intriguing--but come on, can it really be achieved? I can see where it could possibly be effective for dealing with life's little aggravations and setbacks, but what about major tragedy? I mean, I have a close friend; his son was killed in a terrible accident. That's over five years ago, and the guy's still seriously depressed, he can barely drag himself to work. If I told him about this autotelic personality stuff, he'd laugh in my face, and I think he would be right in doing so."

Untraditionally, Dan did not immediately respond to James's statement. He just smiled and remained silent. He appeared to be in deep contemplation. Finally, he spoke.

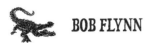 **BOB FLYNN**

"My son was killed in a boating accident four years ago, so I can certainly relate to your friend's state of mind."

The group was openly shocked. James spoke up immediately in a low subdued tone. "Dan, I'm really sorry. I apologize; I had no idea."

"Of course, you didn't, James. It's actually good that you brought it up. I hadn't planned to use such an extreme example in this section, but since it's on the table, let's run with it."

"Dan, are you sure?"

"Yes, absolutely I'm sure. And I'll bet many of you are feeling the same as James. All of us have hurts of varying magnitudes that interfere, even totally rob us of our happiness. Often, we cling to them and wear them like badges of honor. We fall victim to the 'if only' syndrome. If only this hadn't happened, if only I'd taken action, if only I'd not done that stupid thing, and so on. Development of the autotelic personality does not mean we won't have to suffer. It doesn't mean we won't have to grieve a tragic loss. It does mean that we can be happy in spite of anything that happens. And the catalyst for achieving this revered state of mind is 'meaning.'

"What is the meaning of life? The answer to this age-old riddle is astonishingly simple:"

The Meaning of Life Is Meaning...

"It's a unified purpose that gives meaning to life and restores or creates happiness. People who make their lives meaningful develop goals that are meaningful and challenging enough to take up all their energies, goals that have the potential to give significance to their lives.

"When my son Daniel was killed, I was in total shock, and then my shock turned to grief and then to anger—rage, really. I cursed God for allowing this to happen. This was a good kid, why Daniel? Why Daniel? That question haunted and consumed me. And James, just like your friend, I fell into a deep, dark depression. Unlike your friend, I knew the way out. I knew the quicker I could give meaning to Daniel's death, the quicker I could give meaning to my life. I knew this was essential to eventually transcend the vice-like grip of grief and depression. Through my *12 Absolutes* training, I knew the power of meaning. I gave my life meaning by determining to help others who had experienced

AIN'T NO SUCH THANG AS
A PURDY GOOD ALLIGATOR RASSLER

similar losses. I knew in order to be effective I would have to 'walk my talk.' I could no longer be depressed and despondent. If I wanted to give others hope, I would have to project hope in all my undertakings."

"Mr. Composure," as the class affectionately called Dan Hardee, revealed his humanness as he openly wept. Regaining his composure, he continued.

"I've thrown myself into helping others deal with serious personal tragedy, and my life is happy beyond my wildest imagination. I miss my boy every day, and the hurt is there, and it's big, but the difference is--

"I Gave My Hurt Meaning."

"Dan, I'd like to add to that."

"Sure, Jack," Dan responded as he wiped his eyes.

"Thanks. I'm beginning to see how Hannah does it, how she stays so positive and truly happy. I told you Hannah is the happiest person I know, and she is. I live with her and I witness her attitudes and behaviors in all kinds of situations. She's the autotelic personality all right. I don't care what seemingly goes wrong; she gives it meaning, sets her goal, and gets on with it. But Hannah also hurts, especially for her family, and most especially for her mother—who, by the way, was anything but a mother to her. Just the other night we were home alone sitting in front of the fire and chatting. She began talking about her mother and the tears started flowing. Once again, she described her mother's treatment of her dad, her siblings, and herself. Through the tears she smiled, then laughed and said, 'I really hurt for Mom because she has missed so much of life, especially the joy of a happy contented family. I'm so thankful that I gave my terrible upbringing meaning by becoming determined to create a peaceful, happy home.'"

"Thanks for sharing that story, Jack. It helps to solidify the point I've been trying to make.

> **"The development of an autotelic personality is tremendously effective no matter how serious or trivial the situation or circumstance.**

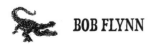 **BOB FLYNN**

"See, folks, the integrity of the self depends on our ability to take neutral or destructive events and turn them into positive ones. With practice and effort, most negative events can at least be neutralized, and possibly even used as challenges that will help make us stronger and happier."

Dan's heaviness abated and he sounded like his usual self as he continued. "In the lives of effective people, there is always a unifying purpose that directs their actions day in, day out – a goal upon which all lesser goals depend. This goal clearly defines the challenges the person will need to overcome to give life meaning and thus create happiness. Without such a purpose, even the best-ordered consciousness lacks sufficient meaning. People who lead their lives in this manner stay in harmony no matter what is happening to them. A person who has given life meaning knows that his energies are not being wasted on doubt, regret, guilt, and fear. Inner congruence ultimately leads to personal effectiveness. We admire people who have come to terms with themselves."

The Job

"I'd like to change gears a little. So far, we have been discussing happiness predominantly as it pertains to our personal lives. Now let's apply it to our work situations. In our studies, we have often encountered a strange inner conflict in the way people relate to the way they make their living. On the one hand, subjects report that they have had some of their most positive experiences while on the job. From this response, you would think they would look forward to working, that their motivation on the job would be high. Instead, even when they feel good about their jobs, people generally report that they would prefer *not* to be working, that their motivation on the job is low. The converse is also true: when supposedly enjoying their leisure, people generally report surprisingly low moods, yet they keep on wishing for more leisure. Behavioral psychologists call this a "contradictory" pattern."

"I can certainly relate to what you're saying, Dan," said Mary. "When I'm on the job, I often think about being off the job, and when I get off the job, I usually find myself bored without much to do. The other side of the coin is that when I do something that I have fantasized as fun and exciting, it often falls far below my expectations and leaves me disappointed, not to mention poorer. In looking back, I've had actually been happier on the job than in my leisure. Why do you suppose that is?"

"Well, Mary, what you just described seems to be commonplace in our society. There are several possible explanations, but one conclusion seems inevitable: when it comes to work, people do not heed the evidence of their senses. They disregard the quality of immediate experience and base their motivation on the strongly rooted cultural stereotype of what work is supposed to be like. They think of it as an imposition, a constraint, an infringement of their freedom, and therefore something to be avoided as much as possible."

William spoke up. "Dan, that's a plausible explanation, but why our discontent with leisure? I often find myself in the same mental predicament as Mary. Gaining a degree of happiness at work yet longing for leisure, getting there only to be disappointed."

"Again, William, the feeling you just described is commonplace in today's society. Leisure often doesn't meet our happiness expectations because of numerous factors. However, there are two that surface most often. First, many leisure activities are engaged in at the expense of higher- priority responsibilities, such as success on the job or quality time with family. And secondly, many people engage in leisure time activities they simply cannot afford."

Dan continued. "One thing is for sure. Some of the most detailed information about who we are as individuals comes from our work, and not so much from our leisure activities. This may explain why even when we're away from our work responsibilities, we're still drawn to them."

The People

"Another thing that our studies on happiness revealed are that more than anything else, our happiness depends on two factors: how we experience work, and how we experience our relations with other people. Our self is largely defined by what happens in those two contexts. When they were asked to list pleasant activities that improve their mood, the kind of events people most often mention are 'Having my work praised,' 'Having people show an interest in me and what I say,' 'Being noticed as attractive.' One of the major symptoms that set happy and unhappy people apart is that unhappy people rarely report such events happening to them. A supportive social network is essential to a person's overall feeling of well-being and happiness. Whether we agree or not, it is a fact that our happiness is dependent to a large degree on the approval of others, and we are extremely vulnerable to how we are treated by them. Therefore, the person who learns to get along with others has taken a giant step toward creating happiness."

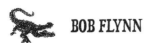 **BOB FLYNN**

"Conflict is huge clutter. I remember you saying that, Dan."

"That's right, Hank, but it goes beyond transcending conflict. We must know in our deepest heart that we can get along with a wide variety of people. In fact, the behavioral psychologists tell us that we are happy to the degree that we can create contentment no matter who we're with."

The Summary

"Well, it's no secret that happiness is a complex subject. I think we have explored it thoroughly, but in conclusion I'd like to throw it open to the group and ask each of you to tell me what you gleaned from this Absolute."

"Like the other Absolutes, happiness is a paradox. It can't really be sought for its own sake; it's a derivative of a lot of other things, especially being true to ourselves and giving our best to our passion, something or someone we really love. Happiness results from how we interpret experiences and we can control that interpretation--that's what the happiest and most effective people do. "

"Thanks, James."

"It became obvious to me that a major key to happiness is to set and work toward goals-- goals that represent our authentic selves. I was intrigued by the concept of molding external conditions so that they match our goals. I was equally intrigued by the concept of changing how we experience external conditions so that they better match our goals. I haven't been doing that, but now I will."

"Much appreciated, Mary."

"This was very eye-opening, a process for happiness, I thought it was like love, it just happened. And yet it is just like love, because love is an action as well as a feeling, and so it is with happiness. Total involvement with every detail of our lives--that's where happiness resides, and in a personal commitment to something other than and greater than oneself. Like I said, eye-opening."

"Poetry as usual, William."

"Well, I was just reminded of something that I already knowed but plum forgot. Our happiest moments aren't always when they're happening. Often, they occur when we have stretched ourselves physically or mentally, or both, pushed ourselves beyond what we consider as our limitations. When we do that, we create a new reality for ourselves, we've raised the high bar. We expand our minds and once expanded the mind can never go back. Ole Russell James taught me that, and now ole Dan's done reminded me of it, and I'm much obliged."

"Clyde, you've got your own form of poetic expression."

"This absolute was quite revealing to me. I sincerely took so much out of it; I really don't know where to start. When I thought about it, I had to agree that it is when we are growing that we are happiest. Not sitting around doing nothing-- that's when we're unhappy, unless we're resting from having sustained a growth spurt. "

"Very astute, Hank; thanks."

"Transmutation, that's my goal. I want to control my mind to the point where happiness occurs of my own volition, like Paul and my wife Hannah. I desire to create happiness in an ever-widening sphere of circumstances. I want to always be looking for that pony and pay no heed to the manure pile. Yeah, the autotelic personality--that's where I'm headed."

"Thanks, Jack, and thanks to everyone. See you next week."

Dan concluded the afternoon by discussing the assignment for next week's session. As usual, it was extensive and quite challenging, especially given Jack's new responsibility and the events that were right around the corner.

Jack didn't know, but he hadn't seen anything yet.

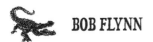 **BOB FLYNN**

Absolute #8

CREATE HAPPINESS

There is no duty we so much underrate as the duty of being happy. By being happy we sow anonymous benefits upon ourselves and the world.

ROBERT LOUIS STEVENSON

KEY POINT

Twenty-three hundred years ago, Aristotle concluded that, more than anything else, men and women seek happiness. While happiness itself is sought for its own sake, every other goal – health, beauty, money, knowledge, or power – is valued only because we expect it will make us happy. The secret to happiness is continually being sought. Contrary to what most people believe, happiness is not found in passive, receptive, relaxing times. We are exceedingly happier when our bodies and minds are stretched to their "limits" of voluntary effort to accomplish something challenging and worthwhile.

❏ Happiness occurs through the interpretation of your experiences.

❏ Happiness is a side effect of your dedication to something other than you.

❏ Only goals that are yoked with your authentic self produce happiness.

❏ It is self-growth that is the ultimate happiness experience.

❏ Transmutation / the autotelic personality is a major catalyst of happiness.

❏ Goals, activity immersion, focus, and experience conversion are the keys.

❏ How you experience work and people is major.

❏ Effective people have a unifying purpose, their #1 priority.

❏ Conflict, especially with family or friends, is huge clutter.

❏ Give your hurt meaning.

❏ Spend zero time in the victim role.

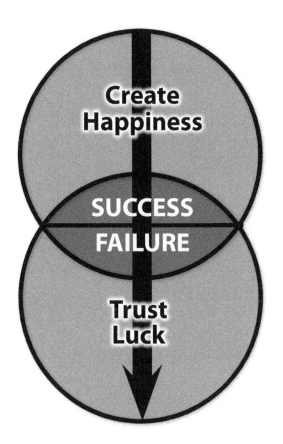

MAJOR POINT

Unless you develop the ability to give order to your thoughts, your attention will be attracted to whatever is most problematic at the moment; your mind will focus on some real or imaginary pain, on recent grudges, or long-term frustrations. The normal state of the mind is CHAOS. Without training and without compelling goals, sustained happiness is very unlikely.

THE SHAME IS THAT IT USUALLY TAKES INTENSE, SUSTAINED EMOTIONAL PAIN TO CAUSE ANY APPRECIABLE EXAMINATION AND CHANGES TO ITS CAUSES.

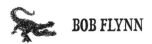 BOB FLYNN

Absolute #8

EXERCISE

Based on what you've learned in Absolute #8, what lifestyle changes, thought processes, and /or behaviors will you change, add, or cease to enhance your happiness?

_____

_____

_____

_____

_____

_____

_____

_____

_____

_____

_____

_____

_____

_____

_____

_____

_____

_____

_____

_____

_____

_____

_____

_____

_____

AIN'T NO SUCH THANG AS
A PURDY GOOD ALLIGATOR RASSLER

CHAPTER TEN

The Adjustment

ABSOLUTE #9
Adopt the Gratitude Attitude

ABSOLUTE #10
Control Your Emotional State

Champions Adjust!

RUSSELL JAMES

The Adjustment

Jack was excited.

He was eager to start his week, as he wanted to immediately begin implementing the motivational and management skills he had learned from Dan and Pete. Sitting in his motel room at 5:00 a.m., he began reviewing the plant's production figures. Unlike his former operation, these numbers, though not stellar, were at least acceptable. To his mind, the challenge was how he should go about creating synergy and getting the Dallas plant producing to its maximum.

Jack would soon have his answer, and it would come from a very unexpected source.

He hustled to get dressed, because he wanted to arrive at the plant before the shift change. Bypassing his office, he headed out on the plant floor.

"Mr. Williams," came a call from across the huge facility.

Jack recognized Ralph Gonzales, the popular Operations Manager, approaching rapidly.

"Hello, Ralph; how's it going?"

"Pretty good. We had a good weekend. There was a slight problem with the robotics, but we got it corrected and didn't lose much time."

"That's great, Ralph."

"Jack, if you have a minute, I'd like to speak with you in private."

From Ralph's voice, tone, and body language, Jack sensed this might be a difficult conversation.

"Sure, Ralph, let's go to my office."

"Thanks Jack."

 **BOB FLYNN**

"So, what's on your mind?"

"I've had it. I'd like to transfer to another plant."

"This sounds serious. What's the problem?"

"Don't take this personally. I don't even know you, but I feel like I got a bad deal. I'm convinced that I deserved the plant manager's job, and I was expecting to get it. As it turns out, I don't think I was even considered. I've been here seven years, Jack. I've worked hard, the people like and respect me, and I've got four years' experience as Ops. Manager. I've proven that I can do the job. It's an embarrassment to be totally overlooked like this."

Ralph's tone reflected controlled anger and disappointment. Jack knew he needed to handle this delicately. He had heard positive things about Ralph, and he didn't want to lose him.

"First of all, Ralph, thanks for getting this on the table. I appreciate your openness, and you know what, if I were in your shoes, I'd probably feel the same way. As far as a transfer, that's beyond my authority. But I'll tell you what; I'll take it up with Pete Morrison this afternoon. What else would you like me to do?"

"I can't think of anything else. Sorry to get your week started off on a bad note."

Ralph was calmer now and more open, so Jack decided to probe deeper.

"You haven't gotten my week off to a bad start. In fact, I see this as an opportunity not a problem."

"You do? An opportunity?"

"Well, I think you have a right to know why you were not offered the position, and I'll do my best to find out. When I do, we'll discuss it and then both of us will be in a better position to determine the best alternative."

"Okay, that makes sense."

"Good, and Ralph…."

"Yeah Jack?"

AIN'T NO SUCH THANG AS
A PURDY GOOD ALLIGATOR RASSLER

"Don't do or say anything rash. I'll get back to you very soon."

"I hear you. I'll keep my cool until we talk again, but please make it soon."

"Will do."

"So that's it, Jack," said Pete. "Those are my reasons for not selecting Gonzales as plant manager. And I'll be glad to discuss it with him, if you'd like."

"I appreciate the offer, but I feel that's my responsibility."

"Great, I'm glad you feel that way. If he wants to transfer to your old position, I think that's a viable alternative. I'll wait for your recommendation. Now, I've got some really good news for you."

"I know, you just saved a bunch of money on your car insurance. Sorry, Pete, I couldn't resist. Go ahead and lay it on me; I need it."

"I'm going to send Mickey to help you get your feet wet. You can have him for a month, longer if you need him."

"Pete, have you discussed this with him yet?"

"No, I wanted to tell you first."

"Hold off, will you Pete? I want to talk with Gonzales first."

"Will do."

"So that's it, Ralph; that's why you weren't offered the promotion."

Gonzales sat in stony silence for what seemed like an eternity until he finally spoke. "I still don't get it. I did my job, that should be enough to at least be considered."

"From Pete's perspective, you had several opportunities to 'step up' to take more responsibility and you didn't seem to want it."

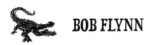 **BOB FLYNN**

"I guess Pete's referring to the time last year when our former plant manager Phil Wheeler had surgery and I was asked to run the plant."

"Yes, that's one incident he cited. Pete said you were reluctant to assume the interim responsibility and when you finally did, production nose-dived."

"Yeah, well, that wasn't my fault. Our people slacked off. I can give you the names of the people that flat out didn't do their jobs. They just kicked back when Phil was out. When I tried to push hard, they all but laughed at me. I thought these people were my friends. If they'd done as I told them, production would have increased. I'm telling you, if everybody worked as hard as me, this plant would be in the top 5%, not in the middle of the pack. And there's another thing--did Pete check the weather during the time I was running the plant?"

"Pete's very thorough, so I'm sure he did."

"Well then, he forgot to tell you that we had a near blizzard. It was terrible. Nobody could have made production during those conditions."

"Gordon Adams in Winnipeg did, and they had one of the worst winters in the last fifty years."

"Yeah, well--Gord was lucky."

"Ralph, no doubt you faced some adversity, and certainly that had an effect on performance, I'll give you that. Let's take the focus off the weather, your teammates, and unpredictable circumstances. Think back and give me some examples of where you could have taken responsibility and improved outcomes."

Without hesitation, Gonzales spoke up. "I can't, because I wasn't responsible. I don't control the weather or the work ethic and attitudes of others."

"I see. So, Ralph, where do we go from here?"

"Again, don't take this personally, but I want to be transferred to another facility."

"I won't recommend that."

"Why not?"

"You're not going to like what I'm about to say, and it gives me no pleasure to say it, but I'm quite concerned about your reluctance to assume responsibility for anything beyond the task right in front of you. Your focus is totally off yourself and on circumstances and other people. See, Ralph, to run a plant you must assume responsibility for everything. And you're probably asking yourself how I would know, since I've never managed a plant."

"It has crossed my mind."

"Of course, it has, and that's understandable. I may not have any experience managing a plant, but I do have experience in learning how to take personal responsibility. You see, I had the same mindset as you. I'd be responsible for my stuff, and that's it. Because of a wakeup call Pete gave me, plus some other training I've had, I saw the folly in that attitude. It's the attitude of the masses, the wannabes, and the chronically complacent. I can tell you this; at best, that attitude leads to behaviors that will keep you stuck right where you are. I know because I was there.

"You're a good man, and if I'm any judge of ability, you have tremendous potential, certainly the potential to run a plant. I'm going to take the responsibility to make sure your potential isn't permanent. I want you to stay here, assume more responsibility, and help me get this puppy in high gear. If you really want to manage a plant, I'll see to it that you'll have the best training and guidance to prepare you for that level of responsibility."

"Sounds like you're telling me it's this or nothing, and that a transfer is not in the cards."

"It's in your best interest, Ralph, and in the best interest of the organization. Why don't you sleep on it? We can discuss it in more depth after you digest what we've talked about today. Will you do that?"

"Okay, I'll think it over."

"That's great. And one other thing; I expect you to continue doing a great job and to project a good attitude. Leaders must often mask their pain. Champions adjust, Ralph. Will you do that? Do we have a deal?"

"We have a deal."

Jack smiled to himself as Gonzales turned to leave. Not long ago, that was me, he thought.

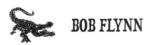 **BOB FLYNN**

Instantly he realized just how far he'd come in such a short period of time. "Amazing what we can do when we officially decide," Jack said out loud.

The ringing of his cell phone startled him back into the moment.

The Call

"Jack Williams."

"Jack, it's Tony from *The 12 Absolutes* class."

"Tony, good to hear from you. To what do I owe this pleasure?"

"Do you recall the conversation we had at the break last week?"

"Sure, Tony. It was interesting to learn that you had managed an operation similar to mine. And I really appreciated your offer to help me in any way you could."

"Well, for some strange reason, you've been on my mind this week. I know how we guys are, we're often reluctant to ask for help and advice, especially from people we don't know all that well, but I just wanted to let you know that my offer still holds."

Jack knew that Tony was a very successful business executive, so he was delighted that he had taken an interest.

"This is ironic, Tony, because I'm in the middle of a challenge, and I'd appreciate your insight. If you have a minute, I'd like to tell you about it, and of course I would appreciate any guidance you could offer."

Tony listened carefully and then responded. "No doubt Jack, Ralph Gonzales presents an interesting opportunity, but let me make sure I've got a clear picture. Here's what I heard you say. Gonzales is a good worker, experienced, well-liked by his teammates, maintains good focus on his personal productivity but seems more concerned about his popularity and the political climate than he does about the performance of others."

"Yeah, that's about it. He is very reluctant to take on responsibility out of his sphere of personal control. And he's not at all comfortable holding others

AIN'T NO SUCH THANG AS
A PURDY GOOD ALLIGATOR RASSLER

accountable. When confronted in that area he immediately looks for scapegoats and fixes the blame on circumstances and others."

"Look, I've certainly been down that road before. Rather than take up your time on the phone, why don't I email you my suggestions and we can discuss it Saturday."

"That would be much appreciated. Thanks again for this unexpected pleasure."

"You may not be so appreciative when you read my suggestions, but we'll see."

"I'm sure they will be quite helpful."

"See you Saturday, Jack."

"I look forward to it, Tony."

The Email

Early Thursday morning, Jack pulled up his emails and the first one was from Tony.

Hello Jack:

Here are my thoughts regarding your situation with Ralph Gonzales.

I think he was both glad and irritated that he wasn't considered for the plant manager's job. If he had been truly interested, he would have immediately and emphatically started lobbying for the position. I also believe he's under considerable peer pressure. His fellow workers have asked him a lot of questions as to why he didn't get the job. I think part of his irritation is an attempt to save face. But I also think Ralph might be taking a look at his life and may be ready to make some positive changes. I suggest that you provide him with clear expectations. He needs to understand exactly what his responsibilities are, especially as they pertain to managing others. By taking that approach, I believe you'll force him to get on board or seek greener pastures.

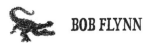 **BOB FLYNN**

I do not suggest that you offer him a transfer, because he needs to produce where he is. With his experience level, he is capable of becoming a tremendous asset to you and the company. Of course, be fair, but be fair fast. It's been my experience that these things turn around rapidly, or they don't turn around at all.

Here are some facts relating to managing the productivity of others that you may want to convey to Ralph during your meeting:

- Management has long been concerned with the debilitating effects of creating too much anxiety relative to productivity gains; this is a legitimate concern. What management has failed to realize, however, is the equally destructive effects of too little anxiety.

- People are not at their keenest when life is too safe, too predictable. When people receive without having to achieve, they are protected from failure. There are no consequences for not achieving. At first glance, that may seem like a good thing, but it's not. By protecting people from risk and high achievement, management can severely limit their potential as well as lower their self-esteem. Overprotection robs them of the opportunity to become strong, competent people.

- When people are not held accountable for performance levels, they don't perform. Instead, they become complacent.

- It often takes a shock to wake people from their chronic complacency. Competent managers provide that shock.

- Alhough past achievements are commendable, only today's achievements will carry an organization into a secure future.

- Good managers teach others to accept risk. They accomplish this by demonstrating the benefits of risk and by helping their team develop techniques to cope with the stresses associated with those risks.

- People sincerely prefer accountability, and they respect managers who hold them accountable. They want their work to be judged, because it's the only way they can feel their work is significant.

- Great managers instill the belief that trying is not enough. They do not allow it to earn their respect; accomplishments and results are the requirement for respect.

- People do not solve problems, move forward, change, and adapt when anxiety is removed. They simply cling to bureaucratic security blankets and profess their "rights."

- Big breakthroughs occur only when people "break set," that is, see things differently. Breaking set involves taking risks. This won't occur where management is overprotective.

- Making things easy for people simply doesn't make them happy, and of course it doesn't enhance productivity. Psychological research tells us that motivation is highest when the probability of success is 50%. We don't get involved if the task is too easy or too hard. Many managers strive to make the task easy, believing it will prove motivational.

Jack, I think Gonzales has become very complacent, even lethargic. The only way, in my estimation, to energize him and your operation is to lead him into the psychology of earning. It will take some shaking up. Ralph is going to resist leaving the comfort of paying attention only to his personal productivity. He's going to be especially reluctant to hold the team to a higher standard. But if he won't, he's of no use to you or the company in his current role.

I've found that it takes great courage and toughness to sustain the pressure long enough to make people realize that the current level of productivity is not acceptable. Most managers give in to the seemingly constant complaining, delaying, and resisting, and that's why most managers are mediocre.

Hope this helps. Let me know what you decide.

Tony's right, Jack thought. *I can procrastinate, but sooner or later I'm going to have to get Mr. Gonzales on track. I might as well find out as soon as possible whether or not he wants to play at this level.*

Jack walked out on the floor and asked Ralph to meet with him at 8:00 the next morning.

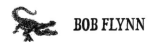 **BOB FLYNN**

The Meeting

It didn't go well.

Jack had hoped that Ralph would rise to the occasion and accept responsibility for holding himself and the team accountable for increased productivity. When Jack laid out the plan, complete with stringent but fair incremental productivity expectations, Gonzales quickly disengaged and retreated to a defensive posture.

"Jack, we've never achieved that level of productivity. Our people simply will not accept it. You can't come in here and make those kinds of demands. These people are my friends. They're already anxious over the acquisition, and now you're asking me to put additional pressure on them. It won't work."

Jack attempted to explain that the increases were incremental and quite doable, and if administered correctly would motivate rather than hurt morale. He advised Ralph that he would provide additional training and incentives. It didn't work.

"This is quite a disappointment, Ralph. I was anticipating a collaborative meeting where we could reach a mutual agreement and set the wheels in motion. What I'm hearing is all the 'reasons' why we can't improve. I simply can't have a management person with that mindset on my team. It's totally unacceptable."

Gonzales seemed shocked. He turned pale and appeared to be in a state of total disbelief. He had always gotten by with his charm and likeable personality, and now that it wasn't working he had no idea what to do. He didn't want to lose his job, so he decided to be totally honest.

As he spoke his tone was subdued, almost humble. Jack detected a genuineness he'd not sensed before.

"I know I've been too soft, that I've let things slide. I think I've been afraid that the people wouldn't like me and that morale would suffer. We've been doing okay, making production, and although I knew we could do better, I didn't want to rock the boat. I got lulled into complacency and didn't even realize it. Now that you've come aboard, I can see those days are over. Jack, I don't know if I can give you what you want, but I also don't want to leave the company."

"Well, now we're getting somewhere. The question is, do you want to help me take this plant to a higher level? If you sincerely do, then I'm confident you've got what it takes to get this job done. If you're willing to stretch your comfort zone, face your fears, and move forward, we'll put this baby on the map.

"You've heard the plan, and you know what I expect in terms of productivity. That's not going to change. If you really want to step up to the plate, I'd be willing to entertain that possibility. I want you to think about it over the weekend, and if you still feel the same way on Monday, I want to hear specifically what you're going to do in order to reach our new production goals. Fair enough?"

"Fair enough. Thanks, Jack. See you Monday."

Absolute #9

ADOPT THE GRATITUDE ATTITUDE

Gratitude unlocks the fullness of life. It turns what we have into enough and more. It turns denial into acceptance, chaos into order, confusion into clarity. It can turn a meal into a feast, a house into a home, a stranger into a friend. Gratitude makes sense of our past, brings peace for today, and creates a vision for tomorrow.

MELODY BEATTIE

It had been a hectic but eventful week. Jack was glad to get back in class; he was looking forward to Absolutes #9 and #10.

"Good morning and welcome."

Jack smiled to himself. There was something soothing and comforting about Dan Hardee's voice. It was like a warm blanket on a cold night.

 **BOB FLYNN**

"This morning we will be covering Absolute #9, Adopt the Gratitude Attitude. This afternoon we'll turn our attention to Absolute #10. If there are no questions or comments, let's get going.

"To date, we have invested considerable time in talking about your future. We have paid particular attention to goal-setting, which is totally oriented toward the future. Additionally, we have for the most part caused your focus to be directed internally. Absolute #9 seeks to change your focus from internal to external. It is a 'pause and reflect' respite on your journey to personal effectiveness. It's so seductive to focus on the future, and while that's certainly advisable, it can cause us to miss pleasures and opportunities that are currently underfoot. As with all of the Absolutes, this one tends to be counterintuitive. Our natural inclination is to take for granted what we already have and seek 'bigger and better' things. Certainly, this isn't all bad; in fact, it's quite good. All accomplishments large and small are rooted in varying degrees of dissatisfaction."

James interrupted. "Is this stop and smell the roses, Dan?"

"Oh no, James, this is keep going while simultaneously giving thanks for the roses. I think it will clear up for you as we proceed."

Jack chuckled to himself and thought, *Dan has a diplomatic and effective way of telling James to shut up and listen.*

Dan continued.

"Ironically, when we give appreciation to things we already have, it opens the door to bigger and better things. You see, the more we focus on what we *don't* have, the more 'lack' will permeate our thinking, creating negativity and even depression. The more negative and depressed we become, the more we will focus on lack—and, well, you get the picture. What we all hunger for is an inner peace that the world and its ever-changing circumstances cannot take away. There's no better way to find that inner peace than to be sincerely grateful for what we already have.

"The fact is…

"The universe will not give more to you until you appreciate what you already have.

"And…

> **"If you don't appreciate what you have, you'll lose it.**

"So not only will we not get more until we are grateful for what we have, we're also in danger of losing what we are taking for granted, and that's a pretty sobering thought indeed. Again, cause and effect, the supreme law is in control. And the more we understand and obey it, the more effective we become.

"I've often heard Russell James say…"

> **"'The more you appreciate and give thanks for what you have, right now, this minute the more the world will give to you – maybe not all at once or the way you expect it – but when you give thanks for what you have and give your very best, the very best will come back to you.'"**

Clyde jumped right in. "Hey Dan, I don't want to be no horse's behind like James—only kiddin' Jim—but does this mean that if we show appreciation for our problems, we'll git more of'em? See, I don't want that, because I've got a stable full right now."

"That's an astute observation, Clyde. Actually, whenever we show appreciation for what we consider problems we are rewarded, not with more problems but with solutions."

"Now I'm trackin' with you, Dan."

"Glad to hear it, Clyde."

Dan continued. "People who take this class, people like you, tend to be ambitious, future oriented, and filled with varying degrees of discontent relative to their current state. As we've discussed, these are primarily good attributes, because they serve as motivators. But there's also a downside; folks like you often take for granted the blessings they already have and as a result don't take time to appreciate them. I'm going to suggest a very simple yet highly effective exercise that will not only get you in touch with your many blessings, but if pursued, will open the door for many more."

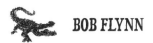 **BOB FLYNN**

Dan suggested that each class member begin keeping a daily gratitude journal. Each night before going to bed, he suggested that each individual write down five things to be grateful for about that day. He said that in his opinion, the gratitude journal was not an option, because after about two months, no one would be the same person. Dan said that after consciously giving thanks each day for the abundance that exists in his or her lives, everyone would undergo a serious attitude change (even if a person's attitude was great to begin with it will get much better). He reminded the class that by taking this action they would set into motion one of nature's immutable laws…

The more you are grateful for, the more will be given you.

He continued by telling the class that as the weeks passed, they would fill their journals with daily blessings and an inner shift in their reality would occur. Soon they would discover how content and hopeful they would feel.

Dan concluded the morning session by saying, "As you focus on what you have right now, you won't think about what you consider lacking in your life. By ingraining this habit of the mind, you'll be designing a wonderful new and exciting blueprint for your future. You will feel a constant sense of fulfillment. This sense of fulfillment is gratitude at work, transforming your dreams into reality.

"A French proverb reminds us that 'Gratitude is the heart's memory.' Begin today to explore and integrate this beautiful, life-affirming principle into each day, and the miracles you have been seeking will unfold to your wonder and amazement."

Dan went on to outline a few key points.

• The more abundance you see and acknowledge in your life, the more you will experience.

• To experience less than abundance in our lives, we must actively resist it.

People tend to hold on to things or accumulate them because they feel that otherwise they might not have what they need at the time they are ready for it. In other words, they do not trust the natural abundance of the Universe to provide them with appropriate things at the perfect time.

When we do not trust the Universe to function perfectly, it reciprocates. It continually gives us what we expect, whether it be shortage or abundance.

• Whatever you focus your thoughts on expands. The more you notice and acknowledge all of the things that you have, the more you will receive.

• The converse is also true. If you dwell on what you do not have and put energy into scarcity, you will receive more of it.

"Let's break for lunch."

Jack quickly found Tony and thanked him for the advice and counsel. The two agreed to continue staying current regarding Jack's new assignment. Jack made a mental note to put Tony's name in his gratitude journal.

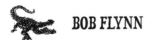

Absolute #10

CONTROL YOUR EMOTIONAL STATE

The key to maximizing personal effectiveness is getting into the right emotional state.

RUSSELL JAMES

"Jack, thank you for sharing the gratitude attitude with me," said Hannah. "I'm starting my journal tonight. My first entry is going to be my gratitude for my wonderful husband and the fact that he's always learning and growing; good-looking, too. Now Jack, tell me about Absolute #10."

"Well, Hannah, as usual it was very interesting and informative. Control Your Emotional State is Absolute #10, and I can tell you one thing; it really opened my eyes to the many myths surrounding personal effectiveness.

"Dan began this session with a question: Is the ideal performance state the result of good performance, or is it the cause of good performance?

"The answers were mixed. One thing for sure, as a class we just didn't know. Dan's answer clarified things.

"He told us that If we think feeling great is a result of doing well, we have got it backward. Because of the configuration of the human nervous system, the proper emotions have to be in place first."

Reading from his notes, Jack continued. "The ideal performance state is characterized by strong *positive* emotions. When our state is positive, performance is good. When our state is negative, performance suffers.

"The relation between your emotional state and your personal effectiveness goes like this:

"1. Your level of performance is a direct reflection of the way you feel inside: When you feel good you perform well.

"2. Performing at the best of your abilities at any given moment occurs

AIN'T NO SUCH THANG AS
A PURDY GOOD ALLIGATOR RASSLER

without conscious deliberation when the right internal conditions have been established.

"3. To maximize personal effectiveness, you must develop the ability to master your negative emotions regardless of the circumstances.

"The critical understanding, which many people miss, is that they are physically and chemically different when they change emotional states. When you change your emotional states, you change your ability to perform. Establishing the right internal climate has the same effect on potential performance as the changing of the seasons has on potential plants."

The Dozen

Much of what has been learned about emotional states and their connection to personal effectiveness flies in the face of conventional wisdom. The constellation of feelings [states], that form the ideal effectiveness state is not a common experience – neither is maximum personal effectiveness.

When five hundred top performers and their peak performances were analyzed, more than four hundred descriptions of their emotional states during these performances surfaced. Out of the four hundred, twelve distinct categories formed a pattern of ideal emotional states.

Mental Calmness
There is a characteristic inner stillness associated with consistent personal effectiveness. Many people believe that the best way to be effective is to psyche themselves up into a fast, accelerated mental state. This is not the state of consistent effectiveness. We are most effective and influential when we are experiencing internal calm and quiet.

Physical Relaxation
Our physical state is a reflection of our mental state, and vice versa. Physical tenseness hampers effectiveness, no matter what you're doing. When muscles are relaxed, not taut, we are at our optimum.

Freedom from Anxiety
Myth has it that some anxiety helps; it motivates you, perhaps. And yes, sometimes we should promote anxiety in others to get them focused, but

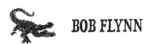

in our ideal effectiveness state, anxiety leads to physical and mental tension and provokes an undesirable shift in focus from our performance itself to its outcome or possible repercussions. There is an exception: when you feel lazy and just can't get going, anxiety will provide a source of energy, a "jump start," so to speak. Just keep in mind that anxiety is negative energy, and no performance motivated by anxiety will be as good as one motivated by a positive source.

Energy

This is the single most important ingredient of the twelve, and the most misunderstood. It is energy that is produced when you are loose, calm, and free from anxiety that produces the optimum effectiveness.

Optimism

Maximum personal effectiveness occurs when you develop a strong belief that whatever the challenge, you will find a way to meet it. Top performers never deplete their options, and their optimism reflects this belief. All top performers know that negative feelings, attitudes, and emotions impact the physiology in *dramatically* different ways than positive emotions do.

Enjoyment

The principle is simple: When you find joy in what you're doing, you perform well. When it ceases to be fun, effectiveness suffers. If you believe you enjoyed it because you did it well, then you've got it backward. You did it well because you enjoyed it, you had fun. This state of fun is all important to personal effectiveness; it represents a limitless source of positive energy.

Effortlessness

When your mind and body are working in harmony, no matter how hard the task, it almost seems easy. When the biochemistry is right, achieving great goals and overcoming major obstacles seems nearly effortless.

Automaticity

During great performances, the action is automatic, almost intuitive or instinctive. The optimum response comes naturally, without hesitation or deliberation. It's when we begin to focus on the mechanics that performance lessens. During maximum performance periods, instinct is always more effective than conscious, deliberate thought.

AIN'T NO SUCH THANG AS
A PURDY GOOD ALLIGATOR RASSLER

Alertness

Peak performances always include an extraordinary awareness and a heightened sense of self. During this state, we accurately sense the pulse of our surroundings yet stay simultaneously riveted to the task at hand. This alertness almost seems like mind reading because the responses are so quick and appropriate.

Focus

The focus of personal effectiveness does not result from a conscious effort at concentration; instead, it is a product of the mixture of calmness and positive energy. In this state, the focus is on the performance itself, not the score, standings, profits, or possible repercussions.

Self-confidence

The self-confidence of the personal effectiveness state is the strong internal belief that one can meet life's challenges. This produces calm when the circumstances might otherwise evoke panic, anxiety, anger, or tension.

Control

Personally, effective people feel that they are in control of themselves and their response to events.

The Myths

Personal effectiveness (good performance) leads to a positive emotional state. This is the traditional concept of top performance. Russell James's findings support a different paradigm....

Positive Emotional State Leads to Personal Effectiveness.

Consistently achieving high levels of performance is nothing more or less than knowing how to maintain a special kind of emotional control. Once the proper emotions are in place, your genius – your brightness, quickness, talents, and intelligence— will emerge.

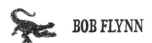 **BOB FLYNN**

Hannah interrupted. "So, Jack, this means that negative emotions are bad, right?"

"Funny that you should ask that question, Hannah, because that's my next point."

"Proceed, Professor."

"Dan advised us that there are two myths surrounding negative emotions. Myth number one is. That negative emotions are entirely out of our control, they just 'happen' spontaneously, usually to events in our lives that we label bad.

"And myth number two is that negative emotions are bad.

"Let's take a look at myth number one."

"Yeah Jack, let's do."

"You're not going to like the answer, Hannah. I didn't, and neither did anyone in the class. The fact is…

"<u>You</u> are the source of all your negative emotions, <u>you</u> create them, and <u>you</u> choose whether or not <u>you</u> deal with them or let them deal with <u>you</u>. <u>You</u> choose whether or not to dwell on them or learn from them and move on."

"Sounds like taking personal responsibility to me."

"Oh yeah, Hannah, that's the challenge. Myth number two, negative emotions are bad, is equally erroneous. Emotions that seem so painful are truly like an internal compass that can point you toward the actions you must take to lead a happy, personally effective life. In other words, emotions that you label as negative are really a call to action. They become negative when we fail to heed the call."

"Elaborate on that, will you?"

"Well, if we continue to suppress or deny the message our painful emotions are trying to send us, they will escalate into full-blown crises."

"So, Jack, you're saying that negative emotions are only potentially negative. If we pay attention to what they are trying to tell us, they become positive."

AIN'T NO SUCH THANG AS
A PURDY GOOD ALLIGATOR RASSLER

"That's it, Hannah, that's the point. Dan said that negative emotions give us the gift of pain; they advise us that we've not dealt with something. But there's another side to this coin."

"Another side?"

"Yeah. See, in many cases, instead of dealing with our negative emotions, we magnify them until they lead to destructive behaviors, even addictions that have the potential to control our lives."

"Give me an example, dear."

"We will go to great, and often destructive, lengths to avoid dealing with the feelings that negative emotions can bring. Drugs, alcohol, overeating, gambling, and so on are mechanisms used to avoid feeling the pain of negative emotions. While these are obvious signs of avoidance, there are others that are 'hidden' but are equally destructive."

"More examples, please."

"Okay, let's take your favorite topic: relationships."

"Yes, let's do."

"In order to avoid feelings, people will often attempt to simply stop feeling. When they do, they harm, even destroy, their most meaningful relationships.

"Here's another example. Fear of rejection is a major fear in our society. People harboring this emotion will shy away from and even totally avoid any activity that could lead to rejection. They won't do things like apply for challenging jobs or ask for what they really want.

"What these people don't realize is:

"Experiencing an emotion and trying to pretend it's not there only creates more pain. Labeling an emotion as 'wrong' won't make it go away or even become less intense because… whatever we resist tends to persist.

"By cultivating an appreciation for all emotions, you'll find that they begin dissipating almost immediately."

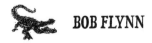

BOB FLYNN

The Truth

"Dan concluded the session by telling us that controlling our emotional state is not a form of magic. There are three factors that determine our personal effectiveness: talent, practice, and attitude.

"Emotional state cannot replace talent, or the skills developed through practice.

"However, emotional control can give us the stamina required to practice and the power to stay with self- improvement, along with the attitudes required for performing at the upper levels of our abilities.

"Controlling our emotional states will greatly assist us in exploiting our talents. It will allow us to consistently put forth our best efforts and perform with excellence.

"The bottom line is:

"Developing the ability to control our emotional state will give us the capability of summoning our best whenever we want or need to."

"Thanks, Jack. These Absolutes are great! Once again, we've been exposed to some very valuable information. I know that I'm going to begin working on my emotional states right now. I see some areas where I'm holding myself back. I hate it when I do that."

"I don't know about you, Hannah, but I'm ready to turn in."

"Me too, Jack. I'm very excited about going to Dallas with you next week. It's been a while since I've been house-hunting, but I'm sure looking forward to it."

Absolute #9

ADOPT THE GRATITUDE ATTITUDE

Gratitude unlocks the fullness of life. It turns what we have into enough and more. It turns denial into acceptance, chaos into order, confusion into clarity. It can turn a meal into a feast, a house into a home, a stranger into a friend. Gratitude makes sense of our past, brings peace for today, and creates a vision for tomorrow.

MELODY BEATTIE

KEY POINTS

It is so seductive to focus on the future, and while that's certainly advisable, it can cause us to miss the pleasures and opportunities that are presently underfoot. As with all the Absolutes, this one tends to be counterintuitive. Our natural inclination is to take for granted what we already have and head for greener pastures. Ironically, when we give appreciation for what we already have it opens the door to bigger and better things.

❏ The more we focus on what we "don't" have, the more we hinder progress.

❏ Being grateful for what you have is the best way to find inner peace.

❏ The universe will not give you more until you are grateful for what you have.

❏ If you don't appreciate what you already have, you'll lose it.

❏ The more you are grateful for, the more will be given to you.

❏ Being future-oriented is a double-edged sword.

❏ Keep a gratitude journal.

❏ A focus on what we don't have creates negativity, even depression.

❏ Gratitude is the heart's memory.

❏ When you dwell on what you don't have, you put energy into scarcity.

❏ The more abundance you acknowledge in your life, the more you will get.

 **BOB FLYNN**

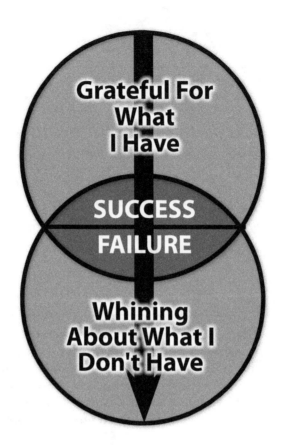

MAJOR POINT

People tend to hold on to things or accumulate them because they feel that otherwise they might not have what they need at the time they are ready for it. In other words, they do not trust The Law of Natural Abundance to provide them with appropriate things at the perfect time.

WHEN WE DO NOT TRUST THIS LAW TO FUNCTION PERFECTLY, IT RECIPROCATES. IT CONTINUALLY GIVES WHAT WE EXPECT, WHETHER IT BE SHORTAGE OR ABUNDANCE.

AIN'T NO SUCH THANG AS
A PURDY GOOD ALLIGATOR RASSLER

Absolute #9

EXERCISE

**Let this be the start of your Gratitude Journal —
List 20 things you are currently grateful for.**

1. _____

2. _____

3. _____

4. _____

5. _____

6. _____

7. _____

8. _____

9. _____

10. _____

11. _____

12. _____

14. _____

15. _____

16. _____

17. _____

18. _____

19. _____

20. _____

 **BOB FLYNN**

Absolute #10

CONTROL YOUR EMOTIONAL STATE

The key to maximizing personal effectiveness is getting into the "right" emotional state.

RUSSELL JAMES

KEY POINTS ─────────────────────────

Consistently achieving high levels of performance is nothing more or less than knowing how to maintain a special kind of emotional control. Once the proper emotions are in place, your genius – your brightness, quickness, talents, and intelligence – will emerge.

❏ Personally effective people have mastered the 12 key emotional states.

❏ You are the source of all your negative and positive emotions.

❏ Negative emotions are messengers: a call to action.

❏ Emotional control gives us the stamina to stay with self-improvement.

❏ Controlling our emotional states greatly assists us in exploiting our talents.

❏ Mastering emotions give us the capability of consistently being at our best.

❏ Emotional state cannot replace talent or skills developed through practice.

❏ Labeling an emotion as "wrong" won't make it go away.

❏ Denying painful emotions leads to withdrawal or crisis.

❏ If you believe you enjoyed it because you did it well, you've got it backwards.

❏ Energy is the single most important emotional state ingredient.

AIN'T NO SUCH THANG AS
A PURDY GOOD ALLIGATOR RASSLER

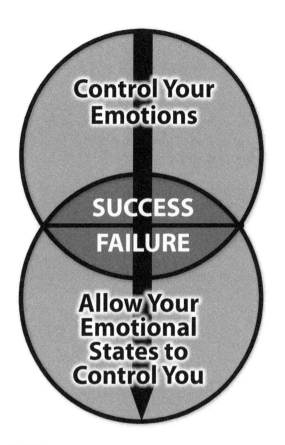

MAJOR POINT

The critical understanding, which many people miss, is that they are physically and chemically different when they change emotional states. When you change your emotional states, you change your ability to perform. Establishing the "right" internal climate has the same effect on potential performance as the changing of the seasons has on potential plants.

IT IS YOUR RESPONSIBILITY TO TAKE RESPONSIBILITY FOR YOUR EMOTIONAL STATES.

Absolute #10

EXERCISE

Based on what you have learned in this module, list the emotional states you need to improve, state your plan for improving, and commit to a specific date you will initiate your plan.

EMOTIONAL STATE: _____

IMPROVEMENT PLAN: _____

_____

_____

_____

_____

_____

_____

DATE: _____

EMOTIONAL STATE: _____

IMPROVEMENT PLAN: _____

_____

_____

_____

_____

_____

_____

DATE: _____

EMOTIONAL STATE: _____

IMPROVEMENT PLAN: _____

_____

_____

_____

_____

_____

_____

DATE: _____

AIN'T NO SUCH THANG AS
A PURDY GOOD ALLIGATOR RASSLER

CHAPTER ELEVEN

Ain't No Such Thang
AS A PURDY GOOD
Alligator Rassler

The Dissapointment

ABSOLUTE #11

Revere Time

I have been too familiar with disappointment to be very much chagrined.

ABRAHAM LINCOLN

AIN'T NO SUCH THANG AS
A PURDY GOOD ALLIGATOR RASSLER

The Disappointment

All signs are pointing to the fact that it's going to be a great day, Jack thought as he headed to the plant for his 9:00 a.m. meeting with Ralph Gonzales.

The flight was uneventful, both he and Hannah got a good night's sleep, and Hannah was off on her house-hunting venture with the real estate agent. *Yes sir, this one's off to a fine start!*

Unfortunately, it wouldn't last.

"So that's it, Jack, I can't accept your offer. I think your plans are far too aggressive. You call them incremental, but I see them as--well, like I said, aggressive. Also, I appreciate the offer of additional training, but in my estimation, I'm ready for the plant manager's position now. You're new in the role, so even if you do a great job, it's not likely anything will open up here for at least three years. I'm willing to take a transfer, but I'm not interested in staying here as operations manager."

Jack didn't allow the silence to force him into a premature response. Carefully considering his words, he remembered that questions are the answer.

"Ralph, your attitude has changed dramatically since we discussed this last Friday. What happened?"

"Well, I talked it over with a trusted friend and he told me that your offer sounded like a ploy to keep me in the same job simply to help you succeed."

"I see. What makes you think that's my strategy?"

"My buddy says you sound like one of those 'fast track' types that uses others for personal gain."

"Ralph, how did this man gain so much influence with you?"

"He's my older brother. He wouldn't steer me wrong."

"Well, I'll have to confess that I'm quite disappointed. I was anticipating your accepting the position. I was convinced we'd make a strong team. I can now see

that you can be persuaded to change your mind rather easily, and that can be quite detrimental to the effectiveness of a leader. Based on what I'm hearing, I think you've made a wise decision."

Then Jack dropped the bomb.

"We're going to miss you, Ralph."

"You're going to miss me? You mean that's it?"

"Keep in mind that you made the decision."

"Well, yeah, I know that. So, Jack, do you want a notice or anything?"

"I'm going to leave that up to you, Ralph. You tell me and I'll make the arrangements with HR."

"Okay. How about the standard two weeks?"

"Fine, I'll make the necessary arrangements. And I wish you all the best."

Jack stood up and extended his hand. Ralph stared at him sheepishly, then shook his hand, turned, and walked slowly out of the door.

"So, Pete, that's it. Ralph will be leaving in two weeks. I just couldn't allow his indecisiveness to continue. I need total commitment, and he was just too easily influenced. I can't afford a person in a leadership position to send that message to our team. Now what I need to know from you is whether that offer to have Mickey assist me still holds?"

Pete paused for a second before replying. "Before I answer that Jack, let me say I'm very proud of your decision and the manner in which you handled it. Most managers fail because they can't make the tough people decisions. As I've said so many times, if we err, we must err on the side of fairness. You were as fair as you could be and made the best call for all concerned. And yes, of course you can have Mickey, but you're gonna have to give him back. So be on the lookout for Ralph's permanent replacement."

"Will do, Pete, and thanks."

AIN'T NO SUCH THANG AS
A PURDY GOOD ALLIGATOR RASSLER

"So, Hannah, that's my day. I spoke with Mickey about an hour ago and he'll get things in order on his end and join me next Monday. Now, tell me about your house-hunting adventure."

"An adventure it was, Jack, and productive. I looked at five houses and liked some aspects of all of them. I didn't like any one of them enough to seriously consider, but I did get an idea."

"Hannah, you've always got an idea."

"Let's build."

"Build?"

"Yes. You know we've been working very hard to get our lives and our lifestyle the way we want it. Since you've been involved in the *12 Absolutes* program, we've planned harder than we ever have, and it's really made a difference. Why settle for part of what we want when we can have exactly what we want? Let's design and build our own home."

"Wow, Hannah, that's a big decision. I've heard horror stories about people trying to build their own homes."

"There's risk involved in anything worthwhile, but as a team I know we can do it."

"Okay, I know how you are when you set your heart and mind on something. But I gotta tell you, you're going to have to do a lot of the work, because I've got my plate full with this plant."

"I know that, and I'm prepared to do what it takes to build the home that suits our lifestyle."

"Done deal, then. Are you hungry?"

"I'm starved."

"Okay, I'll take you to a place I know you'll like, and we can toast our big decision."

 **BOB FLYNN**

Jack's week was quite hectic, but considering all that was taking place things progressed remarkably well. Production kept pace, Ralph worked reasonably hard, and Hannah met with several builders. Friday came fast and both Jack and Hannah were anxious to get home and see the kids. Jack was especially looking forward to getting back in class. The Absolutes were paying off and Jack was ready to sink his teeth into numbers 11 and 12.

Absolute #11

REVERE TIME

Time once spent has no refund option.

DENNIS WAITELY

Dan Hardee began the Saturday morning session in his usual "get down to business" style.

"In studying the lives of successful and unsuccessful people for over twenty-five years, Russell James discovered that the one most common differentiating factor was that successful individuals had the ultimate respect for time. These people had a distinct understanding of the difference between being productive and simply being busy."

Quoting directly from Russell James's book, Dan continued.

"The more I studied success and successful people the more obvious it came to me that they all had one thing in common. They placed a very, I mean a very high value on their time, and they continually worked at becoming better organized and more efficient. They revered time and it really paid off.

"Here's the bottom line:

No meaningful success is possible without excellent time management skills.

"The ability to increasingly enhance your time management skills has multiple payoffs because time management is really life management. As you learn to master your time, you simultaneously master your life and take

complete control over your future. Benjamin Franklin once said, *'Do you love life? Then do not squander time, for that is the stuff life is made of.'"*

The Start

"The starting point of excelling in time management is desire. You must want results badly enough to overcome the natural inertia that keeps you doing things the same old way. Effective time management behaviors are very much a matter of choice. You choose to squander your time on low-payoff pursuits, or you choose to apply your efforts to matters that matter. One main difference between highly effective people and people who seem to produce very little is that…

"Top performers focus on <u>results</u> while average performers focus on activities.

"Top performers focus on *outputs*; marginal performers focus on inputs. The more you focus on outputs—results--the better and more effective you will become. Everything you accomplish, or fail to accomplish, depends on your ability to use your time to its best advantage. You can increase the quality and quantity of your results only by increasing your ability to use time effectively.

"Time is inelastic; it cannot be stretched. Time is indispensable; all work and accomplishment requires it. Time is irreplaceable; there is no substitute for it. And time is perishable; it cannot be saved, preserved, or stored. Once it is gone, it is gone forever.

"A focus on time management is an absolute to personal effectiveness because it forces you to be intensely *results-oriented,* and…

"Results-orientation is the key quality for achieving personal effectiveness.

"Your ability to focus single-mindedly on the most important results required of you is the fastest and surest way to become a highly effective individual. This is true because…

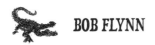

"You grow as a person in direct proportion to the demands that you place on yourself.

"The self-discipline of good time management is a source of energy, enthusiasm, and a positive mental attitude. It builds character confidence and an unshakable belief in yourself and your abilities. The more tightly you manage your time, the more you are guaranteed that it will translate into a great life that is hallmarked by purpose, power, control, and worthwhile accomplishments."

The Focus

"So, as I said," Dan continued, "the first step in effective time management is desire. Once you establish a burning desire to become effective in managing your time, your next challenge is to become highly focused. The most important word in personal effectiveness is the word clarity. Effective time management absolutely requires that that you develop total clarity about your goals and objectives.

"The most common time waster and biggest obstacle to success is never establishing or losing sight of what you are trying to accomplish.

"Most people that you pass on the street work hard every day, but they accomplish little because they have no clear goals and objectives in mind.

"Organizing your goals and objectives clearly, and by priority, and then working with single-minded focus on the most important things that you can possibly do to achieve them, is essential to using your time effectively and well.

"Clarity of goals and objectives requires that you write them down and then arrange them in order of priority. From that point, you select the one goal that will have the most impact on all the rest. To arrive at this conclusion, ask yourself, 'If I could achieve any goal on this list, which one goal would give me more happiness, satisfaction, and rewards than any other?' This goal then becomes your top priority. Continue asking this same question

AIN'T NO SUCH THANG AS
A PURDY GOOD ALLIGATOR RASSLER

about the remaining goals and objectives, and you will establish a priority order. From this point, you develop and write down detailed plans of action essential for the achievement of each goal. Discipline yourself to establish from ten to twenty action steps per goal. When your list is completed, you once again ask the question, 'If I could do only one thing on this list, which one action would help me to achieve this goal more than any other?' Continue this process until you have prioritized your list of actions relative to each of your goals.

"Refuse to allow yourself to make excuses for not engaging in this critical exercise. Avoid any form of rationalization. Do not focus on your problems and obstacles. Instead, take total responsibility for completing this exercise. By doing so, you move yourself into the top 3% of all human beings on planet Earth. This is vitally important, because when you accept complete responsibility for developing, prioritizing, and creating action plans for achieving your goals, people will emerge to help and guide you along the path to goal achievement. But when you make excuses, blame others, and expect them to help you, they will ignore and avoid you."

The Step

Dan continued. "Okay, you've developed a burning desire, become centered and focused, now it's time to take the step. And that step is the step of *faith*. You now must act as if it were impossible for you to fail. A key component of stepping out in faith is to do something every day that moves you toward your major goal.

> *"When you do something every single day that moves you closer to your goal, you eventually develop an unshakable faith and belief that your goals will ultimately be achieved.*

"If you do just one thing each day, no matter how big the goal or how far away it may be, this single action will keep you focused and motivated. It will keep your subconscious mind stimulated and active. Daily movement toward your goal will keep you energized and confident."

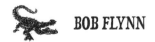

The Duo

As the class listened closely, Dan continued.

"Between you and your goals, there are obstacles. These hindrances can usually be boiled down into two categories: people, including you, and circumstances. Part of your time investment will be identifying and making plans to eliminate or mitigate the barriers keeping you from accomplishing your goals. It is important that you write down every obstacle or difficulty that you think is limiting your ability to achieve the goals that you have defined. These may include internal obstacles, or obstacles within yourself. They may be external obstacles, or obstacles that are created by circumstances and persons other than yourself.

"Once again, prioritization is key. In every goal-seeking attempt, there is almost always a single problem that must be resolved before any of the other problems can be solved. Your job is to identify the biggest single problem or difficulty holding you back, and then focus on solving that before smaller problems and difficulties sidetrack you.

"Human nature causes us to focus outside of ourselves, to 'fix the blame' on others or the environment around you. While these are certainly factors, they are rarely the predominant factors. Usually 80% of the reasons you are not achieving your goals are contained within yourself.

"When you look into yourself you will almost always find that it is the lack of a particular skill, quality, or behavior that is the main constraint on achieving an important goal or result.

"This is the 'what' you need to work on before you do anything else. Ask yourself, 'What else do I need to learn? What else do I need to know? What is the most important additional knowledge, skill, or experience that I require before I can achieve my goal?'

"From this point, you should look at people in two dimensions: the people who are hindering your goal achievement, and the people who can help you to achieve your goals. Sometimes they will fit both categories. Ask yourself: 'Who is standing in my way to goal achievement? Who is impinging on my time? Who is blocking me?' Conversely, ask yourself: 'Who can help me reach my goals? Whose cooperation do I require? Who will benefit when I reach my goals?'

"Never forget that all time management skills require a clear, unambiguous vision concerning your goals and objectives. Decide exactly what you are trying to achieve, and then focus on it single-mindedly. This is a major step toward excellent time management."

The Hallmark

"The difference between average people and highly effective people is that highly effective people are much better organized. Excellent personal and professional organization is the hallmark of highly effective, exceptionally productive people. The top 5% of all high achievers are all persistent, continuous planners and organizers. They are forever writing and rewriting prioritized to-do lists. They think on paper and are continually evaluating and re-evaluating their plans and strategies. The payoff for effective planning is huge.

"Each minute invested in planning and organizing saves ten minutes in execution.

"This means that when you invest in planning and organizing, you receive a 1,000% return on the time and energy you invest. The only way you will ever free up the time you need is by carefully planning your activities in advance.

"Taking action without proper planning is the reason for most failure. If you look back over mistakes and failures you've experienced in your life, you'll discover that almost all of them had one common denominator: that you rushed into a decision or situation without proper planning and organizing. Conversely, when you examine the successes you have experienced, you'll find that you invested in well thought out planning and organizing."

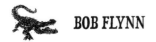 **BOB FLYNN**

The Ideals

Dan went on to discuss that in his study of the key habits of successful, highly effective individuals, Russell James learned that there were four common threads that that ran among the vast majority.

1. Neatness

If order is Heaven's first law, it stands to reason that order is Earth's first law as well. We all require a sense of order to feel relaxed and in control of our environment and our life. You've learned what a huge negative impact clutter has on your effectiveness. Effective people are neat people, period.

2. Evaluate

Effective people are constantly evaluating their processes. They look at everything through the eyes of a neutral third party. They look in their purse or briefcase and ask, 'What kind of a person would have a purse of briefcase like that?' These people know that each time you put an aspect of your life in order, productivity goes up.

3. Non-Acceptance

Results-producers simply do not accept sloppiness; they hold themselves to a very strict standard of organizational quality. They know that every viable time and motion study ever conducted clearly proves that productivity is in direct proportion to cleanliness, neatness, organization, and planning.

4. Clear Desk/Workspace

"I know my desk/workspace is messy, but I know where everything is." Effective people see this as an excuse for disorganization and laziness. As it turns out, the person who claims to know where everything is spends an inordinate amount of time and energy trying to remember where he put things. That's a waste of valuable time that could be invested in productive pursuits.

The Habits

Dan then turned the group's attention to habits they should cultivate. There were other key habits that 92% of overachievers said were essential to maximizing time utilization. They included:

- Assemble everything needed in advance.

- Handle each piece of paper only once.

- Delegate everything to its lowest level of competence.

- When finished, put everything back in its proper place.

- Complete everything you start.

- Use a time planner.

- Work from a prioritized list.

- Plan your next day the night before.

- Schedule your time.

- Get an early start on the day.

- Use an organized filing system.

- Do important work during prime time.

The Wasters

"The only way you can get enough time to do the things that can really make a difference in your life is by conserving time that you would normally spend somewhere else. For most people, there tend to be seven major time-wasters that interfere with the truly productive activities they could be engaged in. These seven common time robbers include--" and Dan turned and wrote the points on the white board.

1. Telephone Interruptions.

2. Unexpected Visitors.

3. Meetings.

4. Fire-Fighting.

 **BOB FLYNN**

5. Procrastination.

6. Socializing and Idle Conversation.

7. Indecision and Poor Decision-Making.

"Here are some proven strategies to effectively deal with these insidious time- wasters:"

Telephone Interruptions:

- Get on and off the phone fast. Don't socialize; instead say: "I've got to get back to work."
- In a professional manner, ask the caller to state the purpose of their call.
- Set aside periods in your day when you do not accept calls.
- Set clear times that you prefer to be called, and advise frequent callers.
- Batch and make all your calls at once. Don't spread calls throughout the day.
- Bullet-point the key agenda items in advance of your calls.
- Take good notes so you don't have to call back for clarification.

Unexpected Visitors:

- Stand up quickly when they enter into your work area.
- Say, "I've got time for one more item then I've got to get back to work."
- Arrange specific times for meetings.
- Avoid wasting the time of others.

Meetings:

- Determine the cost of all meetings.
- Always ask: "Why is this meeting necessary?"
- If the agenda doesn't have "hard" start and stop times, then there is no meeting.
- Cover important items first.
- Summarize each conclusion.
- Assign specific responsibility.

Fire-Fighting:

- Plan for the worst, and develop contingency plans to handle it.
- Identify recurring crises, examine and change the process.
- Plan before acting.
- Delegate responsibility.
- Get the facts.
- Find and eliminate the cause.

Procrastination:

- Develop a keen sense of urgency.
- Separate the relevant from the irrelevant.
- Start with your most important task.
- Set worthwhile, exciting goals.
- Visualize your tasks as completed.
- Set clear deadlines for yourself.
- Reward yourself for task completion.
- Refuse to make excuses; discipline yourself.
- Accept full responsibility for task completion.
- Create a detailed plan of action.
- Clean up and organize your workspace.
- Assemble all materials and work tools before you begin.
- Do one small thing to get started, then move to the task you fear most.
- Think about the consequences of not getting the task completed on time.
- Think about how you will benefit from getting the task completed on time.
- Resist the tendency toward perfectionism.
- Maintain a fast tempo.
- Develop a compulsion for closure.
- Keep saying, "Do it now! Do it now! Do it now!"

 **BOB FLYNN**

Socializing and Idle Conversation:

- Socializing and idle chatter proves you have time to get the important things done.

- Too much socializing is a major cause of career derailment.

- Socialize only at appropriate times.

- Keep track of the time you spend chatting and socializing. [You'll be shocked.]

- Keep saying to yourself; "Got to get back to work and do it now!"

Indecision and Poor Decision-Making:

- 80% of all decisions should be made the first time they come up.

- 15% of all decisions require additional thought and planning.

- 5% of all decisions need not be made at all.

- Delegate decisions to the lowest level of competence.

- Set deadlines for all decisions that cannot be handled the first time they come up.

- Get the facts before deciding.

- Remember that successful leaders and managers are decisive.

- Fear of failure is the biggest foe of timely decision-making.

The Predictor

Dan paused and look around the room and then continued. "Russell James believes that there is one major factor that can accurately predict whether a person is going to move upward and onward financially and socially. He calls it time perspective. He defines time perspective as the period of time that a person takes into consideration when making day-to day decisions and planning their lives. He found that successful people were those who had a long-time perspective. They planned their lives in terms of five, ten, and even twenty years into the future. They evaluated and determined their choices and actions in the present in terms of how those choices might affect them in the distant future, and the consequences that might occur as a result of what they did right now.

"His bottom-line conclusion is:

"The well-rounded high performing person recognizes time as the one invaluable, indispensable, irreplaceable ingredient of a successful, happy, personally effective life.

"This business of time perspective is quite critical if you want to significantly improve your personal effectiveness. See, the longer your sense of time perspective, the more likely it is that you will do the sorts of things and make the kind of sacrifices, in the short term, that will lead to greater successes in the long term. Your thoughtfulness about time today will tend to increase your effectiveness in the future. Economists and sociologists agree that the primary reason for economic failure and underachievement is the inability to think beyond the short-term and delay gratification. It turns out that when the careers of 180 successful top executives, religious leaders, teachers, and business owners were studied, in depth they all treated time as a scarce resource. They saw it as an indispensable ingredient of personal effectiveness, achievement, and accomplishment. They all allocated their time very carefully.

"It turns out that the smaller the unit of time in which you think when planning your day, the more successful you are likely to be. Marginally effective persons think in terms of whole days, or mornings or afternoons. Highly effective people think in terms of ten-minute blocks of time, and they apply every minute to relevant tasks.

"All of life is the study of attention. The more attention you pay to the way you are using your time, the more efficient and productive you are likely to become. The more aware you are of the fleeting nature of time, the better you will use it.

"The more you evaluate how you are spending your minutes and hours, the better and more precise you will become at time management and the more you will revere it.

"As you move down the socioeconomic ladder, the time perspective at each descending level becomes shorter. Often the time perspective of people at the bottom of society is only a few minutes. They don't think beyond the moment."

 **BOB FLYNN**

The Confessions

"Once again, one of the major culprits interfering with good time management is the ego. The Big E causes even the best intentioned to be unwilling to admit mistakes, cut their losses, and move on. This unwillingness is a major source of unhappiness, because it keeps people locked in unhappy, unsatisfying, unproductive situations year after year. And It's a huge time-waster.

> *"Once you have admitted a mistake, you no longer need to explain or justify yourself. You can quit covering up and faking it and get on to something productive. You can quit squandering your precious time on a low- or no-payoff venture.*

"No matter what you've done or failed to do, your future can be unlimited, but you have to let go of the marginally productive use of your time. This is especially true as it pertains to relationships. Many time management experts share the opinion that the wrong relationships are the biggest time- wasters of all.

"So, how can you tell if you are in the wrong kind of relationship? Well, since questions are the answer. Ask yourself:

"• Would I be happier, more effective, etc. if I was not in this relationship?

"• If I had not gotten into this relationship, knowing what I know now, would I get into it today?

"• Am I hoping this relationship will get better, or am I doing something to change it?

"• Is this relationship standing in the way of me becoming a better person?

"Throughout our lives, because of the desire for approval and the fear of rejection, we bend our personalities and adjust our behaviors so that others will like and approve of us. We constantly think about what we need to do to be liked and accepted. If we're not careful, we'll waste huge amounts of time trying to please someone who can't or won't help us be all we can be.

"One of the marks of the 'fully functioning person,' as defined by acclaimed psychologist Carl Rogers, is that they are not unduly influenced by the opinions of others. A fully mature, fully functioning adult takes the likes and dislikes, and

AIN'T NO SUCH THANG AS
A PURDY GOOD ALLIGATOR RASSLER

the opinions of others into consideration, but then makes their own decisions and go their own way. If others do not approve of a course of action, they ignore it and carry on regardless."

Dan concluded Absolute #11 by advising the class that there were only four things that individuals could do to improve their time management.

1. Identify their top-payoff items, their priorities.

2. Identify how much time would be required to bring their priorities to fruition.

3. Identify the actions they must take to stay focused on their priorities.

4. Identify the people and circumstances that are interfering with their actions.

5. Make plans to mitigate or eliminate this interference.

6. Identify and stop doing the things that waste their time.

7. Identify and start doing the things that will increase their time efficiency.

Dan then gave the group a Time Planner and had them do an exercise, taking these seven critical points into consideration.

After the class had completed the exercise, Dan closed the session with a few additional comments.

"You cannot manage time. You can only manage yourself. Time management is life management. Time management requires self-control, self-mastery, and self-discipline. Time management is a lifestyle that must be practiced every hour, every day, all the days of your life. It is the one habit, the one discipline that is essential to everything else you want to achieve.

"With excellent time management skills, there are no limits.

"Now, team, I've got a very special announcement. Your teacher for Absolute #12 will be Russell James. In fact, he'll be joining us for lunch."

 **BOB FLYNN**

Absolute #11

REVERE TIME

Time once spent has no refund option.

DENNIS WAITELY

KEY POINTS

No meaningful success is possible without excellent time management skills. The ability to increasingly enhance your time management skills has multiple payoffs, because time management is really life management. As you learn to master your time, you simultaneously master your life and take complete control over your future. Benjamin Franklin said, "Do you love life? Then do not squander time, for that is the stuff life is made of."

❑ Effective time management behaviors are very much a matter of choice.

❑ Top performers focus on results; average performers focus on activities.

❑ Everything you accomplish depends on your time management ability.

❑ Good time management produces energy, enthusiasm, and confidence.

❑ Desire and focus are the two absolutes of excellent time management.

❑ Single-minded focus on top priorities is essential to managing time.

❑ Each minute spent in planning and organizing saves ten in execution.

❑ Taking action without proper planning is a major time-waster.

❑ The longer your sense of time perspective, the better you will manage time.

❑ Time management requires self-control, self-mastery, and self-discipline.

❑ Plan your time in small units, around top priorities.

AIN'T NO SUCH THANG AS
A PURDY GOOD ALLIGATOR RASSLER

MAJOR POINT————————————————————

You grow as a person in direct proportion to the demands that you place on yourself. Marginally effective people waste considerable time because they never establish clear prioritized priorities and demand a single-minded focus on these priorities. The most important two words in time management are clarity and focus.

WITHOUT CLARITY AND FOCUS YOU WILL UNDOUBTEDLY SQUANDER NOT ONLY TIME BUT YOUR LIFE AS WELL.

 BOB FLYNN

Absolute #11

EXERCISE

Clarity and Focus are the keys to effectively managing your time.
You have established your top five priorities and goals around those
priorities, you've got the clarity piece covered.

To establish and maintain focus identify the activities that waste your
time, develop plans to get these time wasters out of your life, and commit
to a date you will begin taking action.

TIME WASTER: _____

ELIMINATION PLAN : _____

_____

_____

_____

_____

DATE: _____

TIME WASTER: _____

ELIMINATION PLAN : _____

_____

_____

_____

_____

DATE: _____

AIN'T NO SUCH THANG AS
A PURDY GOOD ALLIGATOR RASSLER

TIME WASTER: _____

ELIMINATION PLAN : _____

_____

_____

_____

_____

DATE: _____

TIME WASTER: _____

ELIMINATION PLAN : _____

_____

_____

_____

_____

DATE: _____

TIME WASTER: _____

ELIMINATION PLAN : _____

_____

_____

_____

_____

DATE: _____

BOB FLYNN

TIME WASTER: _____

ELIMINATION PLAN : _____

_____

_____

_____

_____

DATE: _____

NOTES

_____

_____

_____

_____

_____

_____

_____

_____

_____

_____

_____

_____

_____

_____

_____

_____

_____

_____

AIN'T NO SUCH THANG AS
A PURDY GOOD ALLIGATOR RASSLER

CHAPTER TWELVE

Ain't No Such Thang
AS A PURDY GOOD
Alligator Rassler

The Hoax

ABSOLUTE #12

It's Not About You / It's All About You

*You can fool some
of the people
some of the time.*

CLYDE

AIN'T NO SUCH THANG AS
A PURDY GOOD ALLIGATOR RASSLER

The Hoax

Dan had promised that Russell James would be joining the class for lunch, since lunch was half over and there was no sign of Mr. James, Jack's curiosity got the best of him, so he walked over to Dan's table.

"Say, Dan, where's Russell James? I thought he was joining us for lunch; I was looking forward to meeting him."

"He's here, Jack."

Again, Jack's eyes panned the room.

"Dan, there's no one in here other than our class members."

"You're right, Jack. Like I said, Russell James is here, in this room, having lunch with us."

"Come on, Dan! Is this some kind of joke, cause…wait a second, do you mean Russell James is one of our class members?"

"Well, Jack you're mighty sharp today; that's exactly what I mean."

"Okay, which one of us is Russell James?"

"Don't be so anxious; you'll find out soon enough."

"Well I'll be darned--it's you, isn't it, Dan? You're Russell James. I should have known. Well, don't worry about me telling anyone; it'll be our little secret."

As the class gathered back in the training room, Dan stood up and announced…

"Well, folks, it gives me great pleasure to introduce a good friend, the author of *The 12 Absolutes of Personal Effectiveness*, and your instructor for Absolute #12, Mr. Russell C. James."

Everyone looked around. It seemed like hours passed, and finally one of the class members stood and began walking to the front of the room.

 **BOB FLYNN**

It was Clyde!

The class sat in silent disbelief. Finally, Clyde broke the silence.

"Here's hoping y'all ain't too mad at me. Let me explain why I pulled this little ho-ax."

From the back of the room came James's voice.

"Yeah Clyde, I mean Russell, you've got some explaining to do."

"I know, I know, now I got a good reason and here it is. It has been over three years since I have actually participated in a *12 Absolutes* workshop. I wanted to experience the program first hand, as a participant, not an observer. I wanted to make sure we were providing a challenging, enlightening, life-enhancing experience. So, Dan and I cooked up this little scheme. My middle name is Clyde; it's the name I went by until I reached young adulthood, so we figured that a little 'white hoax' wouldn't be so awful. The bottom line is that I wanted to make certain that the *12 Absolutes* workshop was continuing to get the job done. So come on guys, give ol' Clyde a break and forgive me for my well-intentioned farce, okay?'

Before anyone could respond, Dan broke in.

"I'm part of the scam too, so I am begging forgiveness as well."

As usual, James spoke up first.

"Personally, I think it was a great idea. I mean how better to evaluate the program than to roll up your shirtsleeves and get involved? I applaud your creativity."

"Yeah," Tony spoke up. "You guys really pulled it off; I didn't suspect a thing, Clyde kept us in stitches--no way I would have ever figured that he put this program together."

"So, Tony, all is forgiven?" Clyde asked with a sly grin.

"Absolutely."

"Mary, are you still on the team?" Clyde asked sheepishly.

AIN'T NO SUCH THANG AS
A PURDY GOOD ALLIGATOR RASSLER

"You guys are something else, I'm still in shock; on the team? Of course, I'm still on the team, in fact I'm more on the team than ever."

"Oh, why is that?" Dan queried.

"Because of you and Clyde—I'm sorry, Mr. James; you're always going to be Clyde to me."

The entire class, Dan included, nodded their heads in unison.

"Anyway, as I was saying, I'm more on the team than ever because you cared enough to experience the program as a student and not an expert. It shows me that this program is more to you than a source of income. You're sincerely committed to helping people lead happier, more productive lives."

"I agree," William said. "Like Mary, I'm still in shock. Clyde, you played your role to perfection. I never suspected a thing. I like what you did, and I'm looking forward to learning from you this afternoon."

Clyde smiled and thanked both Mary and William.

"Well, young man, let's hear it; what's your take on this ho-ax?"

Hank chuckled as he began speaking. "Fellows this little ho-ax, as Clyde put it makes all the sense in the world. It's not only not a problem It's made the *12 Absolutes* experience even more meaningful."

"How about you, Jack? You knew all along, didn't you?"

"Sure, Clyde, sure I did. My wife almost made me quit the program because of all the 'Clyde sayings' I conveyed to her. No, I gotta tell you, you sure fooled me."

"So, Jack, have you had it with me?"

"No way, Clyde; you're still my man, even more so. One thing that had bothered me about the program is that I was certain that Russell James was this 'always do the right thing' kind of guy, a born overachiever. Even though Dan told us that he came from humble beginnings and had lots of personal struggles, I just got the feeling that he couldn't relate to a person like me, an average man. Oh, I know that Clyde was somewhat of an act, but I also believe that much of what you projected through Clyde is real; I'd bet on it. Now, I'm

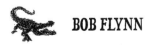 **BOB FLYNN**

convinced that Russell James, Clyde, relates very well to a guy like me. I'm even more encouraged that I can effectively apply the *12 Absolutes*."

Clyde was openly appreciative as he spoke.

"Thanks, Jack—and thanks, everyone else; I feel more better now." Clyde paused and collected his thoughts. "We have a very important afternoon, so I'm not going to invest a lot of time talking about myself."

"Yeah, Clyde; that would be in violation of nature's immutable Law of Indirect Effort."

"You're exactly right, James. I'm gonna keep the personal stuff real short." Clyde continued.

"I come from a little town in North Carolina, grew up on the other side of the tracks, learned how to work hard, but I also learned a lot of other things-- non-productive, self-destructive, dysfunctional things. By my early twenties, I pretty much had my life in a mess. Finally, the pain got so bad that I committed to take action.

"I was introduced to a program called *Lead the Field*. That's where I began learning about nature's laws. As I applied some of the principles of the program, things got better. I was hooked! From that point, I read and studied everything I could get my hands on that related to self-improvement and success. Not only did I read and study; I also applied. That's when the transformation miracle began to occur.

"I was so appreciative of the things that I learned that I wanted to share them with others. I knew that if I could get people to learn and apply these principles, they would, like me, be able to enjoy the abundant harvest. It was from my experiences that *The 12 Absolutes of Personal Effectiveness* was born.

"Now I have another confession…

"The ideals of this program are not mine. I learned them from Jesus; I borrowed them from people like Socrates, Franklin, Carnegie, Truman, Ringer, Nightingale, and Solomon. I stole them from 35,000 pages of the classics. I paraphrased the lessons I learned from my Mom and Dad, my wife Austine, Pastor Ross Rhoades, Coach Harold Bullard, and my mentor, Bob Fisher.

"Clyde isn't smart enough to know all this stuff; no one person is. It's when we learn and apply the wisdom of the ages, wisdom that remains unchanged by current events and personal circumstances, that we can and will truly become effective.

"We'll save the other details of my life for another time. So, if it's okay with you, I'd like to get right into Absolute #12."

From the expressions on all the participants' faces, it was apparent that they were more than ready to hear about the final Absolute.

Absolute #12

IT'S NOT ABOUT YOU - IT'S ALL ABOUT YOU

Teach him to deny himself.

ROBERT E. LEE

"Absolute #12 is a paradox, no doubt. Let me explain what it means."

Clyde still had his southern drawl, but his demeanor was decidedly different. He had dropped the "everything's a joke" persona and was quite serious and focused as he continued speaking.

"When we engage in putting ourselves and our needs first, we minimize our effectiveness. It's when we lose ourselves in service to others, to a cause, to something other than our self-centered laziness, greed, ambitions, and narcissism that we really begin to make significant progress. That's the 'it's not about you' part.

"It is your sole responsibility to take the responsibility to ensure that you get the absolute most out of your potential. That's the 'it's all about you' part.

"The purpose of *The 12 Absolutes* is to guide you on a path that keeps you focused on providing ever-increasing levels of attention and service to others. As a result, you will achieve personal effectiveness, success, and happiness far beyond the self-centered orientation of the masses. In this final Absolute, I'm going to tie the entire program together so that you will have a thorough understanding of a lifelong system that will lead to increasing levels of effectiveness in all that you endeavor. There will be some review and new stuff, too."

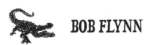 **BOB FLYNN**

The Inclination

"We must first understand that it's a person's natural inclination to busy themselves in trivial matters at the first sign of personal dissatisfaction. This approach seems to work, at first. The problem is it can rapidly become habitual. Rather than deal with their nagging apprehensive feelings, they go to the movies, take up a hobby, try drugs, drink more and sleep later, on and on it goes. The key is to listen to your feelings, they are messengers trying to get through your busyness and lead you in the right direction.

"It all gets back to taking personal responsibility. When we attempt to fix the blame on anything outside of ourselves--the government, the weather, the boss, the job, the company, the competition, the economy, etc.--we are giving control to things outside our sphere of influence. Chronically ineffective people call these things facts, label them as problems, and use them as excuses for failing to take personal responsibility. You can't blame me! Look at all these things that aren't my fault; there's nothing I can do about them; I'm a victim. By assuming this attitude, they're violating one of nature's most powerful laws, The Law of Achievement, which is…

> **"You will always rise to the level of achievement in direct proportion to the degree of personal responsibility you take in any given situation.**

"You and I are always going to be confronted with opportunities; they will wear many disguises such as: change, disappointment, setbacks, unfairness, misunderstandings… they won't look like opportunities; they will look like problems. Potentially effective people become ineffective when they remain focused on the problem and not the solution. See, it's in seeking the solution that we uncover the opportunity. The ineffective person when confronted with a 'problem' focuses on changing their circumstances instead of capitalizing on the real opportunity, which is to…

> **"Take the personal responsibility of changing themselves.**

"It all hinges on the master decision. I think we say it best in the question on our website. Remember when you pulled it up prior to deciding to take the course? Here's the paraphrased version:

AIN'T NO SUCH THANG AS
A PURDY GOOD ALLIGATOR RASSLER

"Are You Ready to Make
THE MASTER DECISION?

"Most people never make it--the Master Decision, that is--and as a result lead lives far below their God-given potential. Decisions determine destinations; there's something empowering, almost magical about the words

'I Have Decided.'

"Not you have decided or they have decided, but 'I have decided.'

> *"Until you can honestly and decisively without equivocation say 'I have decided,' you are forever caught in the web of mediocrity that gray twilight where the icy fingers of 'IF ONLY' encircle your potential and limit your future.*

"But what's on the other side of 'I have decided?' What is the master decision? It's a decision the masses never make, and so they are destined to march forever in the ranks of the average. They become the also-rans, never stretching, pushing, or challenging the status quo. They remain bound by the confines of their self-imposed comfort zones, never daring to break free of their imagined limitations, ultimately realizing that it is in seeking comfort and security that causes both to flee. The comfort-and-security-seeker finally understands that neither comfort nor security can be captured like a butterfly in a net, for both must be attracted, not pursued This attraction is accomplished by the supreme initiative…

> *"Taking total PERSONAL RESPONSIBILITY for who you are and everything you will become.*

"The acceptance, without reservation, that you are where you are and what you are because of yourself, your sowing and reaping to this point. It's the full realization that there's no such circumstance as the problem being 'out there,' and that you cannot change anything but yourself.

> *"The personally responsible individual knows full well that if they want things to change, they must change first.*

"They have come to the complete understanding that the seeds they sow today are the only influence they have on tomorrow. They know that they have been programmed from infancy to believe that someone or something else is responsible for their accomplishments in life. They accept this as a natural phenomenon, and it will become a chronic problem only if they allow themselves to come into adulthood with the expectation that anyone other than themselves are responsible for their place in society.

"So, gang," Clyde continued. "Taking total personal responsibility and accepting full accountability for every aspect of our lives is the master decision that gives life to the Twelve Absolutes. Without continually holding yourself accountable, you'll slip back into the ranks of the ineffective."

CAN DO – WILL DO

"Certainly, by now we are all immersed in the importance of taking action, can do versus will do. One of the key things we need to always be applying the will do step toward is the enhancement of your skill level. You must always keep in mind that…

> *"Your future depends on what you learn and apply from this moment forward.*

"It's back to personal responsibility; it's up to you to keep learning and applying. The *12 Absolutes* are built on nature's laws, and…

> *"Nature is neutral. She is no respecter of persons, not you, not me. She plays no favorites. She gives you back what you put in, no more and no less.*

"What you can do really doesn't matter; it's only what you put in that counts. So, it's all about you to constantly be putting in, not thinking about putting in, not committing to putting in, not assessing what to put in: putting in, that's your responsibility. Yes, of course, you have to do all those preliminary things, but after you do, it's time for the will do step."

Pre-Determine Your Focus

"In this first absolute, you began applying your personal responsibility toward a specific initiative, the things you focus your mind on. You learned this is critical, because until you pre-determine what you focus on, you'll spread your thoughts over to many areas, thereby dissipating your energy, wasting time, and creating confusion. You simply cannot let your mind go its own way. You must master your thoughts, and the best way to accomplish this is to pre-determine what you are going to think about. Our focus drives our attitudes, which drives our behaviors and actions. I've studied the thought processes of hundreds of successful and unsuccessful people there is a clearly discernible contrast…

> **"Successful people focus their thoughts, energy, and efforts on high-payoff items they can influence. Marginally successful people squander their thoughts, energy, and efforts on low-payoff things over which they have little or no influence or control.**

"When we fail to take the personal responsibility of controlling our thoughts and focus on things over which we have no control, we set ourselves up for failure, because…

> **"When we focus on trivial things or things over which we have no control, we empower those very things to control us!**

"See, the person who refuses to change the very fabric of their focus will never be able to change their circumstances and will make only minimal progress, if any. Every significant personal breakthrough is first a break with trivial things. It's simply critical that we're constantly thinking about what we're thinking about."

Clutter

"Clutter is a focus 'robber.' Clutter is any recurring thought that keeps popping up in our thoughts. Our personal responsibility is to categorize clutter into one of two classifications.

"1. Concerns that we *cannot* control, influence, or get help with but continue thinking about.

"2. Concerns that we *can* control, influence, or get help with but continue putting off.

"Our responsibility is to stop thinking about Category 1 clutter. And do something about Category 2 clutter. It's only when we stop procrastinating and take action on the Category 2 stuff that we free up our minds to focus on our high-payoff, pre-determined focus areas.

 **BOB FLYNN**

"Do you remember the seven most common forms of clutter? Remember Dan called them focus killers? I know William does because he did such a fine job of recapping them right before we launched into Absolute #2. William, are you up to it again?"

After thumbing through his workbook William responded. "Yes, Clyde, I am." This time, he gave the short version.

The seven most common and insidious focus killers are…

1. **Intolerance:** This is obsessing on the beliefs of others, especially if they do not agree with your own.

2. **Revenge:** This gives the power to the subject of your revenge, and takes the focus off the one thing you can control, yourself.

3. **Greed:** This violates the Law of Reciprocity; greed has at its roots the desire to take without giving.

4. **Envy:** This is the desire for something that someone else has.

5. **Egotism:** This is an attempt to mask insecurity.

6. **Suspicion:** This causes over security and excessive cautiousness.

7. **Procrastination:** This is the mother of all clutter! The longer we put things off, the larger they grow, and the more room we make for other clutter items to accumulate.

Clyde said, "Great job, William, thanks. Dan, I'll bet you've got something to add to William's recap, because I know how passionate you are about eliminating these seven focus 'killers.'"

"I sure do, Russ, I mean Clyde. Now as Clyde said back in our second session, when it comes to these seven focus 'killers,' we need to take a 'mental enema.' This is especially true as it pertains to procrastination. Here's why…

"The ability to take action is the most important attribute an individual can possess. Procrastination is the killer of focus, and it's our focus that is the catalyst for action."

Dan went on to recap the important points about focus.

REMEMBER THIS

Here's all you have to remember about pre-determined focus…

- It's not about you; focus on losing yourself in service to others and/or a worthy cause.

- What you focus your mind on, you create in your circumstances.

- What you focus on transfers into your life's conditions.

- When you change your focus to your desired reality, you begin moving toward it.

- Progress and focus are "joined at the hip."

- Get rid of the seven focus "killers," especially procrastination.

- You are bound forever to the essence of your focus.

From the time you crystallize your focus, your mind begins both consciously and unconsciously gathering and storing the information required for you to make intelligent and accurate decisions.

Focused Action

Clyde took over again. "As you learned in Absolute #2, there's simply no substitute for taking action. Not just taking action for action's sake but taking pre-determined *focused action* aimed at your goals and priorities. Ineffective types wait until they feel motivated, then they take action. Often the action they take is scattered and not directed toward a pre-established end. So, quite naturally, their results are minimal. Waiting for motivation to appear is an illusory, inconsistent, and unreliable motivational catalyst. You just can't count on it to get you to swing into action. Here's the secret of motivation…

"Motivation results from taking action, not the other way around.

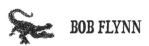

"The most effective people on planet earth consistently take action in their pre-determined focus areas, and – they take action whether they feel motivated or not. They know that action primes the motivational pump, and once they begin taking it, motivation will appear. Just as there are 'killers' of focus, there are 'saboteurs' of motivation. Anyone remember them?" James raised his hand. "Okay, James, tell us about these 'bad guys.'"

"Clyde, I remember the five 'saboteurs' vividly because I struggle with every one of them." James continued with his recap.

1. **Poorly Defined Goals:** Your heart and mind need clear and purposeful goals to continually summon the drive and energy required to achieve them.

2. **Inadequate Plans and Strategies:** If our plans and strategies are ill conceived, the actions we take will not move us swiftly toward our goals, and we will give up.

3. **Unrealistic Expectations:** Motivation problems occur when we develop grandiose short-term expectations and then fall short.

4. **Negative Influences:** Overexposure to negative influences destroys self-discipline, the essential ingredient to consistent action.

5. **Lax Personal Accountability:** Personal accountability is the pain of discipline, and it's a good pain. Without it you will suffer the bad pain, the pain of regret.

"Thanks, James, great job. By the way, how are you doing with the five action saboteurs?"

"Much better. I'm now conscious of all of them and work hard to consistently keep them from sapping my drive and motivation. Number four especially hindered me, and I've taken decisive action and removed significant negativity out of my path to personal effectiveness."

"Glad to hear it, James. Now, who remembers the 'Godfather' of de-motivation? Okay Henry, tell us about it."

"It's expedience, Clyde, trying to reap before we sow, and it will completely destroy our action initiative.

"Expedience is so devastating because it violates nature's most powerful law, the Law of Cause and Effect. We learned that expedience, failing to pay the price in advance, is the root cause of disillusionment and sub-par, ineffective lives.

> **"Just like procrastination is the major killer of focus, expedience is the major saboteur of action."**

"Dan, I remember you hit expedience real hard when you covered Absolute #2. What would you add to Hank's comments?"

"Not much, Clyde. Hank covered it quite well. It's just important, no…

> **"It's critical that we make the connection between expedience and negative consequences, because until that linkage is firmly ingrained in our subconscious mind, we'll keep repeating past mistakes."**

Indirect Effort

"Serve Others, Absolute #3, epitomizes counter intuitiveness; it's just not natural to put others before ourselves; to serve them. Counterintuitive, natural or not, it's backed by law, The Law of Indirect Effort. This law is best defined like this…

> **"What you sow in the lives of others you reap in your own.**

"Be impressed by others, and they will be impressed by you; to be happy make others happy; give respect, get respect. It's not about you; it's about them. When you make it about them, it comes back to you. It's all about you to make it all about them. It's not easy to practice The Law of Indirect Effort; in fact, it's downright hard. Who remembers the two things that make it so difficult to obey this law?"

"Timing and ego."

"Very good, Mary. Care to elaborate?"

"Sure, Clyde. I'd like to talk about this one because I've struggled so hard

with it. I know everyone remembers our class discussion; our opinions of serve others was all over the charts."

"Yeah, Mary, it's the one that sent Joanne packing."

"That's right, James. I didn't think you were too far behind her. Anyway, it's so tough because we know the law works; it's a law, right? We just don't know when others will reciprocate, when we'll reap what we've sown. Usually we bail out too soon. We want instant gratification, and when we don't get it, we go back to serving self. We start making it about us again. As Dan put it, 'If we don't get value for value on the spot, we abandon serving others and proclaim, 'This stuff doesn't work.'

"The second impediment to serving others is the ego. Our need to be right, to have justice, to be heard, to control, to receive immediate value for value; all these things and many more are ego driven."

"At the feast of the ego everyone leaves hungry.

"Right, Mary?"

"That's right, Jack."

"Dan gave us a list of tricks the ego plays on us; it's scary, really, the damage this trickster can do to our effectiveness."

"Well done, Mary. Dan left us with an admonition relative to ego. Anyone remember what it was? Okay, Jack."

"Work hard at not arousing the ego of others; this is best accomplished by keeping yours in check."

"Correct--he also left us with another one; who's got it?"

"Forgiveness is the gift you give yourself."

"That's right, William."

"You know, Clyde I really fought that one; I got the wrong end of the deal in my divorce."

"We've got a song back home that sums it up, William; it's entitled *She Took Everything but the Blame.*"

William snickered and said, "Clyde's back."

"Sorry, William, I couldn't help myself."

"No problem, Clyde. As I was saying, I struggled with forgiving my ex-wife. She was so nasty in court and made it so hard for me to see my children. But I kept saying, 'Forgiveness is the gift I give myself.' I wanted out of this self-imposed prison, so I kept working at it. I stopped fighting it; I did battle with my ego. I began giving her respect, even though I didn't feel she deserved it; I stopped trying to win every point. I finally got it; forgiveness is the gift I give myself.

"There were two other points that Dan made that really helped me. Do we have time for those?"

"We sure do, William."

"It struck a chord with me when Dan said…

> *"Insecure, ineffective people think all reality should conform to their point of view.*

"That described me; I wasn't willing to address my role in the mess my ex and I had made of the relationship.

"Here's the other point Dan made that got me moving in the right direction…

> *"You can serve others to the degree that you look deliberately for the good in each person and situation. If you first look for the bad in people and circumstances, you will not be motivated to serve them.*

"I discovered that I am judgmental to a fault. I'm looking for the flaws, so, of course, I find them."

"Sounds like real growth to me."

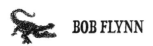

BOB FLYNN

"Thanks, Clyde. Okay, Dan, I know you have something to add."

"One thing, Russ, uh Clyde…

> *"The most important and most highly paid form of intelligence in North America is social intelligence, the ability to get along with an expanding sphere of people. Fully 85% of your personal effectiveness is going to be determined by your social skills, by your ability to interact positively and effectively with others, and by your success in getting them to cooperate with you in helping you to achieve your goals."*

Clyde continued. "Dan's commentary really sums up the power of serving others. It's not only the right thing to do, it is also the most personally advantageous thing to do.

"When *it's not about you, it's about you.*"

The Answers

"Well, y'all havin a good time?" Everyone nodded affirmatively to Clyde's question. "Glad to hear it," he continued. "Cause y'all look like you been weaned on a pickle, like you swallered a bucket of spark plugs and washed'em down with a gallon of Texas Pete."

"Clyde's definitely back," Jack said as everyone agreed.

"Determining how to best serve others is best accomplished by asking ourselves questions-- questions like…How can I be of service to this person? What does this person need that I can supply? How can I help this person with this problem? What's the most effective action I can take to help these people capitalize on this opportunity? Now let me ask you guys why questions are so powerful in determining how to best serve others. Yes, Mary."

"Because strategically placed self-questions stimulate our brains to search for answers. Just like we learned in Absolute #4, Questions Are the Answers."

"Thanks, Mary; well said. Now as we learned in the 4th Absolute, Questions Are the Answers is not simply a play on words; like all the other Absolutes, law backs it. In this case, it's The Law of Balance, which is…

"There are equal and offsetting positives to every seemingly negative situation.

"To truly maximize your personal effectiveness, it's vital that you understand and practice this business of asking questions when faced with what first appears as a negative occurrence. When marginally effective people encounter a 'problem, they do the intuitive thing…'"

"That's THANG, Clyde; please pronounce your words correctly."

"Thanks, Tony; I knew I'd put some culture in this class before it was over. Like I said, faced with a seeming problem, the marginally effective do the intuitive THANG, and that is to make negative statements to themselves, statements like… I knew this would happen. What a week, it just keeps getting worse! Here we go again! And so on. Not only do statements like these make you feel worse, they alert your subconscious mind to actually convert the negative statements into your reality.

"Conversely, personally effective individuals question everything—uh, scuse me; that's everythang, sorry gang--and their questions focus on two primary areas: problems and opportunities. Highly effective people know that all problems contain opportunities. How do they know that?"

"Because of the Law of Balance."

"Co – rrect, William. So, when they encounter a problem, they start looking for what?"

"The pony in the manure pile."

"Right again, William."

"Remember, this has little to do with positive thinking and nothing to do with blind optimism; it's very practical, because…."

Clyde shrugged, waiting for an answer from the class…

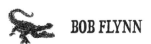 **BOB FLYNN**

"Because it's based on law!" the participants answered in unison.

Clyde laughed as he asked, "And all the people said?"

"Amen!" came the resounding response.

"Effective people, like you, have disciplined their minds to automatically link opportunities with 'problems'— they know this process contains tremendous power."

"Clyde, don't get me wrong; I've already seen the power of the Law of Balance in my life, so I'm a raving advocate. However, you mentioned something that I don't quite understand. You stated that we should ask questions about opportunities as well as problems. Help me with that one."

Clyde looked at Dan and smiled. "Dan, help James with that one, will you?"

"James, that's a great question. When we first encounter an opportunity, it's our natural inclination to immediately begin attempting to capitalize. This can prove detrimental, because there's usually a lot more potential than first appears. Questions help uncover the 'hidden' potential."

"Dan?"

"Yes, Tony, I have an example."

"Great; let's hear it."

"You all know--"

"Scuse me Tony, that's y'all know."

"Touché, Clyde, I'll try again…

"Y'all know that I'm in the training and consulting business. We often get inquiries from prospective customers relative to our services. The prospect calls and says something like: 'I understand you have a sales-negotiation training program. We need something like that in our organization. What's your price for this program and when can you make one available to us?'

"In the past, I would have quoted a price and provided available dates. Ninety-five percent of the time, the deal closes. Before I learned to question

AIN'T NO SUCH THANG AS
A PURDY GOOD ALLIGATOR RASSLER

opportunities, I would have simply accepted the deal at face value. Not bad, but far from optimal. Now that I understand the process, I don't jump through my shorts every time I get these type inquiries. I don't quote prices and available dates; I ask questions."

"Give me an example of the questions you would ask, Tony."

"I'm fixin' to, James, I'm fixin to."

"Well said, Tony!"

"Yeah, thanks, Clyde."

"James, here's an example. 'Mr. Prospect, I'll be glad to provide dates and pricing, but before I do, I'd like to ask you a question. What's going on in your company that caused you to conclude that you need a sales-negotiation training program?'"

"By asking questions about opportunities, I've discovered that…

"The opportunity on the surface is the mere tip of the iceberg.

"When I ask these types of questions, I uncover the 'real' blockbuster opportunities that are masked as problems. These 'problems' then become personal opportunities of a magnitude that far exceed the original issue, the one I used to think was the real opportunity."

"I'm telling you that once you catch-a-holt of The Law of Balance, you're going to uncover opportunities that will shock, amaze, and delight you."

"Thanks, Tony; that clears it up. I can see immediate application."

Clyde re-entered the conversation. "Okay, now keep in mind that…to improve the quality of our lives and become increasingly effective we must change the quality of our self-questions because…

"It's our questions to ourselves that direct our focus.

"Now we all know that what we focus on expands, so if we ask ourselves questions that direct our focus toward opportunities instead of problem, then we expand our opportunity focus. You see, the main difference between

BOB FLYNN

effective and ineffective people is that effective people ask better questions of themselves and as a result… get better answers. Another major difference between the effective and the ineffective is that effective people realize that…

❚ *"Questions to ourselves are the primary way we learn.*

"Positive affirmations are powerful, effective self-motivators. Saying things to yourself such as: I can do it, never give up, and so on are certainly much better than negative self-talk. There is, however, an even more potent method of self-motivation, and you guessed it, it's the proper use of strategically positioned self-questions, like: What can I do right now to improve this situation? What will I gain by completing this project with excellence?

"Again, we are continually asking ourselves questions. By controlling those questions, we significantly increase the resources we have at our disposal. Please understand that our resources are limited only by the questions that we ask ourselves. Gang, thinking is nothing more than asking and answering questions, so to control and focus our thinking we are personally responsible for controlling our questions.

"*It's not about you* to control people and circumstances. *It's all about you* to control your thoughts through the effectiveness of your self-questions."

The Constant

Clyde changed gears as he transitioned into a new topic.

"Because our ability to handle the inevitable changing conditions of life is essential to becoming a high-performance individual, we learned the importance of Embracing Change. Somebody tell the class why this business of capitalizing on change is so important, yet so difficult.

"Okay, Jack."

"Important because nothing is as constant as change; it's going to happen no matter what. So, to maximize our potential as effective people, we must not only cope with change, we must learn to benefit from its many opportunities. Embracing change is counterintuitive. The majority fight and deny change; they perceive it as threatening, an aggravation that, if ignored, will go away."

"Why is that, Jack? Why the universal resistance to change?"

"Well, Clyde, it requires us to do things differently, it messes with our routines and comfort zones, and mostly causes us to look directly in the face of our reality."

"That's the center of the target, Jack; change is flat uncomfortable. The paradox is that discomfort is good, or at least potentially good. See, discomfort tends to take us one way or the other. Either we decide to deal with our discomfort by making the opportunistic changes, or we slip quietly into the effectiveness-killing trap of denial."

"Yeah, I recall Dan saying that it usually requires huge doses of discomfort to get us to deal with change. Sometimes it even may take a crisis."

"True, and who remembers the nine most common pitfalls that keep us from embracing change?"

"Okay if I read from my notes, Clyde?"

"Absolutely, Hank."

Hank gave his effective summary.

1. **Deciding Not to Change:** It takes more energy and effort to cling to the old ways than it does to make the advantageous changes. Stubbornness and denial have the high price of ineffectiveness.

2. **Acting Like a Victim:** Change is totally non-caring; it simply doesn't care if we whine and behave like a spoiled child. Change is going to happen; we can't stop it.

3. **Trying to Play the New Game by the Old Rules:** You think adapting to change is tough? Try not adapting and see how tough things get.

4. **Easing into Change:** Easing into change is a very bad strategy. This strategy just postpones tough times for tougher ones.

5. **Trying to Control Change:** When it comes to change, the more you're out of control, the more you're in control. Good luck trying to push change back into the bottle.

6. **Remaining Neutral to Change:** There's no neutral when it comes to change; either you're moving forward or backward. Change knows no status-quo.

7. **Failing to Abandon the Expendable:** We must abandon the expendables because that creates valuable space and makes room for the new skills that are needed to facilitate change.

8. **Failing to Speed Up:** There's no chance of change slowing down. If we do not, change will overtake us.

9. **Expecting Others to Protect Us From Change:** Change respects no one, and no one can protect you from it. Sooner or later, they as well as you will have to deal with it.

"Thanks Hank, well done. As I recall, Dan concluded this Absolute with this simple admonishment…

| *"Constantly identify the changes you need to make…. Constantly make them."*

The Mastermind

Clyde moved on to a new topic.

"When we make the decision to take full personal responsibility for our success, life has a way of testing that decision. I know from my personal experience that anytime I decided to better my circumstances, it seemed that obstacles quickly appeared in my path to test my commitment. As you continue moving forward in the *12 Absolutes*, I think you can count on the same. For that reason, you'll need what Napoleon Hill calls a 'mastermind alliance.' I've found that many have gone before me and that I can learn invaluable lessons from them. It's really pretty simple; all we have to do is decide what we want to accomplish, then find others that have already accomplished what we're seeking and do what they did. By taking this advice, you'll save yourself significant trial and error and move in a more direct line toward your goals."

"Clyde?"

"Yes, Jack."

"I had a dream about a mastermind alliance—mine."

"That sounds interesting. Tell us about it."

"I was having some struggles at work, and I dreamed that this group of teachers provided information that helped me convert my problem into an opportunity and taught me many other things about myself."

"Who were these teachers, Jack?"

"The first one was Dr. Alfred Adler."

"Oh yeah, the author of *Understanding Human Nature*. It's as relevant today as it was in the twenties."

"Yeah, well—Dr. Adler told me that I had a control issue and that people would do almost anything to escape from control. He went on to explain that my controlling efforts were having the exact opposite effect of their intent. I learned that I must develop full trust in my own capabilities, then, and only then will I break my dependence on controlling others.

"My next teacher was a fellow from Lebanon, Kahill Gibran."

"Sure, the author of *The Prophet;* must reading, folks, must reading."

"Clyde, this guy was remarkable; he explained work in a way that I'd never considered. He convinced me of just how important it is to love our work. I'd just never thought of work as an expression of love."

Speaking in a very excited tone, Jack continued. "Listen to the last part of what he told me…

"Work is love made visible.

"And if you cannot work with love but only distaste, it is better that you should leave your work and sit at the gate of the temple and take the alms of those who work with joy."

 **BOB FLYNN**

"So, Jack. who did you meet next?"

"Dale Carnegie."

"*How to Win Friends and Influence People*. Right, Jack?"

"That's right. Have you read the book, Clyde?"

"I have, and I was so inspired by it that I took the Dale Carnegie Course and became an instructor. So, what did Mr. Carnegie have to say?"

"This was pretty incredible. Many of the things he taught me were reintroduced in Absolute #6, Build Rapport. Mr. Carnegie—Dale, as he asked me to call him--taught me seven ways to become more effective with people. The most personally applicable was... how to go about getting people to see things my way. He said to always show understanding and respect for the opinion of others, when I'm wrong admit it quickly and emphatically, begin all encounters in a friendly understanding way, especially when there's considerable differences of opinion, let the other person do most of the talking, and challenge in a friendly way.

"Now the next teacher I met was quite a character, heavy New Your accent, very animated and excited. His name is Lester Levenson. And Clyde, the name of his book is—"

"*Happiness Is Free.*"

"Co-rrect, Mr. James. Mr. Levenson taught me that most people, including him. spend their lives trying to get love. Though he didn't use the term, he told me The Law of Indirect Effort, that is giving love, was the way to health and happiness. He made a very strong case for his advice.

"Now my final teacher was one tough cookie. Mr. Baltasar Gracian. He wrote a classic, *The Art of Worldly Wisdom*—right, Clyde?"

Clyde nodded in agreement.

"You thought Dan was adamant about taking personal responsibility? Wait till you get a load of this Spaniard! He said stuff like... 'I will teach you nothing Mr. Williams. Even assuming a person can be taught anything is but human folly, and I have an undying disdain for that oh so common malady. You see Mr.

AIN'T NO SUCH THANG AS
A PURDY GOOD ALLIGATOR RASSLER

Williams, in the final analysis you and you alone decide whether or not you will learn!'

"He gave me much good counsel, when I thanked him, he said…

> **'With your puny words you have thanked us all. Words are easy; words alone are the tools of the uninitiated. Thank us with your discipline and your actions, your commitment and resolve, your love and passion. Thank us with a determined dedicated life lived for the purpose of attaining excellence in a worthy cause.'"**

"So, Jack," Clyde asked, "you're a big advocate of a mastermind alliance?"

"Yes, absolutely. When we learn and apply the wisdom of those who have achieved what we're seeking to achieve, we are doing things smart. People like the ones I encountered have paved the way for the rest of us. They have learned that the world operates by law. They've learned and applied the laws, and they've passed their experience and knowledge to folks like us."

Clyde picked up where Jack left off. "Well said, Jack. You know, it's amazing to me that people will devote time, energy, effort, and money pursuing things that have no long-term pay off. Countless hours in front of the TV, hobbies at the expense of their professional growth, novels and newspapers that add little to their body of useful knowledge. This is a shame because there are books, CD's, and tapes that offer tremendous insight into any subject of interest. The price of personal effectiveness must be paid in advance. And it must be paid by immersing oneself in things that are of value, things that are worthy of the time and effort, investment required for mastery. Ah, but I'm preaching to the choir; you guys have learned the vital importance of investing in yourselves. My point is…

> **"People, books, tapes, CD's, and courses are available to serve as your mastermind alliance. You don't have to be pioneers and take the arrows. Tap into the immutable laws of the ages and let them be your teachers."**

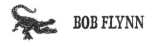

The Resource

After a ten-minute break, Clyde continued.

"People are your greatest resource. Personal effectiveness requires that you learn and apply a process that enables you to build bonding rapport with a wide diversity of people. In Absolute #6, Build Rapport, we learned such a process. Let me give you a brief refresher...."

"Clyde?"

"Yes, Mary."

"This Absolute was tremendously meaningful to me; would you mind if I attempted to recap it?"

"Mary, you're on."

"Like I said, this Absolute shone a bright light on one of my major deficiencies, establishing and building rapport with people. I tend to be somewhat of a loner; I mean I'm friendly enough on the surface, but I'm so analytical that my natural skepticism comes into play and prevents rapport from happening. I mean, once I encounter someone that is different from me, my ego takes over, and I decide they don't know much. Absolute #6 taught me that it's not about me; it's about the other person. It is about me to suppress my ego, to not be so judgmental on the front end, and to seek out what I like about others, not what I don't like."

"Mary, this is huge growth!"

"Yes, definitely, and it's already paid astounding dividends. But I digress... here are the key things I learned from this Absolute.

"Only 7% of communication takes place through our words. Over 50% occurs through our body language, and the other 40% or so occurs through our voice tone. Now I had heard that before, but when Dan said...

"People desiring to become skilled at building bonding rapport must be continually aware and sensitive to the impact they are having on others and take personal responsibility for managing it.

AIN'T NO SUCH THANG AS
A PURDY GOOD ALLIGATOR RASSLER

"I realized just how meaningful those percentages are. I never consciously measured my impact on people; I just saw things from my perspective.

"We also learned that we should encourage others to talk by asking open-ended questions that begin with what, when, why, which, who, where, and how. It was enlightening to learn that when we listen, we are building trust, and when we respond to the other person's interests, we are building credibility. This was all great information, and when Dan suggested we compare this type of behavior to our usual approach, I knew I was on to something! The contrast was stark; I knew I had work to do.

"Having taken the Myers-Briggs and DISC assessments, I was familiar with the various behavioral styles, my own included. In the past I found it interesting but really saw no practical application to my day-to-day effectiveness. What really opened my eyes was when Dan took us through the action exercise. I know you all—uh, that's y'all—remember when we examined the actions that are most effective with the four behavioral types. Dan asked us to circle in red the behaviors we were not taking. I'd say I circled about 85%. No wonder I was having difficulty connecting with people! Since taking the exercise I've continued studying the behavioral types, how to recognize them, and the specific actions to take, and to avoid, to initiate and build rapport. The results are amazing!

"Being introduced to the non-verbal's, body language was awesome, certainly I'd heard of body language, but I thought it was some sort of vague concept. It was edifying to learn that this art form is quite practical in reading what a person *really* means. When we become proficient in reading body language, we can capitalize on agreement and recognize potential problems before they become chronic.

"When Tony told the story of how he combined behavioral styles with non-verbal's to prevent a potential misunderstanding and close a big deal, my analytical side accepted the concept as viable, and I've been hooked ever since."

After Mary's commentary, Dan said, "Mary earlier you mentioned that the ideas you took out of Absolute #6 have already been of benefit to you. Please share some examples."

"I'll tell you about one, a big one. I don't know if the class remembers, but one of my goals in taking the *12 Absolutes* was to motivate my husband to become more ambitious. I'm telling you, I tried everything; I cajoled him with every method I knew. Not only did it *not* work, it seemed the harder I tried, the

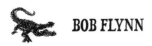 **BOB FLYNN**

worse it got. He basically withdrew and if anything became even more passive.

"Sam's an Amiable, and when I learned that Amiables are passive-aggressive, 'bingo,' the lights went on. When I examined the action steps relative to effectiveness with his behavioral style, I immediately saw that I wasn't doing a single one of them. Basically, I was taking the wrong actions and withholding the right ones. No wonder we were stuck! So… I realized my ego was in charge, got rid of that, and started entering into the behaviors that Dan recommended. The progress is truly remarkable. Our relationship has greatly improved, and Sam's showing signs of taking charge and realizing his wonderful potential. And you know what? I'm not even very good at rapport-building. Think of the progress I'm going to make when I master the concept!

"I'm getting it, Clyde…It's not about me – It's all about me."

"Mary, that was a brilliant recap. I don't think we need to add but one thang… keep your noses in the *12 Absolutes* workbook. Keep learning and applying – keep taking personal responsibility."

The Impediment

"Fear--the very word has an ominous sound. It bubbles up thoughts of doom and gloom, underachievement and failure."

Clyde paused to allow his analogy to take root… then he continued. "What would you do if you knew you could not fail? Every time I ask myself that provocative, penetrating question I gain deeper insight into myself, and I get a better look at the things that are preventing me from realizing the very essence of my potential. Oh yeah, it's true…

> *"Your fear of failure is the greatest impediment to your personal effectiveness.*

"It keeps us right where we are, it prevents us from dreaming and planning big, it stops us from coming anywhere near our God-given potential, it keeps our gifts and talents on the shelf, it blocks us from achievement, it steals our drive and ambition, it cause loss of faith and courage, it motivates us to accept much less than we deserve, it is the root cause of our ineffectiveness!

AIN'T NO SUCH THANG AS
A PURDY GOOD ALLIGATOR RASSLER

"Other than that, fear of failure really isn't so bad."

"What drives fear of failure, Clyde?"

"What do you think drives it, William?"

"Ego?"

"Yes, fear of failure is driven by our ego, which lies to us every chance we give it."

"Clyde, I thought ego pushed us forward, caused us to try new things, to excel."

"Yeah, Hank, that's the impression it gives, but remember, the ego is a trickster; it appears to be one thing when really it's another.

> **"See, it's the ego that tells you, you can't do that, you're not qualified, you'll just look stupid, you're not smart enough, others are much more capable than you, you've made lots of past mistakes, try that and you're going to lose everything. On and on it goes with its lies and misrepresentations."**

"Why, Clyde? Why does the ego tell us those things?"

"To maintain control, Mary.

> **"The ego wants to master you. Once you start trying to apply the 12 Absolutes, it's going to start whispering to you...Mary, you can't do that, think of what you'll look like when you fail. If that doesn't work, it'll increase the volume.... Hey, don't be stupid, that will never work in a million years! And if you keep pushing forward, it will pull out all the stops....This is going to absolutely ruin you and your loved ones, see you're just thinking of yourself, better get back where you belong, where it's nice and safe, better get back under my command because you're not capable!"**

 **BOB FLYNN**

"Thanks, Clyde. I don't like the ego."

"Good, Mary, very good. You keep on not liking the ego—keep on not liking him until you become his master."

"Clyde, I liked what Wayne Dyer said about failure... 'Nothing fails like success because you don't learn anything from it.' That helped me understand that in order to increase my success rate I'll have to increase my failure rate."

"Then you got a great lesson, Jack. It's when we engage in trial-and-error exploration that we learn and grow. Fear of failure—the ego—warns us against this mindset. It cautions us to stay where we are, not to venture out too far. It's afraid if we do, we'll see that we don't need it anymore. It's petrified that we'll discover a Higher, more intelligent Power, and its fears are well founded. We can't advance if we cling to certainty.

> **"If you have to know the answers before the questions are asked, you'd better like where you are.**

"When we embrace security, we pave the road to complacency and we exacerbate the fear of failure."

Dan concluded Absolute #7, Master Fear, with a key point and a solution: "Dan, if you don't mind, no one teaches this better than you."

"Thanks, Russ; coming from you, that means a lot to me."

"We concluded Absolute #7 with some insight into what might cause the three basic fears, which if you recall are the fear of failure, the fear of underqualification, and the fear of uncertainty. We learned that...

> **"The three basic fears are often grounded in the fear of <u>someone else's</u> disapproval or ridicule.**

"To effectively deal with this situation, we must work hard to uncover the source of this fear, and then execute strategies to overcome it. In other words, we need to identify any persons, living or dead, active or inactive, in our lives whose disapproval and ridicule we fear. When this is accomplished, we need to formulate and execute plans to eliminate these fears forever. If the fear is deep and longstanding, perhaps perpetrated by someone very close to us, we may require professional guidance through the emotional maze. If this is the case,

AIN'T NO SUCH THANG AS
A PURDY GOOD ALLIGATOR RASSLER

it can be some of the most productive work you can ever do… don't hesitate to do it."

The Mystery

"Effectively dealing with our fears is certainly challenging, but the potential payoff is more than worth the effort. Speaking of effort and challenge, lets discuss the mystery of motivation. I think we'd all agree that the ability to inspire and motivate others is essential to personal effectiveness.

Rather than me babble on I'm going to give each of you an assigned topic relating to motivating desired action. Using your notes from that session, develop a recap of the key points and present them to the class. Let's take thirty minutes to prepare."

"Okay, James, tell us about Discretionary Effort."

"Discretionary Effort is the level of effort people could give if they really wanted to, but which is beyond what is required. I call it extra effort, and it's difficult to get these days, and that's too bad because it's the difference between good and great. Extra effort can be attained, but we have to understand and apply antecedents to get it started, and that's their jobs—to set the stage for extra effort to occur. Training, memos, speeches, policies, mission/vision statements are examples of antecedents. Now antecedents in and of themselves have a very limited effect on behavior--in order for them to be effective, that is, to sustain the extra effort, they have to be paired with a consequence. This is a critical point because….

I *"The only way anything gets done is through behavior and behavior is a function of consequences.*

"So, in order to take the mystery out of motivation and achieve extra effort, we have to pair antecedents and consequences."

"Okay, James, that gets us off to a fine start. Now Mary, tell us about consequences."

"Just like James said, consequences are used in tandem with antecedents.

The antecedent gets the desired behavior started, the consequence--sometimes called reinforcement--keeps the desired behavior going. Consequences follow the behavior and cause it to occur more or less frequently in the future. Keep in mind this is for desired behavior. To stop undesired behavior, you simply withhold any form of reinforcement. The rule is simple but profound…

"When *desired behaviors* are *not* occurring, reinforcement *is not* being applied… and… when *undesired behaviors* are occurring reinforcement *is* being applied.

"As Dan said, this is the cold hard essence of motivation.

"There are two types of reinforcement, positive and negative. Both positive and negative reinforcement get results. Negative reinforcement, however, rarely motivates discretionary effort. Here's the difference between the two.

"Positive reinforcement causes both desired and undesired behavior to increase because a positive meaningful consequence has followed the behavior.

"Negative reinforcement causes both desired and undesired behavior to increase in order to avoid or escape some unpleasant circumstance.

"The bottom line is…

> **"The long-term use of negative reinforcement can <u>never</u> sustain high levels of performance."**

"Thanks, Mary; very enlightening."

"So Tony, when we think in terms of motivation, we generally associate it with increasing desired behaviors, but in many cases the challenge is to stop the undesired behaviors. Elaborate on that, please."

"Sure, Clyde. Here's the first thing to remember…

> **"Where management is not making conscious attempts to positively reinforce desired behaviors, the extinction of discretionary efforts is assured!**

"Here's the second thing to remember…

"Where management is getting bad behavior, it is absolutely because they are reinforcing it.

"So, in order to stop the undesired behavior, our job is to immediately stop reinforcing it. It's really simple, Clyde. Determine the behaviors that are undesirable, identify the reinforcers that are sustaining them, remove the reinforcers."

"So, Tony, it's as simple as that?"

"Sure is, as long as you prepare for what's coming. See, after you remove the reinforcers sustaining the bad behavior you can expect some repercussions. When you stop reinforcing the bad behavior, expect an increase in bad behavior. This is where most managers and parents give up and give in. When they do, the cycle starts all over again. Why? Because the bad behavior was once again reinforced. How long will the increased bad behaviors last? That all depends on how long the undesired behavior has been occurring and the amount of reinforcement that the badly behaving person has received. The good news is that it will eventually stop if the reinforcement is withheld."

"Now Hank, you and Jack worked on the common errors of reinforcement; which one of you is going to do the recap?"

"I'm elected, Clyde."

"Okay, tells us why reinforcement doesn't always work."

"There are four errors that hinder the effectiveness of positive reinforcement. The first one is *Perception*. The manager perceives that the recipient will respond to the same reinforcers that they do. In other words, they will like it because I like it. This isn't always the case, and the reinforcer falls victim to the *perception* of the manager.

"The next reinforcer error is called the *Contingency* error. This is the most common error; it happens all the time. When a reinforcer isn't contingent on any behavioral change, it does nothing to enhance motivation. For example, when an organization provides an improved benefit package, motivation stays the same because everybody gets the better package. The top performers, and the whiners and complainers all get the same deal.

"The next error is the *Immediacy* error. Delayed reinforcement is marginally effective at best. The longer the time lapse between the desired behavior and

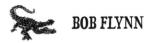 **BOB FLYNN**

the reinforcer, the weaker the effect. For a reinforcer to be effective, it has to come close on the heels of the desired behavior.

"The *Frequency* error studies conclude that a 4 to 1 frequency ratio of positive reinforcers as compared to negative reinforcers is adequate to influence desired behaviors. Most organizations provide feedback reinforcement once a month at best."

"Well, gang, you've done a great job in condensing a rather complex subject; many thanks."

The Duty

"There is no duty we so much underrate as the duty of being happy. By being happy, we sow anonymous benefits upon ourselves and the world.' Until I really contemplated these words by Robert Louis Stevenson, I never saw happiness as my duty.

| **"What a great way to look at happiness, our duty/our personal responsibility.**

"I remember when as a class we did the recap of Absolute #8, how passionate each of you was about it. Happiness is pretty important, huh?"

Clyde paused briefly, obviously thinking about his rhetorical question and collecting his thoughts, and then he continued.

"When I began developing the *12 Absolutes* program, my intent was to provide information that would help people realize their dreams. The more I studied the wisdom of the ages, the more I realized that it's not about realizing dreams; it's about being happy. That's why we dream, plan, and set goals in the first place—to achieve happiness. So, the essence of this program is to help people be happier. Now, you'd think that because of the material luxuries, longer life spans, and the fantastic scientific and technical knowledge of our place in time, we'd be at the pinnacle of happiness, but according to recent surveys, such is not the case. The majority of people you encounter are anxious and bored. Let's make sure we're not among them!

"You and I will never even come close to maximizing our personal effectiveness unless we master the art of being happy. Think about it; do people who are downtrodden influence you? Are you comfortable around constantly complaining, woe-is-me types? There are some people that could get a job posing for cold remedy ads and they are not personally effective, folks. It's your personal responsibility, your duty, not to become one of them.

"Well, right out of the chute let me say, *it's not about you*; happiness is contingent on your commitment to a cause bigger than yourself. Narcissism is alive, not well but alive, and he ain't no happy feller. See, when we focus on what we can do for ourselves, we miss our most prominent happiness opportunity, and that is the opportunity to help others. Yes, *it's all about you* to get your mind off yourself and to concentrate on making others happy. Happiness is not dependent on outside events, and it cannot be achieved by searching for it, see...

> ***"Happiness is found in the midst of intense effort aimed at a worthy cause, a cause that is determined by your <u>authentic self.</u>***

"*It's about you* to determine your worthy cause. Choose wisely, and you are on the road to a happier, personally effective existence. Total involvement in every detail of our lives is where happiness resides.

> ***"If your cause, your goals, dreams and aspirations aren't representative of the 'real you,' your authentic self, you'll create pain, and you'll seek involvement outside of the details of your life.***

"See, this is why the masses are addicted to leisure time activities; this is why the majority is in one place longing for another—that ain't happiness. I know; I've been there. Happiness occurs through the interpretation of our experiences, and if we're not being true to ourselves, then most of our experiences will not be interpreted as happy ones."

The Responsibility

"We've talked about goals until I'm sure you're sick of it. Goals are great, goals are necessary, and goals are what we should be striving for. You've heard all that before and it's all true, but...

BOB FLYNN

> **"You're _authentic_ _self_ must establish your goals; otherwise, even if you achieve them, you'll achieve them at the expense of your happiness.**

"This is where many miss the boat--I know, because I did. Now--"

"Clyde, sorry to interrupt, but how did you miss the boat?"

"William, I don't want to bore you with stories about myself."

"It won't bore us—not me, anyway. I think my goals may not have been developed by my authentic self, and I can see where that would be a huge mistake. Please tell us how you, as you say, missed the boat. I'm sure we all want to hear it—right, people?"

A resounding "YES" went up in the classroom.

"Okay, but it ain't all that pretty of a story.

"I never consulted with my authentic self when I established my goals. I did what almost everybody does; I went straight to my ego. My ego, being a liar and a trickster, bypassed my heart, my authentic self and chose seductive worldly goals: money, houses, women, cars, and self-aggrandizement.

"At forty years of age I had them all: money, a twenty-year-old 'beauty queen' girlfriend--"

"Clyde, you old dog!"

"Yeah, I was a dog alright, Jack, a dog with a capital D.

"Anyway, you'd think I would be a happy boy--I mean, big shot corporate job, luxury condo in the best part of town, BMW Roadster, everybody (at least to my face) telling me how cool I was, and of course the 'queen.' And I was a happy boy, on the surface, for a while. But little by little, I started not feeling so great. Oh, I kept up a good facade; I had it all polished up on the outside, but on the inside, like I say, small cracks started appearing. Then one day I found myself with ten fingers in the dike and a false smile on my face. Clyde was in a full-blown depression. I guess it's easy to understand depression when you're on the bottom; it's a real puzzle when you're on top!

"Well, before all of you break out in tears, let me say that the story has a happy ending. I finally came to the conclusion that the good Lord had brought me to this hard place to let me know that…THIS WASN'T ME. Once I realized that I had been leading a false life, a life that was based on goals that did not represent my authentic self, I started searching my soul to find the real Clyde, and find him I did. I accomplished this by using much of the *12 Absolutes* process. Today, I am my authentic self, even when I'm Clyde, because he's so much a part of my heritage, if I got rid of him, I wouldn't be the authentic me.

"So, that's the short version of a long story. The moral of which is: No one but you can set goals that are true to your authentic self, not society, yo momma, yo daddy, yo boss, and especially yo ego. When we choose the correct authentic goals, we will naturally invest ourselves in them to the limits of our concentration, simply because it's within this concentration that we experience happiness. This effort produced multiple rewards, because once we have experienced this degree of happiness, we will redouble our efforts to experience it again. This, my friends, is the way we grow into becoming truly effective individuals…. Let's take a fifteen-minute break."

The Adoption

"Welcome back. I want to stay on the happiness theme because it's such an integral part of personal effectiveness. But first a story."

"Oh great. We love your stories, Clyde."

"Sure, you do, Mary, sure you do…

"I know you all remember the key components of Absolute #9, Adopt the Gratitude Attitude. We receive hundreds of emails and letters telling us what a magnificent difference this Absolute has made in their lives. Well, here's how it got into the program. I happened to be attending a portion of one of Dan's workshops. He was concluding Absolute #8, Create Happiness, and he began discussing how the Gratitude Attitude enhanced our overall sense of well-being. He spoke for about five minutes. I was hooked! And I knew there was more.

"Remember, Dan, we sat up until 2 a.m. discussing it?"

"Sure, Russ, how could I forget it? I had to teach the next day and you kept me up half the night."

"Boy, was there more; I took over twenty pages of notes. After reviewing the notes several times, *The 11 Absolutes of Personal Effectiveness* became T*he 12 Absolutes of Personal Effectiveness*. Now, who best to discuss how the Gratitude Attitude is not about you, yet all about you, than the author Mr. Dan Hardee."

Dan was openly touched and a little embarrassed when the entire class gave him a standing ovation.

"Russ, how about give me a little warning in the future?"

"What can I say, pal? Clyde's Expressive, he's spontaneous."

"Well, Dan's Analytical, so he ain't! Anyway, adopting the gratitude attitude is certainly an important component of happiness. And, of course, I was honored and delighted when Clyde considered it important enough to become an Absolute."

"Mr. Composure" got right down to business.

"People like you are future-oriented. You invested in this class so you could improve your futures. Quite naturally, varying degrees of dissatisfaction with your present circumstances motivated you to invest the time, energy, and resources into something that would enhance your future. This is all good; complacency is the robber of our futures. There is a downside, however; see, ambitious future-oriented types such as you often overlook all the blessings that currently abound in their lives. It's so easy to do, and yet when we do it, it can negatively affect our futures. Here's why…

> ### *"You rarely receive more until you acknowledge and appreciate what you already have.*

"In actuality, this is only part of the equation. The other part is…

> ### *"If you do not recognize and give thanks for what you have, you stand a chance of losing it.*

"If you recall, I recommended that you begin keeping a gratitude journal. In this journal, you should list five things you are grateful for right before you go to bed. By taking this action, you bring all the things you are grateful for to a conscious level. I promise, you if you will do this for thirty to sixty days,

AIN'T NO SUCH THANG AS
A PURDY GOOD ALLIGATOR RASSLER

you'll begin to see your prosperity multiply, your relationships will improve significantly, and you'll be noticeably happier. It works because…

> **"The more you see to be grateful for, the more abundance you'll receive.**

"And quite naturally, the opposite of this is true. The less we see to be grateful for, the less we will receive. You see, folks, when we do not trust nature's laws to function perfectly, they reciprocate. They continually give us what we expect, whether it be lack or an abundant harvest."

The State

After completing his presentation, Dan started for his seat when the class once again rose to its feet with a round of applause for their teacher who had become their friend. Clyde was all smiles as he thanked Dan for his "usual GREAT job."

"All of us in this room are from different states, but we all live in one state--our emotional state. And it's this state that determines our level of personal effectiveness. I hope we've learned that your level of personal effectiveness is in direct correlation with how you feel inside. It's simple; when you feel good, you're effective. Many people have it backward, they think because they're effective, they feel good. The fact of the matter is…

> **"Personal effectiveness at any given moment occurs without any conscious deliberation when the right emotional state has been created.**

"So, in order to perpetuate personal effectiveness, we must develop the ability to master our negative emotions, regardless of the circumstances. Who remembers the twelve key components of the ideal emotional state from Absolute #10? Okay, William."

William reminded them of the twelve keys.

1. Mental Calmness.

2. Physical Relaxation.

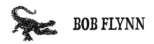

BOB FLYNN

3. Freedom from Anxiety.

4. Energy.

5. Optimism.

6. Enjoyment.

7. Effortlessness.

8. Automaticity.

9. Alertness.

10. Focus.

11. Self-confidence.

12. Control.

"Great, William; thank you.

"Developing our abilities to summon these components will give us the capacity to be at our personal effectiveness best whenever we need or want to. But what about recurring negative emotions that won't go away; what do we do about those?"

"We listen to them."

"Tell us more, Mary."

"Pain in the emotions is like pain in the body--it's trying to get our attention. What we resist persists, so the longer we ignore or attempt to self-medicate it, the more intense it will become. And the more we will find ourselves in negative emotional states."

"So, Mary, what do we do after we listen to them?"

"We acknowledge them, and we begin searching for the root cause. The longer we treat the symptoms, the longer the negative emotion will persist. If it's a longstanding negative emotion, we should get some expert guidance."

"Well, Mary, sounds you've got a little experience with negative emotions."

"Yes, Clyde, tons of it."

"It's for sure we all have negative baggage to deal with. Folks, it's like a roaring lion waitin' under your porch. If you don't deal with him, he's gonna deal with you, usually at the worst possible time and under the worst possible circumstances. Negative emotions negatively affect our emotional states and hinder our personal effectiveness. They do this to the degree that we continue tolerating them. Remember …

| You get what you tolerate.

"It's not about you to be problem free. *It's all about you* to solve your problems."

The Indispensable

"This morning we covered Absolute #11, Revere Time. I know most of the lessons from this Absolute are still very fresh in your minds, so I'm not going to re-plow tilled soil. I am, however, going to review the salient points of this critical Absolute and keep insisting that you continually treat time as the invaluable, irreplaceable, indispensable resource that it is. Why? Because all personally effective individuals revere time."

Clyde moved to the board and wrote…

| Action without planning is a major time-waster.

"Not only is it a huge time waster; action without planning is the major cause of underachievement and failure. Take Action is an Absolute for sure, but our actions must be calculated and focused on our prioritized goals and objectives; otherwise we're going to spin our wheels. It's a fact that all time management skills require crystal-clear focus. And it's a fact that proper execution of all the Absolutes is reliant on excellent management of your time."

Clyde went on to describe the ways in which time management was integral to the Absolutes.

• Pre-Determine Your Focus, or waste time in the land of ineffectiveness.

• Take Action, or watch time evaporate while you sit and wring your hands.

• Serve Others, or use up twice as much time doing it by yourself.

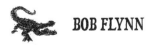

- Questions Are the Answers, or waste time doing it the hard way.

- Embrace Change, or lose time catching up with changing conditions.

- Build Rapport, or spend time learning things others already know.

- Master Fear, or spend time sitting and wringing your hands while others move ahead.

- Create Happiness, or invest your time being miserable.

- Adopt the Gratitude Attitude, or lose time trying to recover your losses.

- Control Your Emotional State, or use up your time apologizing.

- Revere Time, or squander it on the irrelevant.

- It's Not About You to disregard time – It's All About You to cherish it.

"*The 12 Absolutes* are predicated on the value of time. Think about the essence of what we've been studying the past twelve weeks, it can be summarized into one overriding objective…

> *"Personal effectiveness rests on a foundation of taking the responsibility to maximize the use of your time. This is best accomplished by organizing your goals and objectives clearly and by priority and then applying yourself with single-minded focus toward their achievement.*

"We can't manage time; we can only manage our actions within time. When we truly become results-oriented, we naturally gravitate toward the actions that produce the results we've predetermined. This is the key quality for achieving personal effectiveness.

> *"Personally effective individuals rapidly separate the relevant from the irrelevant, then address the relevant with total focus and a keen sense of time urgency.*

"There's no greater discipline than managing your actions within time. Wasting time is wasting life and life is our precious gift.

"Thank you for the marvelous opportunity to serve as your classmate and your teacher. Forgive me for my little guise; it was well intentioned, I assure you.

I plan to be at the graduation exercise in two weeks, and we'll get to know each other on a more personal basis. I'm certainly looking forward to that.

"I'm going to turn it back over to Dan now--thanks again."

All of the *12 Absolutes* participants stood and applauded as Russell "Clyde" James took his seat.

"Thanks, Russ; I'll never forget this class, especially having the one and only Clyde as the mystery student.

"Well, gang, I'm going to email you your final exercise. I'll need it by the seventeenth, so don't let down now. Remember our graduation dinner is the evening of the twenty-fourth starting at 6:00; make sure to let me know how many guests you will be bringing no later than the twentieth. Have a great weekend, and I'll see you in two weeks. Thanks for all your hard work and dedication." The entire class stayed and chatted for over an hour. All expressed their excitement concerning the graduation dinner. It promised to be a great time.

The Dinner

The evening had proven to be absolutely delightful. All the *12 Absolutes* class members were in attendance, and all brought family members and guests. The one-hour social prior to dinner was quite lively, with Clyde keeping everyone laughing uproariously.

There were a few surprises. William brought his ex-wife; they seemed to be getting along quite well. James brought his entire family, including his mom and dad. Jack of course brought Hannah, and Brian, his best buddy from college, the one that had advised him to immerse himself in self-development.

However, the biggest surprise was about to happen.

Just as the group was finishing up dinner… in walked Pete Morrison, Fred Rawlinson, and Mickey Kelly. Jack was caught totally off guard. He'd not invited any of them, not because he didn't want them there, but because of the inconvenience he surmised it would cause.

As they entered the room, Dan was the first to greet them. As Jack approached, he observed them chatting like long-lost friends.

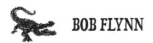 **BOB FLYNN**

"What's going on here? How do you guys know each other?"

"Well now, Jack, try to control your enthusiasm."

"Sorry, Mickey--I'm thrilled to see you guys; I'm just in shock! I didn't know you guys were acquainted."

Dan laughed as he spoke. "Well, Jack, I've known Pete for quite some time. He's a *12 Absolutes* graduate, as you know. This is the first time I've met Fred and Mickey face to face, but we've talked on the phone on several occasions."

"Okay, guys, what's going on?"

Pete smiled warmly as he spoke. "Jack, after every session, Dan and I would have discussion about your progress."

Jack interrupted with a grin. "Yeah, Pete, I know you were checking up on me."

Ignoring Jack's comment, Pete continued, "Anyway, as I was saying, Dan and I would talk after every session--he was lavish in his praise, Jack; he reported that you were totally involved and making excellent progress. In subsequent discussions with Fred and Mickey, I would convey Dan's comments. They both became interested in the program, and I'm proud to announce that they both will be attending a *12 Absolutes* program in the very near future. The bottom line is when I told them you would be graduating on the twenty-fourth, Mickey immediately suggested that we show our support and attend. Fred and I thought it was a great idea, so here we are."

"Man, I'm speechless. Thank you, guys; this means so much to me. Why didn't you join us for drinks and dinner?"

Fred spoke up. "Dan suggested that we wait until after dinner so that you would have the opportunity to mix and mingle with your classmates, their family and friends. He knew you might feel obligated to focus on us."

"Dan is always thinking about the bottom-line implications, Jack. I really admire him in that regard."

"Yeah, Pete, me too."

The tapping on the glass indicated that it was time for everyone to take their seats.

AIN'T NO SUCH THANG AS
A PURDY GOOD ALLIGATOR RASSLER

Dan Hardee walked to the front of the room and addressed the audience.

The Speech

"It is indeed a delight to be with all of you on this special occasion. Support and encouragement are so vital to a person's progress, and there's tons of it here; thank you for caring and demonstrating that caring by being here tonight.

"I have extended an open invitation for all of our *12 Absolutes* graduates to make whatever comments they choose. You will be relieved to know that all speakers are limited to three minutes at the podium; that includes you, Russ."

Dan smiled as he made eye contact with Russell James. Then he continued.

"It never ceases to amaze me when at the conclusion of one of these programs I reflect back on the whole *12 Absolutes* process and see the power of the human spirit. I'm humbled to witness men and women with the courage to come face to face with their authentic selves, recognize and deal with what needs dealing with and then move on with their lives having elevated themselves to a new and exciting level. All can achieve this, but few will. Tonight, we celebrate with what Russell James calls 'The Will-Do Few,' and tonight's six graduates certainly fit that category.

"This group was like no other I've had the privilege to work with. This group represents significant diversity along many fronts including: background, goals, strengths, weaknesses, personality, gifts, age—" (Dan shot a quick glance at Clyde) "--and acting ability. They all worked extremely hard and demonstrated open-mindedness and a sincere desire to enhance their personal effectiveness. They bonded and offered each other encouragement and support. You won't be surprised when I say these are truly exceptional people…

"You knew that already, didn't you?"

Dan paused before continuing.

"I am delighted that all of our six graduates have agreed to speak. I'm sure we will be edified by their remarks. Mary, would you speak to us first?"

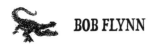 **BOB FLYNN**

All *The 12 Absolutes* participants made positive comments about the program and each of them cited numerous personal gains as a result of the experience.

Mary stated that as a result of the program, she realized that she had a "control issue." And that's good as long as she applied it to controlling her thoughts and actions.

William said that after taking the program, he closely examined his role in the break-up of his marriage. After discussing this with his ex-wife, they had begun reconciliation discussions.

Hank said that the program caused *him* to deal with some major clutter in his life, his relationship with his dad. He and his dad embraced at the conclusion of his comments.

Tony said he got what he came for, a new direction. "My new direction was clearly identified when *I* discovered my Authentic Self. I finally realized my ladder of success was leaning against the wrong wall."

Clyde said as a result of his participation in the program, he had committed to being more truthful and to fight *his* ego with a vengeance.

Jack's comments were particularly penetrating.

"I came here to deal with my complacency and because my wife and boss said I had potential that was becoming permanent. I leave here with much more than I can express in a few minutes.

"It's really easy and real tempting to tell everybody else what they should do. It's altogether another thing to find out who you are and then discipline your focus and actions toward pre-determined, mind-stretching goals. It's very hard, and that's a good thing, because it offers a very special place for those 'Will-Do Few' who exercise the discipline, commitment, and good sense to find their authentic selves and then follow their hearts. Dan, I don't yet consider myself a member of 'The Will-Do Few,' but I know I'm headed in the right direction.

"If I let my authentic self guide me in pre-determining my focus, take action on the relevant and not the irrelevant, control my ego and serve others, keep asking myself positive, penetrating questions, embrace inevitable change, not allow myself to be put off by those different from me and build bonding rapport, confront and master my fears, create continual happiness in my life, control my emotional states so I can always be at my best, revere time so I will use it to my best advantage, and most importantly… always remember that *it's not about me* to control others or to put myself ahead of them, *it's all about me* to learn and continually apply the immutable laws that are contained in the *12 Absolutes.*"

At the end of the presentations, Dan presented the certificates. The class honored Dan with a gift. Russell James said Dan was the best of the best.

Laughter and tears abounded, and people were reluctant to leave. Finally, after midnight, Jack and Hannah said their goodbyes and headed home.

The End?

Hannah smiled big and said, "Jack, your comments were great. I'm so proud of you--you've worked so hard. I know you're glad it's over and you've reached the end."

Jack patted Hannah's growing tummy and said, "Yeah, Hannah, I gotta say it was a lot of work and I am glad the workshop is over, but I feel like it's just the beginning and not the end. Remember what Clyde said?"

"You mean the race analogy?"

"Yeah, you know the part about the three stages of a race."

"Sure, I remember. He said there are three stages of a race: the beginning, the middle, and the end. He went on to say that the easiest part of the race is the beginning and the end. At the beginning you're excited, you've trained hard, you want to see what you can do, you're raring to go! At the end you're tired and exhausted, but you can see the finish line, and that motivates you to push on to completion. He said it's the middle part that's the toughest. You've come a long way, you're pretty tired, and you realize you still have a long way to go, you're only half there. It's at this point that most people either quit or coast."

"That's right, Hannah; that's exactly where I was when you and the kids left for the weekend. You know when I watched that Giants – Redskins football game, and the Skins became complacent. I realized they were only halfway through the race and they were starting to coast. And then I also realized that's

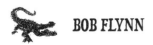

where I was, halfway through the race, complacently coasting. So, that's why I say I'm at the beginning of applying the *12 Absolutes.*

"I really am committed to integrating the *12 Absolutes* into my entire lifestyle; I don't intend to ever coast again. I sincerely want to be a member of the 'Will-Do Few' fraternity.

"Do you think I have what it takes to finish this race, to maximize my potential and become personally effective?"

"Absolutely, Jack. Absolutely!"

Absolute #12

IT'S NOT ABOUT YOU - IT'S ALL ABOUT YOU

Teach Him to deny himself.

ROBERT E. LEE

KEY POINTS

It's not about you to put your wants ahead of others'. When you take that route, you succumb to your ego and place yourself in the ranks of the vast majority, thus minimizing your effectiveness. It's when you lose your authentic self in a cause that's larger than your ego that you really begin to approach personal effectiveness and true distinction. It's all about you to take personal responsibility for controlling your ego for the purpose of maximizing your potential.

❑ Focus on high-payoff areas.

❑ Separate the relevant from the irrelevant; take immediate action.

❑ Help people get what they want.

❑ Ask yourself questions you have never asked yourself before.

❑ Abandon the expendable.

❑ Cease rebelling against those whose perspectives don't align with yours.

❑ Trust yourself to handle anything that life has to offer.

❑ Examine the cause of your pain.

❑ Trust the Law of Natural Abundance.

❑ Establish the "right" internal climate.

❑ Master time management.

MAJOR POINT

Taking personal responsibility is all about you and the acceptance, without reservation that you are where you are and what you are because of yourself, your sowing and reaping to this point. It's the full realization that there's no such circumstance as the problem being "out there." It's not about you to change others; the personally responsible individual knows unequivocally that if they want circumstances and people to change, they must change first. They fully believe that the seeds they sow today are the only influence they have on tomorrow.

DECISIONS DETERMINE DESTINATIONS.

 **BOB FLYNN**

THE 12 ABSOLUTES

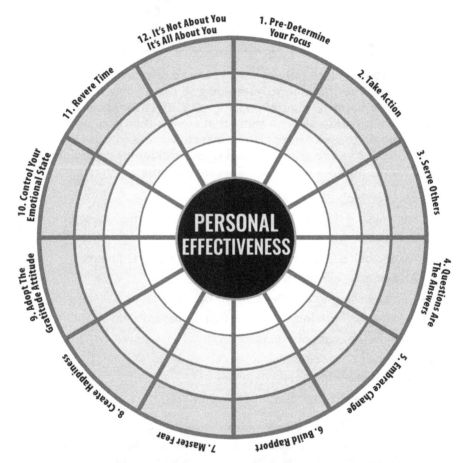

- 1. Pre-Determine Your Focus
- 2. Take Action
- 3. Serve Others
- 4. Questions Are The Answers
- 5. Embrace Change
- 6. Build Rapport
- 7. Master Fear
- 8. Create Happiness
- 9. Adopt The Gratitude Attitude
- 10. Control Your Emotional State
- 11. Revere Time
- 12. It's Not About You It's All About You

PERSONAL EFFECTIVENESS

WHEEL OF EXCELLENCE

AIN'T NO SUCH THANG AS
A PURDY GOOD ALLIGATOR RASSLER

THE CHOSEN FEW

The key to your future is in your hands
You know the rules
Now make your plans
It's up to you to decide, my friend
Just how much you want to win
Your actions and your thoughts of mind
Can turn the tide and make you shine
But if you waver and fail to act
You'd best prepare to face the fact
There will be no special place for you
And you'll not stand with the chosen few
When you decide to give your all
To charge ahead and never crawl
Frustrations will vanish before your eyes
And success from failure will materialize
The sun will shine the clouds will part
As you transcend the faint of heart
And take your place a man among men
Embracing sweet victory as a long-lost friend
I leave you with these parting words
Which skeptics call foolish and absurd
The key to your future is in your hands
You know the rules
Now make your plans
It's up to you to decide, my friend
Just how much you want to win.

Bob Flynn

Bob Flynn

About Bob Flynn

Bob Flynn is the founder and managing partner of PeopleWorks and an internationally respected authority on change management, tactical and strategic selling, sales negotiation, executive coaching, influencing others, personal development, and employee motivation. He has developed and led workshops throughout the United States, Canada, and Europe. Bob has designed numerous programs that have generated millions of dollars for PeopleWorks clients. Mr. Flynn has taught for more than 25 years in both the academic and business worlds. He has helped thousands of senior officials, engineers, marketers, sales executives, and managers improve performance by providing unique, practical, down-to-earth techniques that work. Additionally, he has developed training for and consulted with over 200 organizations, including Shell, ABB, Panasonic, Qualcomm, Ciba Specialty Chemicals, Kraton Polymers, Trimac Transportation, Ingersoll-Rand, The United States Postal Service, The American Heart Association, The Army Corps of Engineers, Dryden Space Center, NASA, and Bechtel.

Prior to founding PeopleWorks, he was Vice President of Sales and Marketing for Overnite Transportation Company, where he led the organization to over one billion dollars in sales. In addition to his executive responsibilities, he founded Overnite Professional Development Institute and personally developed and delivered the key components of training.

Bob is the author of *The 12 Absolutes of Personal Effectiveness*, an adjunct professor at the University of Richmond's Management Institute, a popular speaker at regional and national conferences, and a Certified Professional Consultant.

PeopleWorks, Inc. is a firm specializing in professional development, corporate education, and consulting services related to maximizing business results through people. Our firm helps clients differentiate themselves and grow their businesses through the development of people and the processes and tools they use to do their work.

For information on how PeopleWorks can help your organization, call 804-379-7939 or email peopleworks@aol.com with questions.

CPSIA information can be obtained
at www.ICGtesting.com
Printed in the USA
LVHW111438081219
639816LV00006B/31/P